CHORAL ARRANGING

for

SCHOOLS, GLEE CLUBS and PUBLICATION

A complete guide for the problems of choral arranging for all types of voice combinations and for all kinds of choral groups in schools, churches, communities, or professional organizations.

by

HARRY ROBERT WILSON

Chairman, Department of Music and Music Education
Teachers College, Columbia University, New York

PRICE $ *5.00* in U. S. A.

Copyright 1949

ROBBINS MUSIC CORPORATION
1540 BROADWAY • NEW YORK 36, N. Y.

ACKNOWLEDGMENTS

The author is gratefully indebted to all of the publishers who have kindly permitted him to quote excerpts from their publications, namely: Leo Feist, Inc., New York; Miller Music Corporation, New York; Hall and McCreary Co., Chicago; Clayton F. Summy Co., Chicago; Silver Burdett Co., New York; C. C. Birchard and Co., Boston; Carl Fischer, Inc., New York; G. Schirmer, Inc., New York; Paull-Pioneer Music Corp., New York; Associated Music Publishers, Inc., New York; Galaxy Music Corp., New York; Shawnee Press, Inc., New York; Theodore Presser Co., Philadelphia; Augsburg Publishing House, Minneapolis.

Dedicated
To all my students who have submitted
numerous manuscripts to me for examination.

TABLE OF CONTENTS

CHAPTER I

THE GIST OF CHORAL ARRANGING

The phenomenal growth of the number of amateur choruses and glee clubs during the past twenty years has opened a new field of music writing; and, has turned both the composer and publisher to developing suitable materials to meet the demands of these groups. Since choral organizations are of such varied types and represent many degrees of technical proficiency, the publication of suitable material which will fill the need of every situation becomes increasingly difficult.

Therefore, many choral directors are forced into the necessity of arranging and composing suitable choral numbers for their own individual groups. Also, publishers are turning more and more to arrangers and composers having direct contact with the choral field for compositions which will be suitable for the greater number of choral organizations in schools, churches, and communities.

FOR WHOM THE BOOK IS DESIGNED

Practically nothing has been written which can be used as a guide in writing choral numbers for these amateur groups. Consequently, the creative efforts by amateurs in the field are often clumsy and lack professional artistry, even though they contain good basic choral effects. On the other hand, many professional arrangers fail to realize the limited vocal and technical facility of these groups. They are not familiar with the devices which will obtain the maximum effects without the necessity of elaborate means. Moreover, in response to the increasing demand, many schools are introducing courses in choral composition and arranging, and including many assignments in choral writing in their general harmony courses. Students need a fundamental guide for this work.

This book is an attempt to provide useful principles and devices in choral arranging for amateur choruses of all types and degrees of development. It is addressed to the professional arranger, the amateur who wishes to perfect his creative efforts, and for the student in his growth as a musician and composer.

WHAT THE BOOK IS ABOUT

In the writing of this book it has been assumed that the reader has a basic understanding of the principles of harmony and counterpoint. Without this understanding, musical ideas are bound to appear nebulous and ineffective, if not actually disconcerting when produced on paper. However, the common pitfalls of chord connection, doubling and distribution of parts, and basic devices of good counterpoint will be indicated in the various musical examples.

Only the actual problems of choral arranging will be discussed in this book. *What is choral arranging?* It has to do with every aspect of choral writing except the creation of the original musical idea (which is the realm of musical composition). The arranger must be creative even though he deals with a previously conceived musical idea, which he may change so that it bears little resemblance to the original. Different parts of the same composition may represent both original writing and arranging, such as Brahms' "Academic Overture" or Bach's treatment of well-known chorales in his cantatas.

The arranger with his imagination and technical facility may transport a mediocre musical idea into an effective choral piece. The composer of choral music must not only have superior musical ideas, but also the imagination and technical skill of the arranger if his music is to sound as though it were intended for human voices. The sources of musical ideas are as unfathomable as the depths of the sea but the basic principles of arranging can be learned and put into practice.

SCOPE OF CHORAL MUSIC

Musicians have indulged in many a lively debate about the relative values of orchestral and choral music. The extended means of technical facility, variety of tone color, as well as the pitch and dynamic range possibilities of the orchestra have caused most of the great composers to turn to it for some of their most prodigious musical ideas. Nevertheless, the masters have also turned to the art of choral and vocal writing to express many of their most intimate and sacred emotions, as found in the works of Bach, Mozart, Schubert, Brahms, and Wagner. Moreover, the English, French, and Italian composers have a glorious choral tradition. The Russians have written some of their greatest music for the church. Our American composers are also discovering that instruments, with all their technical advantages, cannot replace the human voice for the expression of many of their most poignant musical feelings.

Choral music must be conceived in terms of the technical and emotional qualities of the human voice. This unique quality is best observed in the style of writing called *a cappella** which is the modern label applied to all un-accompanied singing. There may be an instrumental accompaniment which should enhance the vocal expression. However, sad to relate, when an orchestral accompaniment is used, it often becomes, at least in performance, the tail that wags the proverbial dog.

There are many different combinations of voices which can be used in a complete composition, or, the combinations may be shifted within an individual number to attain musical and tonal variety. The scope of choral music depends upon the technical and emotional scope of the human voice. Any emotion that can be expressed by the voice, which practically includes the entire gamut of human emotion, can be expressed in choral music. The choral composer or arranger has the added advantage of the use of words with their suggested meanings and emotional connotations to support tonal ideas. There is also the possibility of using voices in the manner (not imitation) of instruments for tonal and rhythmical effects, such as humming, neutral vowel sounds and use of consonants. These effects must be used judiciously and in keeping with the general character of the composition or arrangement. They should tend to make the word text more effective or to create mood, and not become an end in themselves.

*NOTE SPELLING

MATERIALS FOR CHORAL TREATMENT

For the choral composer practically any text from the Bible, lyric poetry or suitable prose can be used as a possible vehicle for a musical composition. Even the laundry list has been the source of inspiration to composers in their so-called lighter moments. However, the arranger must turn to existing melodies and texts for musical treatment.

The source of this material which offers the greatest opportunity for creative imagination is the *folk song.* It tends to lend itself to the most effective choral writing, partly, at least, from the fact that it originally sprang from the sorrows, joys, and labors of the people themselves. There are many sources for these songs: the singers of folk songs, editions of folk songs, (be careful of copyrights) and a collection at the Library of Congress in Washington, D. C. This rich source of material is available to any arranger who is free to spend the time examining it. There is still an untapped wealth of folk songs from all lands, especially those of the Latin-American countries, which will make stunning choral arrangements.

The *modern song* of the master composers is another source of material for the arranger. Extreme care and judgment must be exercised in the selection of songs that are to be given choral treatment. Care must also be taken to retain the harmonic texture and musical flavor of the original. Songs with simple melodic line and harmonic structure are the ones which usually can be developed into the best choral arrangements.

There is always the adverse argument that, if the composer had intended his songs for choral singing, he would have arranged them himself. Anyone acquainted with the intimate ways in which composers work will know that this is not necessarily the case. Also, there are many examples where composers have given their own melodies, as well as melodies of others, various kinds of musical treatment.

However, arrangers today should approach the master songs, as well as the lesser songs of Stephen Foster and other writers, with respect and care in their effort to present them in a medium where they may be more widely used. There is opportunity for real musical service here.

The *popular song* of the day usually lends itself to choral treatment of different combinations of voices. This is due to the fact that the melodies are usually not complicated and the harmonic structure is straight forward. When arranging these numbers the harmonic structure should follow, to a considerable degree, the vogue of the day. Rhythmic effects should predominate. Often, the arrangements of these songs are too difficult to warrant the amount of rehearsal time necessary for amateur groups to master them. One should not attempt to "dress them up" entirely out of keeping with the simplicity of the original song, at least, not for amateur groups.

Novel and rhythmic effects are the key to success in arranging these songs. The flavor of the professional arrangements of these songs can be attained with modest harmonic and rhythmical means. Then, amateur groups will enjoy rehearsing them and can prepare them for performance in a short time.

The *arranging of instrumental numbers* for choral groups is a questionable procedure. This objection is not necessarily based on the fact that, since the composer did not originally conceive them for voices, they should remain unmolested. A choral arranger has as much right to arrange instrumental compositions as choral numbers as the instrumental arranger has in taking folk songs, art songs, or popular songs and making instrumental numbers out of them. However, it just so happens that most instrumental melodies do not lend themselves to the addition of a text for a satisfying musical result. The melodies are usually difficult or ungracious for singers when words are added to them. It is for this reason, rather than because they are sacrosanct, that choral arrangers should be cautious and careful in using them.

Certain instrumental numbers, such as the choral section in "Finlandia" by Sibelius and portions of "Les Preludes" by Liszt, seem appropriate to use with words. But these are few and far between and, unless the instrumental number (either piano, violin, or orchestra) has natural choral qualities, it had better be left alone in its original form.

The same objection does not hold true for the *re-arranging of standard choral numbers* for different voice combinations. Granted that it is best for the music to be done in its original form, still, if the voices are not available to sing it, a different version is acceptable. Many composers wrote with specific groups in mind for example, Handel when he composed "The Messiah" for the resources of the Dublin Choral Society. Otherwise, they might have written differently or for another combination of voices.

Some of the old masterpieces for mixed voices sound well when arranged for treble or male voices. If not made available for these voices, then many girls' and boys' glee clubs in this country would be denied familiarity with much beautiful music and suitable material. Many of the songs written by Brahms for treble voices would sound well for SATB. Quite a number of the modern choral compositions and arrangements today are published simultaneously for mixed, treble, and male voices.

CONCLUSION

Remember that, in choral writing the complicated musical treatment is not always the most effective. Choral writing must be more lucid and transparent than orchestral writing. Therefore, look for simple but appealing melodies, texts that offer varied rhythmical and vocal treatment, and songs that invite a contrapuntal line for development of interesting voice parts.

CHORAL RESOURCES

The voice, with all of its technical limitations, is the most expressive of all single instruments. Of course, that statement is a platitude but in essence it is true. Of all the instruments the voice can produce the widest variety of tone color and also numerous sound effects. Some readers may cite the pipe organ to refute this statement but the pipe organ is a combination of many instruments.

The voice is the only instrument to use vowels and consonants to pronounce words. This factor not only gives literal meaning to musical ideas, but also, it affords infinite subtleties of tone color. The choral arranger must understand and explore the tonal possibilities of the human voice if he is to write for it effectively.

TYPES OF VOICES

Voices are classified in accordance with their individual quality and range possibilities. The choral arranger need not concern himself with the former, but rather, with the *normal* tone quality of each *general* division and its range and dynamic possibilities. It may be of interest, however, to point out the types of voices which usually sing a given part. There is no universal practice in assigning voices to parts, largely on account of the difficulty of classifying untrained voices.

Soprano I (1st soprano)
- Coloratura, (brilliant, very high range)
- Lyric, (pure, velvet quality, high range)
- Dramatic, (full, resonant, range usually to high B♭)

Soprano II (2nd soprano)
- Lyric, (those singers whose range is not too high)
- Dramatic, (those voices often too heavy for Soprano I)
- Mezzo-soprano, (full, resonant, approaches contralto quality with medium high range)

Alto I (1st alto)	{ Mezzo-soprano, (especially useful on this part for high notes) Lyric·contralto, (full, velvet quality with low notes)
Alto II (2nd alto)	{ Contralto, (full, resonant, sombre, extreme low notes)
Tenor I (1st tenor)	{ Lyric, (pure, ringing, high range) Dramatic, (full, resonant, used only on this part when high notes are easy and free)
Tenor II (2nd tenor)	{ Lyric, (when high notes have not been developed) Dramatic, (when high notes are strained or voice is too heavy for 1st tenor)
Bass I (1st bass)	{ Baritone, (warm, colorful, wide range)
Bass II (2nd bass)	{ Baritone, (when high notes have not been developed or when rich low notes are in the range) Bass-baritone, (rich, firm low notes) Basso, (contra-bass notes possible)

RANGE OF VOICES

Although the chorus does not have the extended pitch range of the orchestra, due to the physical limitations of the voice, its range is sufficiently wide to offer a wealth of contrast to the arranger. Individual voices of the same type may vary by as much as an octave. However, there is a normal range for each voice part, which the arranger can use without hazarding objections on the part of choral directors.

The pitch ranges indicated below are for adults and students of senior high school and college age. When writing for very young voices of the elementary and junior high school age, it is necessary for the arranger to observe further limitations in the practical ranges of various parts. The degree of these limitations will be pointed out in Chapters V, VI, and VII.

In the following charts, the white notes "o" indicate the range which we are assured is within the range of most amateur choruses who have received adequate vocal training from their directors. The black notes "●" are possible with well-trained groups but they must be used with discretion.

Use extreme low notes only for contra-
bass parts that are doubled one octave
higher.

An aggregate of the normal individual voice parts over a grand staff gives the arranger the following pitch resources.

TESSITURA

The extreme ranges of voice parts may often be used if these extremes are not sustained over too many notes or too long a time. *Tessitura* means the general highness or lowness of a song or voice part. If a part stays in the upper half of its range for a period of time, without any relief by skipping to lower notes, it is said to have a high tessitura; a part that remains in the lower half of the voice range is said to have a low tessitura. Very often it is not the high or low note, but rather the general tessitura, that causes difficulty for amateur voices. This is especially true of the part that has a high tessitura, because the strain is taxing for inexperienced singers. Their voices tire until after a while they are unable to reach the notes without undue strain, if at all.

These musical examples show voice parts with extreme tessituras.

Ex. 1

CHORAL SYMPHONY
LAST MOVEMENT

Note: This entire score is very taxing for both sopranos and tenors.

In the music of the Russian church, such as the following example, effective use is made of a contra-bass part. Although the extreme low notes may be sung an octave higher, much of the sonority is lost when this is done. The ending is also quite low for sopranos, but since the part is written in unison with the altos who are singing in a comfortable range, the sonority is not impaired.

Ex. 2

LET THY HOLY PRESENCE
(S.S.A.T.T.B.B.)

P. TSCHESNOKOFF
Arr. by Noble Cain

Copyright C. C. Birchard & Co., Boston, Mass.
(Used by Permission)

Sometimes singers are unable to reach extreme high or low notes preferred by the arranger. In these cases, optional notes (other harmonic notes) are written for the parts where these extreme pitches occur.

Ex. 3

IN STILLY NIGHT

J. BRAHMS
Arr. by H. R. W.

(1) Choral Program Series, Book IV. Silver Burdett Co., New York.　　Used by Permission.

TEMPTATION

(T. T. B. B.)

Lyric by
ARTHUR FREED

Melody by
NACIO HERB BROWN

Arr. by H.R.W.

*) High notes may be sung by a few selected voices.

DYNAMIC LIMITATIONS OF VOICES

Although well-trained voices have a wide range of dynamics (from *pp* to *ff*), the amateur and young voice usually does not have sufficient control to obtain much contrast between loudness and softness of tone. Practically any choir with proper direction can quickly learn to sing a lovely soft tone but they cannot sing a rousing *forte* without evidences of strain. With proper vocal training the chorus can learn this control but the singing of thrilling *forte* passages are not evident in most of the amateur and school choruses.

Therefore, the arranger must accept to some degree this dynamic limitation and prepare his climaxes accordingly. It is well not to sustain *forte* passages for too long a time without some relief, and great care must be taken to write piano and orchestral accompaniments so that they don't completely cover or "drown out" the singers.

MUSICIANSHIP OF SINGERS

The ability of singers to read music fluently is notably bad. Most choirs learn their music by the rote process or by "picking out each part." Schools and the directors of amateur choruses are taking steps to correct this general weakness but not much success is evident.

Therefore, arrangers must be careful not to write intricate parts when simpler ones will get the effect and do just as well. When complicated harmonic difficulties arise, a passage in unison may be the solution. Canonic treatment is easy to learn and often offers an interesting way out of difficult spots. If complicated parts are written they should be, as in the great compositions of Bach, worthy of the rehearsal time necessary to master them.

CHAPTER III

BASIC TECHNICAL CONSIDERATIONS

Although this book is written on the premise that the reader has acquainted himself with the rules of harmonic and melodic writing, some observations and cautions will be pointed out to correct the most obvious faults usually found in amateur arrangements. These suggestions are not presented as rules because the secret of choral writing is inherent in the music and the choral effects desired. However, before an arranger can feel free enough to experiment with novel effects, he must first be thoroughly familiar with the standard harmonic effects which will be illustrated in this chapter.

HOW TO BEGIN

In arranging a song, it is quite a good idea to block it out (plan it) completely before beginning the details of writing. The usual procedure is to let the melody stand out in relief at the beginning before resorting to changes of key, mode, and rhythmical effects for variety. Then, a return (or a suggestion of a return) is usually advisable before the end to give a feeling of three-part form. Folk songs often lend themselves to this treatment. For the same reason, it is often best to begin a song, especially a popular one, with the chorus, then to the verse, returning to the chorus for the ending. In arranging an art song the form or structure is largely determined by the music as it stands.

One does not necessarily start an arrangement at the beginning and continue on to the end. He may start arranging with the body of the song, or, with some special cadence or middle section into which he wishes to develop the arrangement. Introductions and codas are often written after the body of the arrangement is finished, just as the preface or introductory chapter of a book is often written last.

INTRODUCTIONS OR PRELUDES

What the arrangement should begin with is often a problem. Four or eight measures of piano accompaniment, drawn from the body of the composition, are often used before the voices are introduced. A novel introduction using piano and voices is often effective in setting the mood of a piece. The following example shows the development of a choral introduction from the piano introduction of a popular song. It is written for male voices.

Ex. 5

from the Musical Play "Rio Rita"
THE RANGERS' SONG
(WE'RE ALL PALS TOGETHER)

Lyric by
JOSEPH McCARTHY

Music by
HARRY TIERNEY

Ex. 6

from the Musical Play "Rio Rita"
THE RANGERS' SONG
(WE'RE ALL PALS TOGETHER)
Glee Club T.T.B.B.

Lyric by
JOSEPH McCARTHY

Music by
HARRY TIERNEY
Arr. by H. R. W.

The following novel introduction utilizes sound effects in the basic rhythmic pattern of the song.

Ex. 7

CINDY*
(S.A.T.B.)

The use of humming or neutral vowels is very effective for introductions to set the mood for quiet numbers.

Ex. 8

OFT IN THE STILLY NIGHT
(S.S.A. a cappella)

IRISH AIR
Arr. by H. R. W.

Ex. 9

POOR WAYFARING STRANGER

WHITE SPIRITUAL
Arr. by H. R. W.

From "Poor Wayfaring Stranger" octavo 2528

DISTRIBUTION OF PARTS

Successful arranging depends largely upon writing tuneful vocal lines in compact harmony. To do this, the arranger must be melody-conscious but still not lose the solidity of close harmony. Soprano and alto should stay within an octave as a rule. The same is true for alto and tenor. It is occasionally permissible for tenor and bass to be wider apart than an octave but not for too long a time. Although the following examples are for single chords and do not necessarily represent the distribution of voices in contrapuntal vocal writing, they still remain the basis for compact harmonic writing.

Occasionally; an arranger may disregard the above distribution of parts but only to retain the melodic line of a voice part, or, to secure a unique choral effect. See also Ex. 25 written for treble voices.

Ex. 10

MARY HYMES
(S.A.T.B.)

JAMES STEPHENS   SAMUEL BARBER

she _____ is a rune, she is a rune,

_____ is a rune, she is a rune, she is a rune, she is a rune,

_____ is a rune, _____ she is a rune, she is a rune,

rune, is a rune, she is a rune, she is a rune, she is a rune,

DOUBLING OF PARTS

The usual rules for harmonic writing as to the doubling of parts should be rigidly observed in choral arranging. These rules may be relinquished when writing in contrapuntal style, where the melodic line of the voice part is paramount; or, where some special choral effect is desired.

Briefly, these rules are:

1. Do not double the third of the principle chords of a key (I, IV, V).

Questionable   Satisfactory

2. It is usually best to double the third of the secondary chords of a key (ii, iii, vi). Think of these chords as substitutes for IV, V, I in this order and treat them accordingly.

Satisfactory   Permissible (More minor effect)   Questionable

3. As normal practice, do not double the leading tone of a key.

Questionable   Advisable

4. Dominant Sevenths. It is standard practice to omit the fifth of the dominant seventh chord and double the root when the chord is in fundamental position. In the inverted position, it is best to include all four tones. Today, much more freedom is being exercised in the resolution of these chords. Normally, the seventh of the chord always moved down but now it is used freely in either direction, especially when some other note moves to the note to which the seventh would resolve.

Satisfactory   Normal resolutions   Permissible resolutions

CHORD CONNECTION

Likewise, basic harmonic principles in chord connection should be followed unless relinquished in the use of sequence, contrapuntal line, or special tonal effects.

1. *Parallel Fifths and Octaves*

These bugaboos of the harmony student should be avoided, not so much because they sound badly to the modern ear, but because they destroy independence of parts, a necessary factor in fine choral arrangements. Naturally, octaves appear in unison passages, and fifths, if treated as in the example below, are effective.

Ex. 11

ALLELUIA
CHORUS FOR MIXED VOICES

H. R. WILSON

✱ Two accompanists at one piano are needed.

This composition takes advantage of the possible antiphonal effects between treble and male voices. Unusual rhythmic effects may be secured by following closely the accent marks on different syllables of the word "Alleluia". Sing as fast as it is comfortable for the singers to maintain rhythmic accompaniment.

If only a few tenors are available they may all sing first tenor part.

2. *Nearest Chord Progression*

The old rule of the common tone and moving the other tones as nearly stepwise as possible holds good. The shifting of the melody prevents the retention of the common tone at times but, if so, the other voices should generally move to the nearest chord tones. Wide skips, especially in the inner voices, should be avoided. Overlapping of voices should only be used for special effect. Within the limits of harmonic principles, each part should be made as melodically interesting as possible. This means that there should be no hesitancy to dispense with rules if the parts are harmonically sound and singable.

3. *Harmony Over the Bar Line*

Since the music progresses to a stressed beat over the bar line it is usually best to change the harmony. The same harmony over the bar line is weak and tends to give a monotonous effect.

4. *Difficult Skips*

All parts should be written in accordance with sound melodic principles. After wide skips, it is best to reverse direction unless the melody represents some chord. Do not skip after a stepwise run, as a rule, especially over the bar line. As mentioned above, be careful of wide skips in inner parts; they are usually difficult to sing. Avoid the augmented second and the augmented fourth intervals, especially in inner parts. Most important of all, avoid a descending skip of the seventh in the bass. Work out the passage so the skip down can be an octave. Then the basses will have no trouble since they handle skips of a fifth and octave easily.

SHIFTING OF THE MELODY

It is common practice for the sopranos to carry the melody. As a result, the inner parts often become a succession of repeated notes or otherwise very uninteresting melodically. To give the singers, as well as the listeners, more variety, it is wise to shift the melody between different parts. This practice should not be abused by trying to shift the melody every few notes. The change should usually be maintained for at least the length of a four measure phrase, if not longer.

CROSSING OF PARTS

At times, it may seem unavoidable to cross parts if interesting melodic lines are to be secured. This is often the case with inner parts (alto and tenor). However, it is a fact that any choral arrangement which has much crossing of parts is difficult and confusing to the average amateur singer. It is wise for the arranger to make adjustments so that the parts will not need to cross.

Especially is it unwise, in mixed-voice writing, to take the alto above the soprano and the tenor below the bass. It would be better to shift the melody to a different part before the necessity of crossing these parts arises.

In writing for male voices, since the harmonic spacing is so close, it is often necessary to cross parts, such as writing the second tenor above the first tenor and the interchange of baritone and second tenor parts. However, crossing of parts in male voice arrangements can be kept to a minimum by the judicious selection of keys and the careful shifting of melody at opportune times. Again, however, the arranger is cautioned not to shift the melody just with occasional notes, but for a considerable length of time, at least a musical phrase.

USE OF RESTS

An amateur arrangement can often be detected by the lack of imagination in the use of rests. The loveliest part of the music may be the rests. Don't continue all parts without any interruption. Permit one part to rest and bring it in later, perhaps in canonic treatment. This should not only be done to give the singers a rest, but also, for the musical effect. Dramatic pauses should be utilized in all parts. Make a study of the effective ways in which composers use rests.

CLOSING CADENCES

An arranger should be familiar with the effect of closing cadences. In fact, he should plan the type of cadence that he wishes to use in various sections of the piece and work toward them. He should acquaint himself thoroughly with the sound of the usual cadences as the following:

Preparatory   Cadence

$$\text{VI II}^6 \Big\}\ \text{I}^6_4 \qquad \text{V}^7 \qquad \text{I}$$

$$\left.\begin{matrix}\text{VI}\\\text{III}\end{matrix}\right\}\ \text{IV} \qquad \text{V}^7 \qquad \text{I}$$

$$\left.\begin{matrix}\text{I}^6\\\text{VI}\end{matrix}\right\}\ \text{II}^6 \qquad \text{V}^7 \qquad \text{I}$$

$$\left.\begin{matrix}\text{VI}\\\text{II}\end{matrix}\right\}\ \text{IV} \qquad \text{I}$$

These cadences are common. There are many other possibilities but the arranger must first be at home with these. Notice that the final chord is never used in fundamental position to prepare a cadence. Save it for the end so that it will sound fresh.

At the end of sections or the close of the piece, the arranger should study the effect of rising and falling cadences; the first gives the feeling of excitement or a majestic quality while the latter gives a feeling of repose. The entire character of an ending can be determined by the decision to take the bass up or down.

CLARITY OF WORDS

In vocal music words are paramount. They give precision and mood to the performance. Therefore, in arranging choral music the words must not be so covered by the music that they cannot be understood. The value of counterpoint and rhythmical shifts to make the parts more interesting are questionable if the use of these devices obscure the text, especially where the text is subtle or necessary to the full meaning of the music. Many arrangers resort to humming or a neutral vowel in the harmonic parts instead of the shifting of words to avoid covering the text. This is a moot point with arrangers, however.

CODAS

Just as with introductions, many arrangements seem to need a short ending of some kind beyond the body of the arrangement to give it a feeling of finality;

and also, to make it more attractive in performance. Sometimes this ending may be a replica of the introduction with a different cadence. It may grow out of a deceptive cadence, or it may have an individual character of its own. Compare the following coda with the introduction of the same arrangement in Ex. 7.

Ex. 12

CINDY*
(S.A.T.B.)

Chapter IV

MODERN CHORAL DEVICES

As long as music is written, composers and arrangers will be seeking new ways of expressing themselves. They will continue to experiment with different types of tonal-rhythmic patterns to obtain novel and unusual effects. However, there are no short cuts to mastery of the printed score and it is essential that the novice arranger be familiar with the practices of his predecessors before striking out for himself into unfamiliar and unknown tonal paths. Any creative art is built on experience and no one should seriously try to arrange choral music in a style with which he has had practically no association.

This statement does not mean, however, that an arranger should be satisfied with just the style of writing in which composers of the past have expressed themselves. He should seek different and novel ways continuously and incorporate them into his style as fast as he can master new techniques. This chapter is designed to give some hints to the neophyte arranger seeking more modern patterns of writing.

USE OF MODES

The old Ecclesiastical modes offer to the modern ear fresh combinations which have been partly lost during the past two centuries through almost complete adherence to our common major and harmonic minor scales. A thorough study of these modes are available in many harmony text books. The arranger can quickly get the spirit of them if he will play usual chord progressions using different white notes on the piano as key or tonal centers without employing any accidentals as in the following examples.

Ex. 13   Using only white notes with "D" as tonal center.

Using only white notes with "A" as tonal center.

These progressions give a very strong minor feeling, due largely to the use of the lowered seventh step at the cadence. To offset this quality in the majority of the modes, the early contrapuntal writers often made use of the raised seventh step as in the Ionian mode (which is the same as our major scale). They employed this mixed form of the modes along with the so-called pure form. Carrying this practice a little further, unusual effects can be obtained by alternating between major and minor chords in the normal progressions of one triad to another as in the following example.

Ex. 14

*MODERN CHORDS

Not only may the classic triads be used in fresh combinations and progressions but, in the present century, much experimentation has been carried on by composers in the construction of new chords.

1. Triads with added notes.

The most obvious of these chords is simply the addition of a note, usually the sixth, to a triad. This addition forms a secondary seventh chord without the restriction of the normal resolutions of these chords. Arrangers of popular songs have utilized this system to such a degree that it has almost become banal procedure. The following example shows the harmonic effect of these chords.

Ex. 15

2. Ninth, eleventh, and thirteenth chords.

With the expanded use of ninth, eleventh, and thirteenth chords in instrumental music, a natural development led to the distribution of the notes so that the chords were built on fourths. Only in polyvocal writing do we find chords of the eleventh and thirteenth in choral music and due to the intricacies of intonation they are used infrequently by most arrangers. The following composition makes excellent use of these luscious chords, however, in fine musical taste.

*Anyone wishing a succinct presentation of the newer trends in chord building and harmonic progressions should study, "New Harmonic Devices," H. A. Miller, Oliver Ditson Co., Philadelphia, Penna.

Ex. 16

EVERY WIND THAT BLOWS
FOR CHORUS OF MIXED VOICES
(UNACCOMPANIED)

Poem by
EUGENE PILLOT
By permission

Music by
LEIGHTON LUCAS

3. Chord building on fourths.

Chords built on fourths produce an effect which is very useful when introduced occasionally. The effect becomes too bizarre in choral writing when used for an extended passage. The following examples give some hint of the possibilities.

Ex. 17   Ex. 18

4. NEAPOLITAN TRIADS

The conception of the Neapolitan triad has been extended to include, not only the one for the tonic chord, but also, each chord of a key may have its own Neapolitan triad. The examples show the various Neapolitan chords of the key of C; a resolution of the Neapolitan triad of the tonic chord; and a typical resolution of one of the other Neapolitan chords of this key.

Ex. 19

Neapolitan triads of the Key of C.

Ex. 20

Ex. 21

5. Augmented sixth chords.

The use of augmented sixth chords has also been greatly expanded. The following examples show the usual augmented sixth chords and their traditional resolutions, as well as some of the newer combinations of augmented sixth chords. In fact, if the augmented sixth interval is preserved the inner voices may be shifted around almost at will.

Ex. 22

6. Whole-tone chords.

Closely associated with the augmented sixth chords are the almost inexhaustible combination of chords which can be derived from the whole-tone scales. Since there are twelve notes in the chromatic octave there can be only two of these scales. The notes of each scale can be combined into chords at will. Use of these chords in choral music is limited but they can often be introduced for striking or bizarre effects.

Ex. 23   SCALE I   SCALE II

MODERN PROGRESSIONS

The expansion of harmonic possibilities in piano and orchestral music has opened new vistas in harmonic progressions for the choral composer and arranger.

1. Modern resolution of chords.

One of the most striking changes in harmonic progressions has been the freeing of the rules in the resolution of dissonances. The prepared suspensions of an earlier period became independent notes of the chord itself. More complicated harmonies resulted and more choices in their resolutions followed. In fact, in instrumental music, practically any combination of notes may be used as a chord, especially if their resolution is chromatic or the voice leading smooth. In choral music the arranger must continually ask himself if these ultra-modern progressions are consistent with the idiom used throughout his arrangement; and also, if the progressions are singable by amateurs. The following examples give some idea of the possibilities.

Ex. 24

The use of the diminished octave in the following manner has a special piquant effect.

Ex. 25

LITTLE LAMB, WHO MADE THEE

WILLIAM BLAKE   HARRY ROBERT WILSON

From Choral Program Series, Book II,
Silver Burdett Co., New York   Used by permission

2. Parallel movement of chords.

A very effective choral practice, if not maintained for too long a time, is the parallel movement of the chords in a phrase. The parallel fifths in the bass of example 11 are common practice now. Also, open parallel fifths without the third of the chord have the flavor of olden times as well as a modern touch of the unusual. These liberties with fifths do not excuse the occasional and clumsy parallel fifths sometimes found in arrangements of traditional, classic harmony. These parallel fifths are due to errors in voice-leading, rather than intentional design. The following example shows the effect of parallel fifths and octaves in a sweep.

Ex. 26

ODE TO SOLITUDE

CHARLOTTE CAIN

NOBLE CAIN

Parallel movements need not be limited to fifths and octaves but may be used with any type of chord construction. Here are some whole-tone chords in fan shape, parallel movement.

Ex. 27

3. The Pyramid.

Building up to a full chord, part by part, is often used for special effect, usually at the beginning or end. However, it may be used in the body of the composition and more than one voice may be introduced at a time. Also, the chord may be built upward or downward.

Ex. 28

CONTRAPUNTAL AND CANONIC DEVICES

Since the contrapuntal style of writing is melodic it is especially gracious for choral arranging. The parts are more interesting for singers and also, usually more singable than parts conceived at the piano or those which resemble the instrumental style of writing. In arranging folk songs it is well to arrange at least one verse in contrapuntal style for variety. Also, the shifting of the melody to various parts, as suggested in the previous chapter, and writing contrapuntal lines for the other parts often gives added attractiveness to the arrangement. At the same time, this practice seems to retain the flavor of the simplicity of the original song rather than when it is accompanied with over-rich harmonies.

The counterpoint of today is usually much freer than the strict variety of the sixteenth and seventeenth centuries and it generally has a sound harmonic basis. But the practice of thinking parts melodically is a sound one for the choral arranger.

The arranging of, at least, some of the verses of a folk song in contrapuntal style gives opportunity for bridging verses and consequently, the feeling of continuity. This bridging is accomplished by having one part drop out and rest before the end of one verse, then entering before the part which is carrying the melody finishes that verse.

Ex. 29

WASSAIL SONG

Arr. Vaughan Williams

The choral arranger must be continually on the lookout for passages which can be written in canonic style, either at the unison, the octave, or some other interval. They are easy to sing and effective in performance.

Ex. 30

THE BELLS OF ST. MICHAEL'S TOWER

WM. KNYVETT
Arr. by R. P. Stewart

From *Choral Program Series Book V.* Silver Burdett Co. New York   Used by permission

RHYTHMIC EFFECTS

The modern arranger must study the various rhythmical devices which are effective. One of these devices is in the style of chanting a phrase while one of the parts carries the melody. It is beautifully done in the following excerpt.

Ex. 31

LOST IN THE NIGHT
(MIXED VOICES)

F. MELIUS CHRISTENSEN

Another rhythmic effect that is often used by arrangers is writing the harmonic parts as a choral accompaniment for the melody.

Ex. 32

LI'L LIZA JANE
(T.T.B.B.)

De LACHAU
Arr. by H. R. W.

Also, rhythmical effects may be employed by means of vocal sounds, clapping, or percussive instruments.

Ex. 33

SKIP TO MY LOU
(S.A.T.B.)

American Dance Tune
Arr. by H. R. W.

*)CALLER: Swing your partners all around, Right foot up and left foot down,
Swing your opposite across the hall, You haven't swung her since last fall,

Make that big foot jar the ground, Now promenade your honey 'round.
Now trot home and swing your own, And thank your stars the bird ain't flown.

*) Create an atmosphere of the old square dance. All eyes should be turned toward pianist. This section may be repeated as often as desired and solos on violin, harmonica, or jews'-harp may be introduced. If stage permits, a short dance can be performed by a group of eight in front of chorus. Different calls can be used.

HUMMING EFFECTS

The modern arranger often employs humming as an accompaniment for a solo, for rhythmical sound effects as suggested above, or, in quiet passages for the tonal loveliness of humming voices. The use of humming can be overdone and the arranger should be sure that it is an integral part of the total effect desired. Humming is most effective in *a cappella* work, where it serves as an accompaniment. It is ineffective when used with piano accompaniment unless the piano part is interwoven around the humming. With organ or orchestral accompaniment, humming is practically useless because it is covered up by the sustained harmony of the instruments.

Ex. 34

THOSE HOURS WITH YOU
(S.S.A.)

H. R. WILSON

NEUTRAL VOWEL EFFECTS

As suggested in the previous chapter, choral arrangers often use a neutral vowel in some parts to supply a harmonic accompaniment for the melody. This procedure is gradually replacing the older practice of shifting words and deleting part of the text in harmonic parts, because the singing of words in these parts often covers the complete text of the soloist or the part singing the melody.

Ex. 35

48

Neutral vowels may also be used in providing a rhythmical accompaniment, producing striking sound effects, or for tonal effects where words seem unnecessary.

Ex. 36

SIBONEY
(Glee Club T.T.B.B.)

English Words by
DOLLY MORSE

Spanish Lyric and Music by
ERNESTO LECUONA
Arr. by H. R. W.

THE DESCANT

In the early contrapuntal writing a florid melody, called a *descant* (singing against) often accompanied the more simple *cantus firmus*. In modern writing the descant is more like a countermelody based on the harmony. However, it should retain some of its florid character and is most effective when it is an independent melodic line and does not duplicate other parts. It is generally sung on a neutral vowel, although words drawn from the text may be used.

General rules for writing descants:

1. Make the descant an independent part.

2. Don't duplicate other parts unless it is absolutely necessary.

3. Enter at an advantageous point, usually where the other parts are sustaining a long note.

4. Sustained notes are good when parts are moving.

5. Figuration is good when parts are sustained.

6. The descant can be used to fill in the missing harmonic notes in the parts.

7. Some crossing of the descant with the soprano part is permitted just so long as it does not lose its own individual identity.

8. The top range of the treble voices may be extended somewhat in writing a descant but the *tessitura* must not lie extremely high for too long a time.

Ex. 37 a

SILENT NIGHT

JOSEPH MOHR

FRANZ GRUBER
Descant by Harry R. Wilson

Descant from "Songs We Sing"
Copyright 1940 Hall & McCreary Co., Chicago   Used by permission

Ex. 37 b

O COME, O COME, EMMANUEL

GREGORIAN MELODY
Descant by Charles Ripper

From Twice 55 Green Book, C. C. Birchard & Co., Boston   *Used by permission*

Ex. 37 c

AMERICA, THE BEAUTIFUL

KATHERINE LEE BATES   SAMUEL WARD
                                                 Descant by Harry R. Wilson

From "Songs We Sing" Hall McCreary Co., Chicago, *Used by permission*

THE SOLO VOICE

In early choral writing little use was made of the solo voice, probably due to the fact that there were usually only one or two voices on a part anyway. With the advent of larger choirs and a more harmonic style of writing, the need of solos to secure more variety in choral compositions became recognized. When a solo is used it may either be sung unaccompanied, with an accompaniment of voice parts; with instrumental accompaniment; or with a combination of instrumental and choral accompaniment. In arranging popular or folk songs for several voices it is usually wise to have one verse or, at least, a section of a verse written for a solo voice. However, the solo may be marked "optional" or "for a few selected voices" in case the choir does not have an adequate soloist. (See Ex. 32.)

USE OF SPEECH

With modern poetry there are passages which seem to defy musical settings. Therefore, some composers of choral music are resorting to declamatory passages in choral speech. This is very likely, however, a practice growing out of the desire for newer and more novel expression of creative ideas. At times, it is effective but it can be overdone and thus border on the theatrical. The choral arranger is free to use this device but he should be careful that when he does it is a natural outgrowth of the musical expression.

SUMMARY

In this chapter an effort has been made to point out some of the newer procedures and devices which the modern choral arranger can consider in his search for adequate means to express his musical ideas. Many of these newer trends are an outgrowth of the amazing development in instrumental composition. Therefore, they are not always equally successful in their adaptation to choral writing. It is well to remember that, with the technical limitations of the average amateur chorus, it is wise to avoid extravagant harmonic and contrapuntal means when simpler ones will express the music just as well.

CHORUS OF MIXED VOICES

Mixed choruses are those consisting of treble voices, (female or unchanged male) and changed male voices. The voice parts are labelled: soprano, alto, tenor, and bass. Each part is often divided into two sections (I and II). The number of singers on each part varies with different choirs, the ideal condition being when there is about an equal number on each part. However, the fact, as regards the greater number of mixed choruses is: sopranos are predominant in most groups, altos are usually too weak, tenors are just plain scarce, and basses usually manage to hold their own.

The arranger must consider the foregoing fact when assigning the melody and other important musical phrases to various parts. Nevertheless, balance of voice parts is the director's job and the arranger should not disregard the principles of good writing and produce a badly balanced score when writing for an unbalanced choir.

In arranging for the mixed chorus it is usual practice to use a separate staff for each voice part and the piano. Only one voice staff is usually necessary where a voice part is divided into two sections. However, if the entire composition (or a long section of it) is written *divisi* (divided parts) and the writing is so contrapuntal that words fall on different beats, it is best to use a separate staff for each section. The usual layout for mixed chorus score is as follows:

Ex. 38

Sometimes, to save space in an arrangement in straight harmonic style, the voice parts are condensed on two staves plus piano accompaniment. If the accompaniment is just a duplication of voice parts, it is often omitted altogether. This latter layout is found in all hymn books.

Ex. 39

As will be seen by these examples the old soprano, alto, and tenor clefs

are not used. In modern notation the

G clef is used for soprano, alto, and tenor parts with the tenor sounding one octave lower than it reads. The F clef is used for the bass part at all times; also the tenor part when scored in hymn style (see above). Then the tenor sounds the actual note that it reads. So the "poor" tenors must learn two clefs.

SATB COMBINATION

The combination most usually found in mixed choruses is that consisting of SATB (soprano, alto, tenor, bass). This is the combination used in most church, high school and college choirs. There are many fine examples of music for this combination written by the great composers which every arranger should study and analyze. The principles presented in the preceding chapters must be carefully observed in writing for this combination. The arranger must give constant attention to compactness in the spacing of parts, the range of voice parts, doubling of parts and the writing of parts that are melodically interesting. He should observe caution in the crossing of parts and shifting of the melody between parts.

Even in four-part writing for mixed voices there are times when it is necessary to divide parts for a few chords to express complete harmony. Sometimes division of parts can be avoided by careful voice leading before the necessity arises. When there is a need to divide parts, it is best to divide the soprano and bass parts, rather than the alto and tenor, because there is usually a shortage of altos and tenors in school and church choirs.

SAB COMBINATION

This shortage of tenors in the high school choirs (and almost the total lack of them in the junior high schools) has given rise to another type of mixed chorus, composed of soprano, alto, and bass parts. Since the range of the bass part must be limited, it is often labelled as baritone, although this classification is usually given to a *type* of voice, rather than a voice part.

The staves used are the same as those for SATB with the omission of the tenor part. They are presented here with the advisable range for each part. Notice that the voice ranges are reduced considerably from those given in Chapter II, due to the fact that this combination usually occurs in young choirs where the voices, especially those of the boys, are not developed.

Ex. 40

White notes indicate practical ranges. Black notes are possible, but not advisable.

In writing for this combination, care should be taken to write specifically for the SAB combination, rather than writing for an SATB combination and just omitting the tenor. Here, more movement of the alto and bass parts is necessary than in the four-part combination in order to obtain complete harmony with little or no doubling of parts. Since, in this way, the arranger is obliged to write more melodic parts, writing for this combination is good practice for him.

The bass part should be treated as a fundamental part, rather than as a tenor part with the piano supplying the bass, unless the music calls for this effect. Naturally, the root of the chord in the bass will result in an incomplete chord at the cadence if the melody also ends on the root of the chord. The alto, then, must end on the third unless the open fifth ending is desired. The normal progression of the alto, in some instances, does not lead easily to the third of the chord at the cadence. When such is the case the arranger may write the regular tenor part in small notes at the cadences, with instructions for a few basses to sing these added notes. It will produce a fuller and richer harmonic ending.

Ex. 41

IN STILLY NIGHT
(S. A. B.)

J. BRAHMS
Arr. by H. R. W.

(1) Choral Program Series, Book IV. Silver Burdett Co., New York.   Used by Permission.

In writing for the SAB combination, it is often wise to give the bass part a considerable portion of the melody. First of all, it is easier for the boys to learn; secondly, the incomplete harmonies are not so obvious. Due to the limitations of ranges in young voices, it would seem natural for the voice parts to be more compact; however, since there is no tenor, as in the SATB combination, care must be taken to avoid wide spacing so that the harmony will sound solid.

56

The old masters were adept at writing for mixed combinations of **three** parts such as: SAB, STB, or SAT. They leaned heavily on counterpoint and melodic harmony, which should be a key to the arranger today, even though he is writing for young inexperienced voices. The arranger can well afford to study some of the compositions written for mixed voices in three parts to gain a better understanding of the possibilities of this combination.

Many choral directors and arrangers disparage the musical quality of this combination and, to be sure, it is not as effective as a fuller one. However, music can successfully be written for SAB and there certainly is a need.

SA(A-T)B COMBINATION

Many teachers and directors who dislike the three-part combination of SAB are continually seeking four-part material for the combination soprano, alto, alto-tenor, bass. The problems are the same as in four-part mixed voice writing, except for the limited range of the alto-tenor part. The young fellows with changing voices are given the unusual classification of alto-tenors. Their tone is generally fuzzy in quality and their range extends over about a sixth

as follows: When writing for this

combination the range for the basses is the same as in SAB.

SB COMBINATION

There has been very little written for just a combination of two parts using treble and changed voices, indicated as soprano-baritone, high-low, or girls and boys. However, there certainly is a field here which needs to be exploited because such a combination would ideally fit the needs of many schools. The staff-layout for such a combination is as follows:

Ex. 42 a

The writing that has been done for this combination is in two general styles. The first treats the voices as in two-part writing of the soprano-alto type; however, the soprano range is not so high as when writing for treble voices alone, the baritone singing the harmony notes usually given the alto part. The melody should often be given to the boys for variety and also for the different tonal effect of having the harmony above the melody. The following examples illustrate this style:

Ex. 42 **b**

ODE TO JOY

L. VAN BEETHOVEN
Arr. by H. R. W.

From Soprano-Baritone Choruses, Auditorium Series No. 37 Copyright 1939 Hall & McCreary Co., Chicago, Ill. Used by permission.

Ex. 43

IN THE SILVERY MOONLIGHT
(AU CLAIR DE LA LUNE)

Translation by H. R. W.

FRENCH FOLK SONG
Arr. by H. R. W.

From Soprano-Baritone Choruses, Auditorium Series No. 37
Copyright 1939 Hall & McCreary Co., Chicago, Ill.
Used by Permission

The second style of writing for this combination is to write a rhythmic passage for one part, usually the baritones; and have the sopranos sing the melody. The melody can be switched around in this style, also. The following arrangement is a very effective illustration of this style.

Ex. 44

COMIN' THRU THE RYE

Arr. by Harry Simione

This combination invariably needs an accompaniment unless the group is singing a canon or a section of an arrangement in canonic style. This need is evident because the baritones are not usually singing the fundamental bass and also because the harmonies are incomplete throughout the arrangement.

SATB COMBINATION DIVIDED

In writing for more than four mixed voices, there are two general styles, often referred to as polyvocal (many voices) and polychoric (many choirs). In the first of these styles, each voice part is divided into two or more sections; in the second, the entire group is divided into two or more choirs. Of course, sometimes there is an overlapping and general fusion of these two styles in one composition. The staves for the divided parts are indicated as in the first example in this chapter (Ex. 38).

As mentioned in the explanation of that example, only four staves are necessary, unless the part-writing is so contrapuntal or complicated that the vocal line and words are not clear unless a separate staff is used for each part. In the latter case, eight staves are required. When the music is written for two distinct choirs, two of the regular SATB staves are used and are indicated as Choir I and Choir II.

There are many combinations of voices which may be used in writing the polyvocal style. Here are a few of them:

SSATB—a favorite of Brahms.

SATBB—contra basses give an orchestral quality.

SSATBB—meets the problem of the fewer number of altos and tenors.

SSATTBB—a favorite of popular song groups; a girls' trio with male quartet.

Ex. 45

AT PARTING

S.S.A.T.B.B.

FREDERIC PETERSON   HARRY R. WILSON

The use of two distinct choirs is probably most effective in antiphonal singing in which Choir II, generally smaller and sometimes placed off stage, repeats the phrases sung by Choir I. The most famous example of this style of writing is Palestrina's "Gloria Patri." Bach makes use of two choirs in the final chorus, "Here Yet Awhile" from the St. Matthew's Passion. However, he has both choirs sing the same four-part contrapuntal harmony except in phrases where the music seems to demand a division of the choirs. It is a beautiful example and should be studied by every choral arranger.

The writing of eight parts in homophonic style, where the male voices and treble voices answer each other (in the same manner as the choirs of an orchestra) makes an effective setting. This procedure should not be continued too long because it can become tedious very quickly. Even though this style is polyvocal, most amateur choruses have little trouble with it. Here is a good example: (See also Ex. 11).

Ex. 46

LET THY HOLY PRESENCE
S.S.A.T.T.B.B.
(A Cappella)

P. TSCHESNOKOFF
Edited and Arr.
NOBLE CAIN

Except for the sophisticated arrangements of popular songs, the choral arranger has little use of more than four parts with an occasional *divisi.* Folk songs do not usually need more than four parts for their adequate expression unless they are sung unaccompanied with rhythmic effects. The arranging of art songs seldom calls for more than four parts because they generally have an instrumental accompaniment.

It is the choral composer who sometimes needs a larger combination of voices to express his musical ideas. Of the earlier composers, it is worth studying the works of Giovanni Gabrielli to see how he wrote for large vocal combinations. His "Jubilate Deo" still has a modern ring. The unlimited possibilities in voice combinations can be studied in Vaughan William's "Serenade to Music" written for sixteen solo voices and Healy Willan's "An Apostrophe to the Heavenly Hosts" where he uses two four-part mixed choirs and two 'mystic choirs', one four-part mixed and the other three-part treble.

When a choral arranger decides to use more than four voice parts, except for an occasional *divisi,* he must realize that he is automatically limiting the number of amateur choirs that will have the personnel to sing his arrangements. Therefore, he should ask himself if the added voice parts are necessary for adequate musical expression.

CHAPTER VI

CHORUS OF TREBLE VOICES

The word "treble" is used in this chapter in preference to 'girls',' 'women's,' or 'female's' because the discussion is to include any treble voice group, including boys' choirs of unchanged voices. Moreover, many school treble choirs include both boys and girls. It is true that, of all the types of singing groups, there are far more girls' glee clubs than any other combination. Every high school and college has a girls' chorus, and now many women's clubs, musical and otherwise, are forming singing groups. In fact, writing for treble voice groups is the largest single outlet for a choral arranger's wares. It is probably the fastest way of gaining the attention of the publishers.

Of course, there are definite artistic limitations in writing for these groups. The total range is small and the monochrome (one color) quality of all the parts produces a monotonous musical effect. Therefore, writing for these groups should be limited to rather short numbers, extended arrangements being questionable unless enriched with an interesting orchestral accompaniment or male voice solo. Nevertheless, all choral arrangers and composers should know the problems of writing for these groups because to secure tonal variety in mixed-voice writing, sections of a composition are often arranged for treble voices alone.

Regardless of the number of parts, whether two, three, or four, it is usually best to have a staff for each part. Naturally, G clefs are employed on all staves.

Ex. 47

In writing for treble voice groups, it is safe and usually necessary to extend the normal ranges slightly over those given in Chapter II.

PIANO

If arrangement is to be sung unaccompanied and alto parts are low, they are often written in the bass clef.

See Ex. 53

SSA COMBINATION

Arrangements of treble voices are generally written for Soprano I, Soprano II, and Alto (three staves, one staff for each voice) plus accompaniment. The parts are sometimes indicated as 'High,' 'Medium,' and 'Low' so as to avoid any resentment on the part of the "big fellows" of being labelled sopranos and altos. This combination probably evolved because of the shortages of second altos in the schools. In writing for SSA, it is never wise to take the altos lower than G below middle C, it being best to limit the low range to A♭ except in soft work. Naturally, this limitation necessitates extension of the upper range of all parts one or two semi-tones. However, most treble voice groups are sufficiently well-trained to assimilate this slight increase of tessitura.

All the ingenuity that an arranger has is needed in order to write interesting music for these groups. Special effort should be exercised to make all parts melodic; also, rhythmical variety shall be employed between them. The contrapuntal style is especially needed when the piece is to be sung unaccompanied. Mendelssohn's "Lift Thine Eyes" from 'Elijah' is one of the most excellent examples of music written for this combination without accompaniment. The entire piece is included here in condensed score form for thorough study.

Ex. 48 **a**

LIFT THINE EYES
(S.S.A.)

FELIX MENDELSSOHN-BARTHOLDY

Ex. 48 a

First inversions of triads sound exceptionally well for this combination. Many composers have used them in a parallel sweep, such as the following excerpt of Gaul's "At Eventide It Shall Be Light" from 'The Holy City.' This type of progression has become rather common, however. For the most part, this composition is written in the same style as the foregoing Mendelssohn number and is equally worthy of thorough study.

Ex. 48 b

AT EVENTIDE, IT SHALL BE LIGHT
(From "The Holy City")

A. R. GAUL

From Choral Program Series, Book II
Silver Burdett Co., New York
Used by Permission

When writing for this combination in 'a cappella' style, a 'divisi' of the altos at the final cadence gives a more complete chord if the lower part takes the fundamental note.

Ex. 49

OFT IN THE STILLY NIGHT
(S.S.A. a cappella)

IRISH AIR
Arr. by H. R. W.

Most usually, arrangements for this combination should have piano accompaniments (see Chapter VIII for the various styles). The piano accompaniment provides the fundamental bass, especially for the ending, as well as a richer musical texture for the entire piece. However, where the contrapuntal style is employed (as, for example, in the three preceding excerpts) and the treatment of the parts is sufficiently interesting, no accompaniment is necessary.

When an accompaniment is used, the addition of other instruments, such as one or two violins, flutes, trumpets, etc., creates greater musical variety, as in the following example:

SOMEWHERE A CHILD IS SINGING

Ex. 50

S.S.A.

With optional obbligato for violin (or flute)

and, if feasible, a second violin

Text and Music by
PETER W. DYKEMA

All the devices suggested in previous chapters may be used in arranging for SSA, namely, shifting of the melody, use of canon, contrapuntal lines, rhythmic effects, humming, neutral vowels, discontinuance and overlapping of parts, descants, solos; all contributing to a more interesting arrangement.

SA COMBINATION

Although most choral directors of girls' glee clubs seem to prefer the SSA combination, there have been many fine duets written for soprano and alto which sound extremely well when sung by treble choral groups. An example of most successful writing for the SA combination is found in Pergolesi's, "Stabat Mater," written for soprano-alto with orchestral accompaniment. Here is one short excerpt.

Ex. 51

O HOW MOURNFUL
(O QUAM TRISTIS)

Translation by H. R. W.

GIOVANNI B. PERGOLESI
Arr. by Harry R. Wilson

From Choral Program Series, Book I, Silver Burdett Co., New York
Used by Permission

Another excellent example of writing (in the modern idiom) for this combination is "A Ceremony of Carols" by the English composer Benjamin Britten (pub. by Boosey & Hawkes, Inc.).

Since only two notes of the chord are represented, arrangements for the SA combination should have an accompaniment unless the piece is in canonic style. The accompaniment should be colorful but in keeping with the lightness of the vocal tone. The writing of an optional descant for selected voices introduced near the close gives an added part and a fuller ending without placing unreasonable demands upon the vocal facilities of the choral group (as in the following).

Ex. 52

LISTEN TO THE LAMBS

NEGRO SPIRITUAL
Arr. by H. R. W.

From Choral Program Series, Book I, Silver Burdett Co., New York
Used by Permission

For this combination, it is not wise to write for the alto below A or the soprano above F♯ or G. Often, parts are simply indicated as 'High' and 'Low' to avoid any resentment of the boys for having to sing parts marked 'Soprano' or 'Alto,' which, to them, represents something to be done by girls.

In writing for the SA combination, the most euphonious intervals are the third and the sixth. However, an occasional fourth or fifth, or the dissonance of the second, is often a relief from the continual sweetness of the third and sixth. Contrapuntal and canonic writing are especially gracious in a combination of two voices and part of every arrangement should include one of these styles.

It is questionable taste, except in the folk songs of the Latin-American countries, to use the soprano as a tenor part when the alto is singing the melody. Many of the Latin-American songs employ continual thirds sung by two parts. Such continual use of the same interval obscures the melody and consequently it loses its identity. This style is indigenous with some of the songs of these countries; however, the same device used for the folk songs of other countries will cause them to lose their native character.

There is a need for fine SA arrangements for choral performance aside from the incidental arrangements found in school songbooks. Arrangers will usually find a cordial reception from the publishers if they master the musical limitations of this combination and are able to write effective numbers for it.

SSAA COMBINATION

The most satisfactory sounding combination for treble voices is SSAA. The four parts offer an opportunity for complete chords with the fundamental, although the second alto quality cannot in anyway be considered as a bass. The number of choral groups which will attempt arrangements for this combination are limited. This is due to the shortage of altos who can sing low notes with a deep, rich quality. To offset this limitation, it is necessary to extend the normal range of the first sopranos to G or A♭ in writing for this combination.

Since complete four-part harmony is possible, the SSAA combination lends itself to unaccompanied writing better than any of the other treble voice combinations. Nevertheless, it is not wise to write extended arrangements for SSAA without accompaniment because there still remains the monochrome tonal quality of treble voices alone.

Brahms wrote a number of choral pieces for the SSAA combination, constructed on a sound harmonic bass but each part an interesting and singable melodic line. They are all worth serious study. The following excerpt is a complete verse of one of the loveliest of these pieces. It is written with accompaniment but may be sung a cappella.

Ex. 53

LOVE SONG
S.S.A.A.

English Text Adapted by H. R. W.

JOHANNES BRAHMS
Edited by Harry R. Wilson

From Choral Program Series Book II Silver Burdett Co., New York   Used by Permission

Ex.53 Cont.

love song I sing to-day, For the fair - est,

love song I sing to-day, For the fair - est,

love song I sing to-day, For the fair - est,

love song I sing to-day, For the fair - est,

and the rar - est, Smiles her thanks for my love song gay.

and the rar - est, Smiles her thanks for my love song gay.

and the rar - est, Smiles her thanks for my love song gay.

and the rar - est, Smiles her thanks for my love song gay.

CONCLUSION

Much missionary work is needed to influence treble glee clubs to sing in four parts (SSAA)) instead of the usual three parts (SSA). Many more musical arrangements that are worthwhile should be written for the four-part combination. Any glee club that has the technical proficiency to sing in three parts can sing in four parts if the slightly extended range of the outside parts can be surmounted. If arrangers realize and study the possibilities of this combination, and learn how to write well for it, perhaps they can provide directors with much needed material which their singing groups can master.

CHAPTER VII

CHORUS OF MALE VOICES

When we speak of a chorus of male voices we refer to changed voices. Unchanged boys' voices come under the problem of treble choirs. Although male glee clubs have a monochrome effect (as in treble choirs), the quality of the voices is so rich and vibrant that it is more feasible to write longer works for male voices than for treble.

In writing for a chorus of male voices, it is sometimes necessary to extend the normal range of the first tenors and second basses a semitone beyond the range indicated in Chapter II. The use of the *falsetto* in the tenor voice, for high *pianissimo* passages, not only gives an extended range of several semi-tones, but also, an additional quality of tone which can be used with unique effect. The Russian male choirs are especially adept in the use of the *falsetto* for unusual musical effects. The usual staves and clefs for male voice writing are as follows:

Ex. 54

TTBB COMBINATION (STANDARD)

Of all the combinations of voices, treble or mixed, the four-part male glee club lends itself best to unaccompanied singing. This is due partly to the quality of voices, but mostly, to the compactness of harmony in a low range.

In the standard style of writing for the TTBB combination the melody is normally in the first tenor. When the melody is shifted to one of the lower parts, the upper parts are usually written in a contrapuntal style. It is impossible to avoid continual crossing of parts without shifting the melody because of the closeness of the harmony. To avoid this continual crossing of parts, some arrangers often shift the melody for just a few notes, even for only one or two. When this is done the melody becomes lost. As was suggested in writing for other combinations of voices, it is best not to shift the melody for less than a musical phrase. The crossing of parts is usually found in the first tenor moving below the second tenor to carry the lower notes of the melody, the two parts seeming to interchange for a time. This crossing, when used, should be done gracefully, as regards the melodic lines of the two parts. It occurs most often at the closing cadences when the melody descends. The following example illustrates the crossing of the tenor parts at the cadence:

Ex. 55

AT PARTING
FOR MEN'S VOICES
(A Cappella)

FREDERIC PETERSON   HARRY R. WILSON

Humming is especially effective as an accompaniment to the melody or a soloist. Descants, as such, are practically never written. Canonic writing automatically produces continual crossing of parts which, however, is easy, sounds natural, and is very effective. In writing for male voices there is always the tendency to write the lush harmony produced by over-chromaticism. This gives the effect of "barber-shop" writing and should be avoided unless this effect is deliberately intended. Rhythmical and sound effects seem especially appropriate in writing for male voices and, as a novelty, even whistling might be introduced, although purists would probably say that the arranger was departing from anything that resembled music.

TTBB COMBINATION (BARBER-SHOP)

The famous American style of singing labelled "barber-shop" or "curbstone" harmony is probably the only style of singing which has an association designed to preserve its existence, namely, the SPEBSQSA (The Society for the Preservation and Extension of Barber-Shop Quartet Singing in America). Although this style of singing is often frowned upon by serious composers as being banal and over-saccarine, the fact remains that it is greatly enjoyed by most amateur groups. It is true that the style best fits the old-time popular music and has no place in the more serious style of writing.

In barber-shop writing the melody is invariably in the second tenor, so the parts are often called top tenor, lead, baritone, and bass. In many barbershop quartets the harmonies are faked, that is, sung without the aid of notes. In writing a number in this style to be sung by a male quartet or glee club, the arranger should try to retain the same spontaneous harmonic quality. A little participation on his own part in some barber-shop singing will give him an instinctive feel for the parts.

Humming may be used but very seldom. Canonic and contrapuntal writing have little place. Descants are a foreign language. Close harmony prevails. Chromaticism comes into its own. The *portamento* style of the singing opens up vistas of the possibilities of divided semitones. Keys must be carefully chosen with regard to keeping the melody preponderantly in the lead tenor so as to retain the individuality of this style. All types of rhythmic effects are good. There is a continual crossing of the second tenor and baritone parts but this does not cause confusion. The other parts practically never cross. Occasionally, it is necessary to shift the melody to the first tenor but in so doing the purity of the style is somewhat lost. Here is a typical example of barber-shop harmony:

Ex. 56

TELL ME WHY

ANONYMOUS
Arr. by Harry R. Wilson

From Choral Program Series, Book IV, Silver Burdett Co., New York
Used by Permission

The following excerpts, taken from a modern arrangement in modified barber-shop style, indicate possible devices and procedures:

Ex. 57

THE WHIFFENPOOF SONG
(BAA! BAA! BAA!)
GLEE CLUB T.T.B.B.

Revision by
RUDY VALLEE

By
MEADE MINNERGERODE
GEORGE POMEROY
TOD B. GALLOWAY
Arr. by H. R. W.

(THE WHIFFENPOOF SONG - later section)

Ex. 60 (THE WHIFFENPOOF SONG - 2nd chorus)

Another style of barber-shop writing is for the lead (or second) tenor to sing a phrase as a solo while the other parts join in on the second phrase of the period. This procedure is especially appropriate for humorous or dialect songs. As a rule, all parts join together on the refrain. Here is an excerpt to illustrate this style.

Ex. 61
R. H. H.

WHO DAT A-CALLIN' ME?

RUTH HUFFMAN HUNT
Edited by Harry R. Wilson

From Choral Program Series Book III Silver Burdett Co., Chicago By Permission

It is at the closing cadences that barber-shop harmony comes into its own. All kinds of weird changes may be experimented with. Practically anything goes as long as the final triad is reached by all voices at the same time. Many arrangers, including the writer, are much more conservative in the writing of barber-shop cadences because the style can easily be carried to the point of bad taste. Here are some of the endings often sung by barber-shop quartets.
Ex. 62

✱ From Choral Program Series Book III Silver Burdett Co., New York   Used by Permission

TBB COMBINATION

Due to the shortage of first tenors a considerable amount of experimenting is being done in writing for three-part male choruses. Sometimes the three parts are indicated as TTB (tenor, tenor, bass) but it is more consistent to label the combination TBB (tenor, baritone, bass). Although this combination lacks the fullness and richness of TTBB arrangements, some fine compositions have been written for TBB, as exemplified by the following classic excerpt:

Ex. 63

VERE LANGUORES NOSTRES *
T.B.B.

ANTONIO LOTTI

* Originally in
G minor for T.T.B.

From Choral Program Series Book III
Silver Burdett Co., New York
Used by Permission

Usually the arrangements for this combination are designed for glee clubs of boys and young men, therefore, it is wise to reduce the voice ranges for the various parts. The staves and most practical vocal ranges are as follows.

Ex. 64

All of the various suggestions made in Chapter III to make arrangements interesting are effective in writing for this combination. There need not be as much crossing of parts in the TBB arrangement as in the TTBB, due to the elimination of one inner part which causes the harmony to be somewhat more 'spread.' Since these arrangements are for young voices, it is wise to avoid crossing of parts unless the style is contrapuntal or canonic.

The barber-shop style of writing calls for four-parts; therefore, arrangements for the TBB combination will follow closely the style of writing for the standard TTBB combination. However, a semblance of the barber-shop style can be attained wherever it is desired and appropriate. A considerable amount of unison is good because it is learned more easily by young groups. It is also effective to have different phrases of the melody sung in unison by various combinations of parts.

If the melody is in the tenor and descends, say as low as F, the final cadence may cause trouble since then the baritone and bass parts are too low and a unison ending becomes necessary. When the ending is an ascending cadence, a chord with two roots (tenor and bass) and a third (baritone) is the usual result. A complete chordal ending can be attained by dividing the tenors on the last chord, giving the fifth to the second tenor. When the baritone is carrying the melody, the basses may divide on the last chord to give a complete chordal ending. Since the bass in the TBB combination is treated as a *fundamental* bass, the endings are not written as in the SSA combination. These various endings are illustrated by the following examples. Condensed scores are used to save space.

Ex. 65

From Choral Program Series Book III   Silver Burdett Co., New York   Used by Permission

There is no question that, if a glee club can handle TTBB arrangements, it should not sing TBB numbers except where compositions are especially written for this combination, such as example No. 63. Since many schools cannot handle the four-part male arrangements (because of a serious lack of first tenors and second basses), their male glee clubs are dependent upon TBB arrangements; or, very simple compositions for TTBB with limited voice ranges.

TB COMBINATION

Arrangements for this combination (tenor-baritone) are designed for boys glee clubs that lack the vocal equipment with which to sing TTBB or TBB arrangements. At times, a composition may lend itself to two-part writing for changed male voices, as in songs for tenor and baritone duets. The latter, however, are usually too pretentious for young male glee clubs to perform.

The voice ranges for this combination must be kept as narrow as posible within the scope of the musical expression desired. The following ranges are usable.

Ex. 66

Arranging for the TB combination is usually done in one of two styles. It is often treated as an SA combination singing one octave lower. In this style there is no attempt to make the baritone a fundamental bass but rather to treat it as an alto part. The other style is to treat the TB combination as a male voice combination (TTBB) with the lower parts omitted. Here the baritone part usually carries the melody; the tenor part sings in the usual tenor idiom. Both of these styles can be used in the same arrangement for contrast.

The following examples show the general treatment of the parts in both styles. Of course, the Brahms' number was written especially for this combination. Although part of its beauty is dependent upon the lovely accompaniment, the parts themselves are worthy of concentrated study.

Ex. 67

LOVE SONG
(LIEBESLIEDER No. 14)

English Text by H. R. W.

JOHANNES BRAHMS
Edited by Harry R. Wilson

From Choral Program Series Book III
Silver Burdett Co., New York
Used by Permission

86

Ex. 68

HOME ON THE RANGE

Arr. by H. R. W.

From "SONGS OF HILLS & PLAINS"
Copyright 1943 Hall & McCreary Co., Chicago

Used by Permission

Two-part contrapuntal and canonic devices, which the author has been pointing out throughout the book, should permeate the writing in the two styles illustrated above. These devices are best shown by an example such as the following:

MASTERS IN THE HALL

OLD FRENCH CAROL
Arr. by H.R.W.

From Choral Program Series Book III   Silver Burdett Co· New York   Used by Permission

It is wise to use considerable unison in arranging for the TB combination, to be sung by both parts or shifted between parts. Closing cadence problems occur in the same way as in TBB combination and the same solutions are appropriate. One caution should be observed, that is: writing for TB should never be thought of as just a melody and a fundamental bass with the inner parts missing. Of course, this effect may be used if desired but, as a rule, it is empty and bizarre. The TB combination invariably needs a piano accompaniment except, possibly, for contrapuntal or canonic sections.

CONCLUSION

Good, easy, and singable arrangements are needed for young male glee clubs. It is difficult to interest boys in singing, but one sure way is to organize a male glee club, and the constant cry is for material written especially for them.

There may be occasions where an arranger wishes to divide the male voices into more than four parts to retain the harmony of the original piece. This is exceptional, however, because of the lowness and closeness of the harmony, more than four parts become too "muddy" in color. Besides most glee clubs have enough trouble with TTBB arrangements and compositions. (See "Temptation," ex. No. 4.)

Chapter VIII

THE ACCOMPANIMENT

It is the opinion of the author, after examining hundreds of choral manuscripts submitted to him by students, that it is in the writing of piano accompaniments where most novice arrangers meet their nemesis. The effectiveness of interesting vocal lines can be completely spoiled by an amateurish accompaniment. Every choral arranger should study the vocal and choral works of such masters as Robert Schumann and observe his skill in writing varied types of accompaniments that are musically interesting.

Of course, the easiest way to avoid the writing of 'bad' accompaniments is to arrange all numbers to be sung *a cappella* (or unaccompanied). However, as mentioned in the previous chapters, certain combinations of voices, such as SA, SSA, TB, TTB, SB, and SAB, usually need an accompaniment to fill in the missing harmonies and provide added musical interest. Writing unaccompanied arrangements for any combination of voices requires a skilled hand to make the voice parts sufficiently interesting to stand alone.

ACCOMPANIMENT FOR REHEARSAL ONLY

Usually, when a choral number is arranged for *a cappella* singing, an accompaniment which is a duplication of the voice parts is included on the manuscript. This is only intended as an aid, "For Rehearsal Only" and is often engraved in small notes. The same practice is followed where, in compositions that have an accompaniment, certain sections are to be sung *a cappella.* The following example illustrates this procedure:

Ex. 70

HE NEVER SAID A MUMBALIN' WORD
(EIGHT PART MIXED CHORUS)

Spiritual Arr. by
HARRY R. WILSON

As a rule, few choral arrangers today feel the necessity of an accompaniment which just duplicates the voice parts, except to facilitate learning the piece at rehearsals. Most directors, also, prefer to have arrangements sung unaccompanied when they are so intended; however, because of the flatting in pitch of their singers, they often resort, out of desperation, to the use of a piano accompaniment.

OPTIONAL ACCOMPANIMENT

Some arrangements, notably those for SSA, TBB, and SAB, even for SATB, call for a degree of support of the voice parts, even though they are musically satisfying in themselves. In such cases an optional accompaniment is often written. These accompaniments may or may not be used at the discretion of the director. They usually follow the rhythmical and chordal pattern of the voice parts, but fill in the missing harmonies and further enrich the harmony by using fuller chords in the right hand and often octaves in the bass. The following excerpt illustrates an optional accompaniment for a simple SAB composition:

Ex. 71

GOD BE IN MY HEAD

Words from the
SARUM PRIMER, (1588)

H. R. W.

RHYTHMICAL ACCOMPANIMENTS

Many folk-songs of a lively nature need only a simple rhythmical accompaniment to bring out their spirit. This type of rhythm is sometimes called an "oom-pah" accompaniment. It is often embellished when used as an accompaniment in published arrangements. This favorite play-party song is an example:

SKIP TO MY LOU

American Dance Tune
Arr. by H. R. W.

CALLER: Choose your partners, folks!

(Clapping on two measure introductions of each verse is optional)

Of course, there are other types of rhythmical accompaniment which are appropriate, especially in the arranging of folk dances or popular songs. The arranger must be careful that a rhythmical accompaniment does not become

92

monotonous. He can avoid this by employing figuration while retaining the basic rhythmical pattern. Here are several styles of rhythmical accompaniment:

Ex. 73

HOLIDAY PARADE
Four Part S.A.T.B.

Words by
MITCHELL PARISH

Music by
DOMENICO SAVINO

Ex. 74

A HEART THAT'S FREE
(S. S. A.)

A. G. ROBYN
Arr. by Hugo Frey

BLUE MOON
Three Part S. S. A.

Lyric by
LORENZ HART

Music by
RICHARD RODGERS
Arr. by Hugo Frey

MELODIC ACCOMPANIMENTS

A favorite style of accompaniment to support the voice parts, and, at the same time add a little musical interest, is the practice of playing the melody in either the right or left hand of the piano part. This procedure makes the piano part almost a little composition in itself. It supports the voices and, although not distinct from them, has individual musical interest. This practice is invariably followed in the arranging of popular songs although it is by no means limited to them. The melody is often switched in the piano part in the same manner as in the voice parts. The following short excerpt is typical:

Ex. 76

THOSE HOURS WITH YOU
(S.S.A.)

Words and Music by
HARRY ROBERT WILSON

94

EMBELLISHING ACCOMPANIMENTS

The master composers of song have given us the best examples of florid accompaniments. They are of all types but are usually based upon some kind of *arpeggio* figuration. In writing these types of accompaniments, the arranger should be careful that they are an integral part of the composition and not just a display of piano technique with little relation to the musical expression of the voice parts.

In using *arpeggios* as the basis for accompaniments, the arranger should be sure to hold them in place with a fundamental bass, otherwise, they will seem to be at loose ends and almost fly off of the manuscript paper. In other words, don't depend too much upon the pianist's artistic use of the sustaining pedal to make the accompaniment sound. All the necessary notes and their duration should be plainly indicated.

Ex. 77

DEDICATION
(TO SINFONIANS EVERYWHERE)
OP. 25 No. 1

English Text
by Harry R. Wilson

ROBERT SCHUMANN
Arr. by J. Hubert Liverman

From Choral Program Series Book III
Silver Burdett Co., New York
Used by Permission

DIFFICULT ACCOMPANIMENTS

The foregoing section suggests a caution about the writing of difficult accompaniments. The skill of the accompanist of most amateur choirs is often limited. The arranger who writes piano accompaniments that require virtuosity is borrowing trouble. It is a keen disappointment for a choral director to train his group to render an expressive and musical performance of the voice parts and then have the effectiveness marred by the inability of the accompanist to play the accompaniment. The same is true of band and orchestral accompaniments. Naturally, the accompaniment must be musically adequate but should be playable by the average pianist.

INDEPENDENT ACCOMPANIMENTS

Some arrangers and composers have written accompaniments which are partially, or even totally, independent of the voices and still effect a satisfying musical expression. This type of accompaniment is usually found in original compositions rather than arrangements. As long as the two (accompaniment and voice) form a synchronized whole, the result is musically pleasing. When the accompaniment completely absorbs the musical interest, the singers often have a feeling of futility which distracts from their performance. This type of accompaniment should only be attempted after much experience in composing or arranging.

96

For instance, the accompaniment of the Liebeslieder Waltzes of Brahms
sound extremely well as a piano duet, but still, when the choral parts are
sung with this completely independent four-hand piano accompaniment, the
dual result is a unified artistic composition of musical charm. The following is
an excerpt from one of these waltzes:

Ex. 78

LOVE WALTZ
(LIEBESLIEDER No. 13)

Translated by H. R. W.   JOHANNES BRAHMS

From Choral Program Series Book I
Silver Burdett Co., New York
Used by Permission

FOUR-HAND ACCOMPANIMENTS (ONE PIANO)

The foregoing example illustrates the possibilities of using four-hand accompaniments, a type of accompaniment that has been greatly neglected in choral writing. It is true that another piano staff per page needs to be engraved and publishers are continually thinking of costs and practicability. However, the musical effectiveness of an expanded accompaniment would certainly offset these objections where an arrangement would be enhanced by a four-hand accompaniment. Moreover, every chorus usually has among its ranks some member who can assist the regular accompanist by playing the *secondo* part.

It so happens that one of the most successful choral arrangements of recent times utilizes a four-hand accompaniment of considerable ingenuity. The following excerpts are from this arrangement:

Ex. 79

Ex. 80

TWO-PIANO ACCOMPANIMENTS

There is a similar need in choral writing for arrangements with a two-piano accompaniment. By the use of two pianos, an orchestral solidity can be secured. The problem here *is* practical. It is difficult for many schools to have two pianos that are in tune, or have some semblance of tonal balance available on one stage. Many schools are lucky to have one piano — two are usually out of the question. Thus, a two-piano accompaniment greatly limits the possibilities of performance. Most choral compositions which require a two-piano accompaniment are usually published also in an edition in which the accompaniment is reduced so that it can be played on one piano (by one pianist). Unless this can be done, it seems wise for an arranger to confine his expanded accompaniments to four hands using one piano.

PIANO ACCOMPANIMENT WITH INSTRUMENTS

Most schools have an instrumental organization, either band or orchestra. If not, there are usually a few instrumental players around the school who are eager for a chance to perform. It would be advantageous for choral directors to make use of these players. However, there are very few choral arrangements which call for a small number of instruments with the piano as an accompaniment.

In Chapter VI the advantages of using one or two instruments with treble voices was pointed out. There are unlimited possibilities in this area and, if such arrangements were made available, they would probably be popular with choral directors.

A list of instrumental combinations which could be used with piano to add to the musical interest of choral arrangements would include: two violins; two trumpets; violin and cello; violin, viola and cello; brass quartets of different combinations, especially with male voices; two flutes; flute and clarinet; two clarinets; two French horns; harp; and tympani. It is obvious that the possibilities are practically unlimited. Choral accompaniments which include additional instruments often afford a delightful relief from the uniform color of singing voices. A few examples will show how some composers have made use of such accompaniments:

Ex. 81

SONG FROM OSSIAN'S FINGAL

J. BRAHMS

Ex. 82

BEFORE THE PALING OF THE STARS

S.S.A.A.

(SOPRANO SOLO AND TWO TRUMPETS)

ad libitum

CHRISTINA ROSETTI

ERNEST KANITZ

BAND AND ORCHESTRAL ACCOMPANIMENTS

Music educators are continuously urging directors of choral and instrumental groups to combine their efforts for the added educational and musical values to the participants. This idea is gradually gaining converts and more and more regular programs as well as festival programs contain, at least, one choral number with band or orchestral accompaniment. The author makes a practice of including one number of this nature on the numerous programs which he conducts.

As in the case with the piano accompaniment, the director does not usually have a professional orchestra or band at his disposal. The technique of the players is often limited, and also, there is usually insufficient rehearsal time for the instrumental accompaniment. Moreover, the combined rehearsals of singers and instruments are usually hurried affairs. Therefore, during the *writing* of the instrumental accompaniment, the arranger or composer should use all his ingenuity to insure adequate results with such limited means.

The arranger would be wise to consider carefully a few other cautions. Avoid any accompaniment which may be too heavy for immature or undeveloped amateur voices. Avoid needless technical difficulties when a simpler solution will be just as effective. Avoid the extreme ranges of instruments, which invite "out of tune" playing, especially in the woodwinds. It is well to provide a generous supply of optional, as well as cued-in, parts in anticipation of the instruments which may be missing in the ensemble.

Practically every school has a creditable band although the orchestra may be meager and struggling. Still, orchestral accompaniments are far more available than those for band. Regardless of the musical superiority of the orchestra as an accompaniment for voices, there is a practical need for more choral numbers with band accompaniment. It is beyond the scope of this book to discuss the techniques of arranging for amateur bands and orchestras. The reader is referred to such books as Paul Yoder's, "Arranging for the School Band," Robbins Music Corp., and A. O. Andersen's, "Practical Orchestration," C. C. Birchard and Co.

CONCLUSION

At the risk of being redundant, the author wishes to close this chapter with a statement similar to the one which he made in the beginning. So often in arranging for amateur choral groups (and most of them are amateur) it is the accompaniment which may be the deciding factor in the success or failure of the arrangement. So often the choral arranger is likewise a choral director and has a natural feel for voice lines. Consequently, he needs to strengthen his techniques in writing musical accompaniments if his work is to possess professional flavor. In writing accompaniments the arranger should continually ask himself such questions as the following: Is the accompaniment pianistic? Does it lie well under the hands? Does it have rhythmical flow? Were the choral motives and figurations utilized in the accompaniment (see ex. 52)? A complete book could be written on this subject and so the author urges the reader to make a systematic study of the developments and styles in writing piano accompaniments for voices.

CHAPTER IX

THE TEXT

Since choral music is dependent upon words, the text must receive consideration equal to that given the music. The composer must choose his texts carefully because the literary quality of the words is usually reflected in the musical quality of the music. Fine poems beget fine music. Of course, some of the masters did write glorious music to some rather banal texts but this was because their genius rose above the mediocrity of the words.

SUITABILITY OF TEXTS

As mentioned in a previous chapter, the choral composer can turn to the bible, standard poetic works, or lyrics of recognized worth by modern poets. Some adaptation may become necessary when using literary works for musical settings. This is permissible provided the poetry is not mutilated. Some poetry, although fine as poetry, may not necessarily lend itself to a musical setting and is therefore best left alone. This decision we leave to the composer.

The writing of lyrics for a popular song is a professional job which very few amateurs can hope to do with success. There is nothing as bad as a bad popular lyric and the amateur composer who has ambitions to write in this field should seek professional collaboration.

Unlike the composer, the choral arranger, unless he is both composer and arranger of a song, has the words given to him along with the melody, and so it becomes a matter of the selection of suitable verses and an editorial job.

SINGABILITY OF TEXTS

Some excellent poems, although they are fine as literature, are not singable. All texts should literally sing themselves. Combinations of words containing double consonants are difficult to sing and do not foster lovely *legato* lines. The words must 'flow into each other' as in much of the poetry of Robert Burns. The following poem is an example of one which is so filled with double consonants that to set it to music would be a hazardous task.

Ex. 83

WORLD, TAKE GOOD NOTICE

World, take good notice, silver stars fading,
Milky hue ript, weft of white detaching,
Coals thirty-eight, baleful and burning,
Scarlet, significant, hands off warning,
Now and henceforth flaunt from these shores.
from"Leaves of Grass"—Walt Whitman

Nevertheless, many modern choral composers are turning to the free verse of Walt Whitman to best express their musical ideas. Many of the lines of his poetry have beautiful lyric quality. For example:

Ex. 84

a. 'Look down, fair moon, and bathe this scene.'
b. 'O, a new song, a free song.'
c. 'Out of the cradle endlessly rocking.'
d. 'I hear America singing.'

It is interesting to note that all of these poems have been used by well-known modern composers for musical settings.

As a rule, it is well to be careful of poems with too many sibilant consonants. Try singing, "Let us set sail on the bounteous sea." Try to avoid double consonants of 'd' followed by 'b' or 't' as in 'soothed by' or 'loud tone'; also, words ending in 't' when followed by a word beginning with 't' such as 'last time.' There are countless little rules and things to watch but the best practice is to read the words aloud to make sure they flow; and then, try singing them to a melody.

The following poem is the quintessence of an easy flow of words. So much so, in fact, that it seems like a song without a melody.

Ex. 85

Ode
WE ARE THE MUSIC MAKERS
(First Verse)

We are the music makers,
And we are the dreamers of dreams,
Wandering by lone sea-breakers,
And setting by desolate streams;—
World-losers and world-forsakers,
On whom the pale moon gleams:
Yet we are the movers and shakers
Of the world forever it seems.

A. O'Shaughnessy

When editing a text, the arranger should sing the various parts to see if the words flow easily in each part. Sometimes, the words sing well in one part but, due to the melodic construction of another part, they are clumsy. A slight rhythmical change in the part may correct the difficulty. At times, slight changes in the words, especially the unimportant ones, may produce a more even flow without impairing the poetry. Be as careful with the musical flow of the words as of the voice parts.

ACCENT OF WORDS AND MUSIC

In addition to the attention which must be given to the euphony of words, an equal amount of care must be devoted to having the accent of the words synchronize with the accent of the music within a bar. A composer should read and scan a poem many times until the natural inflection of the words suggests a meter and melodic line for the music.

The arranger must be just as careful, when arranging songs (especially folk-songs) for voice combinations. Securing agreement of musical accent with text presents a marked difficulty especially in contrapuntal writing, where the melodic lines of the lower or inner parts may need considerable rhythmic revision from their original form. If an arranger is careless in this, the inevitable result is an inartistic performance due to the unmusical phrasing and nuance. Also, since the response of singers is more spontaneous when there is a natural accent and rhythm of words, a failure to match accent of words and music often presents actual tonal and rhythmic difficulties.

The following examples may shed a little light on the problem.

Ex. 86 Abide With Me

A - bide with me! Fast falls the e-ven-tide The dark-ness deep-ens

In this old hymn, the accent of words and music do not coincide at places marked X. However, this fact did not deter its popularity.

Ex. 87 It Came Upon A Midnight Clear

And the whole world sends back the song which now the an-gels sing.__

This unnatural accent comes in the last line of the third verse.

Ex. 88

Cradle Song

J. Brahms

Lull-a - by and good-night!

The clumsiness of the word and music accent in this translation at point marked X causes most people to sing the measure in this rhythm.

by   and good

Ex. 89 Yankee Doodle

Fa - ther and I   Fath'r and I

Editors have always been puzzled as to whether to use the original version, No. 1, with its unnatural accent or No. 2 with correct accent but crowded syllables to sing. Neither one is very satisfactory.

RHYMING OF WORDS

Normally, poems that have a pattern of rhyme seem to lend themselves to a musical setting better than poems written in free verse. Because of this, the rhyming dictionary becomes the arranger's best friend when editing the texts of folk songs or in making translations for art songs.

If, however, in an effort to secure a consistent pattern of rhymes, the meaning of the poetry is distorted, or wrong accent of words and music occur, or, unsingable vowels and consonants arise, it is best to relinquish the rhyming pattern momentarily, or, write a smooth text without rhymes. The following poetry, when interpreted correctly, does not rhyme but is so musical and euphonious that it serves as an ideal vehicle for a choral number, especially one in contrapuntal style. In fact, the author came under the spell of its beauty recently and composed a SATB choral number using this poem:*

Ex. 90

A THING OF BEAUTY

A thing of beauty is a joy for ever:
Its loveliness increases; it will never
Pass into nothingness; but still will keep
A bower quiet for us, and a sleep
Full of sweet dreams, and health, and quiet breathing.
from "Endymion"—John Keats

WORDS ON HIGH NOTES

Arrangers unfamiliar with the difficulties which singers have with certain vowels on high notes present added problems in the work of choral directors. In fact, some directors select their music with extreme care with regard to the singable vowels found on extreme high notes. A wise choral arranger will not write high notes using words that contain the vowels, *ee, i,* (especially as in *ing*), *eh,* or *ay* for unchanged treble voices. These vowels must be modified by sopranos from about a top line 'F' on up. Untrained voices who do not understand this literally "choke themselves to death" trying to sing them. On the other hand, the tenors and baritones have little trouble singing these vowels on high notes, in fact, they are often easier than the open vowels of *ah, aw* and *oh.* These latter vowels, especially the *ah,* are the most gracious to treble voices on their high notes. The *oo* vowel is neutral and can be used almost at will, although sopranos need to open it on extreme high notes.

The importance of an easy flow of consonants in the text has been pointed out. This fact is increasingly true in sections of the music which lie high for the part, especially soprano. The difficulty of singing the high section

*"A Thing of Beauty," Carl Fischer, Inc., New York.

of "The Star-Spangled Banner" is well known to all music teachers and directors. The high pitches (when sung in B♭) are only a partial reason for the difficulty. When one examines the unmusical quality of the words, both as to unsingable vowels and consonants of such passages as "The rockets red glare, the bombs bursting in air," the real culprit is evident. It has always been ludicrous to the author that the accepted orchestral arrangement of our National Anthem employs singing strings to express the explosiveness of these words.

EDITING OF TEXTS

Since the choral arranger must fit the words of a folk song or a translation to the music which he is writing, he must be equally adept in editing the texts. It has already been suggested that it is permissible to change an occasional word to secure an easy flow of text; or, to change the rhythmical pattern slightly in various parts to secure a matching of accent with the words.

Some folk songs with a dozen or more verses must be abridged without losing the thread of thought or story. Sometimes, verses need to be combined while others need to be omitted. Occasionally, questionable words need to be changed. In arranging Negro spirituals, the newer practice is to use the regular spelling of words, rather than dialect. The performers can then follow their own preference or discretion as to whether or not to sing the arrangement in dialect. The same practice is followed with most mountain or hillbilly songs.

Words with more than one syllable should be hyphenated to fit the notes, one syllable to a note, such as *moth-er* or *fa-ther*. When in doubt consult the dictionary. A single line, even with the bottom of the word, should be drawn to indicate the number of notes that the word sustains.

It goes without saying that grammatical errors should not occur unless they are typical of a native folk song, in which case it would lose its indigenous character if changed. Care should also be exercised in the punctuation of words in either poetry or prose. The key to phrasing choral music is found in the words and correct punctuation of the text is of untold value to the director in achieving a musical and artistic performance.

CHAPTER X

PREPARING AND SUBMITTING MANUSCRIPTS

The first nine chapters of this book have been committed to the idea that students and choral directors should devote time to making choral arrangements for practical use and, more important still, the growth in musicianship which it will foster in them. The author attributes the greater part of his own musical development to the writing of many choral arrangements and continuous practice of choral composition.

However, every composer or arranger, sooner or later, will have a keen desire to see his name in print. The publication of his creative efforts becomes an ever-increasingly important goal. This desire for recognition and approbation is probably stronger than the anticipation of remunerative reward which is usually rather frugal compared to the amount of time and effort that goes into the writing of choral arrangements. If an arranger is going to write for publication he must first discipline his writing so as to conform with the demand or needs in the field. After he has established a reputation as an arranger, he may then give vent to his own individual creative ideas.

Many amateurs, carried away by stories of fabulous returns from popular songs, try their hand at writing one. There are probably many good unpublished songs floating around the country, but the expense and precariousness of the exploitation of a popular song makes it almost prohibitive for a publisher to take a chance on a novice composer, regardless of the merits of the song. Therefore, he naturally turns to the professional song writer and is reluctant to even look at the songs of amateurs. As suggested earlier, the amateur with ambitions in this area should seek professional collaboration, at first, so as to gain entree to publishers.

Likewise, it is useless for a teacher to make an arrangement of a popular song for his own choral group and, in light of its local success, submit it to the publisher of the song for publication. The fact is that he is breaking the copyright law in making such an arrangement unless he has secured permission from the publisher who owns the copyright. Through correspondence or personal acquaintanceship, he may be able to convince the publisher that he has a unique way of arranging popular songs which would make them very useful to school groups. The publisher then might become sufficiently interested to ask him to "try his hand" at a few and submit them for consideration. On the whole, however, the publishers of popular songs are inclined to turn to their own professional arrangers for publications in the choral field. These arrangers, though highly skilled in various branches of arranging, are not all conversant with the needs of amateur and school choral groups. This is probably the reason for the many popular song arrangements which are not adapted to or usable by school choral groups.

Therefore, it is best for the choral arranger who is bent on the publication of his efforts to turn to the field of the folk song as suggested in Chapter I. Here is a rich field of materials which most publishers, if they are interested at all in choral music, are willing to consider for inclusion in their catalogues. The re-arranging of standard choral works from mixed voices to treble or male voice numbers is also a field which provides an easy and acceptable road to publication.

COPYRIGHT CLEARANCE

Great care must be taken that the words and melody of a song are in public domain (p.d.) before an arranger begins work on a number. In the United States, the copyright of a musical composition or arrangement extends over a period of 28 years. After this period the publisher, the author, or the composer may renew the copyright for another 28 years. Consequently, it is the safest practice to make sure that a song is 56 years old before assuming that it is in public domain and thus free to be arranged.

Of course, this fact immediately eliminates the availability of the present-day popular song (except where permission is granted by the publisher) and leaves only the songs of the gay-nineties and early minstrel songs. Caution must also be exercised in the art song field. The contemporary art song enjoys the same copyright status as the popular song; therefore, the arranger of art songs must turn to the songs of the past century or the canzonettas of an earlier period.

Even the copyright status of folk songs must be established. One would think that anything labeled a 'folk song' would be in public domain, but it is not necessarily so. One collector of folk songs may change and edit a version on which he obtains a copyright and it becomes identified with him. Even though it is not written in voice parts, this version is considered an 'arrangement' and enjoys the same copyright status as an original song. Another collector may come out with a slightly different version of the same song on which he also obtains a copyright. Many arrangers simply make enough changes in a version to avoid copyright infringement.

If the same version of a folk song is published by several different publishers, it is generally safe to assume that this version is in public domain. The usual version of "Home on the Range" is an example. There are some cases where a folk song is in public domain but the arranger has inserted an original (or derivative) middle section which he has copyrighted. The well-known arrangement by David Guion of "Home on the Range" (G. Schirmer) is an example.

Equal care and research must be exercised in the use of texts and translations. The copyright law is as applicable to the words as to the music. In making a translation of an art song, it is always best to go to the original source. Often, the melodies of folk songs are in public domain although the words are copyrighted. Such is the case with some of the Negro spirituals. When in doubt consult the Copyright Office, Library of Congress; American Society of Composers, Authors, and Publishers (ASCAP); or the publisher.

The whole status of the copyright of folk songs needs clarification. As one editor puts it, "If a folk song isn't in public domain, what is?" This is a liberal point of view, for most collectors of folk songs (especially American ones) zealously guard their copyrights. Some of these collectors have a flat fee, usually $10.00, for the permission to make a choral arrangement of one of the folk songs from their collections. It seems that the privilege of labelling anything a 'folk song' should carry with it the responsibility of indicating what is 'folk' and what is 'individual'; or, in other words, what is public domain and what can be copyrighted.

The Business Handbook of Music Education, a manual published by the Music Education Exhibitors Association, an auxiliary of the Music Educators National Conference (MENC) clearly explains the copyright law in the following quotation from this valuable little book. It is addressed to the music teacher but is equally informative to the arranger and composer. An extended and annotated list of publishers which provides the arranger with active outlets to whom he can submit his wares is also included in the book. Copies of this handbook may be secured, free of charge, from the Music Education Exhibitors Association, 64 East Jackson Blvd., Suite 804, Chicago 4, Illinois.

THE COPYRIGHT LAW

Some instructors have gained the mistaken impression that copying of copyrighted material is permissible and legal as long as the copied material is not sold for profit.

Composers and publishers invest their talent, efforts, and capital in publications. They are entitled to the income from the sale of these items. Any practice of copying which deprives the composer and publisher of just and deserved royalties and sales is an unfair practice and is definitely a violation of the copyright law of the United States of America.

Following are phrases taken directly from the copyright laws:
. . . any person entitled thereto, (the person securing the copyright) . . . *shall have the exclusive right* (a) to print, reprint, publish, copy, and vend the copyrighted work; (b) to arrange or adapt it if it be a musical work; (c) to make or to procure the making of any transcription or record by or from which . . . it may in any manner or by any method be exhibited, performed, represented, produced, or reproduced; (d) to perform the copyrighted work publicly for profit if it be a musical composition; (e) to make any arrangement or setting of it or of the melody of it in any system of notation.

That any person who willfully and for profit shall infringe any copyright secured by this Act, or who shall knowingly and willfully aid or abet such infringement, shall be deemed guilty of a misdemeanor, and upon conviction thereof shall be punished by imprisonment for not exceeding one year or by a fine of not less than one hundred dollars nor more than one thousand dollars, or both, in the discretion of the court.

Following is a copy of a statement issued by the Standard Music Publishers' Association of the United States:

Unauthorized Copying of Copyrighted Material Illegal!

Copying by any process — by hand on paper or blackboard, by multigraphing, mimeographing, photostating or any other method — of any part of a copyrighted work, no matter for what purpose or use (religious, educational, theatrical or otherwise), without the permission of the copyright owner, is a serious offense against the United States law, punishable with heavy fines beginning at one hundred dollars, plus minimum damages of two hundred and fifty dollars. The United States copyright laws are very strict in this particular and many actions are now being conducted against teachers, directors and other offenders making unauthorized arrangements or copies. The practice is unfair to composers, authors and publishers.

The law is specific and clear. *In spirit and fact you are guilty of infringement if in any case you through act or sanction, without express permission of the copyright owners, do any of the following*:

(1) Reproduce copyrighted words or music through the use of mimeograph stencils.

(2) Make a song slide of a copyrighted song.

(3) Write the words or music of such a song on the blackboard.

(4) Copy extra parts for your band or orchestra.

(5) Make any arrangement of copyrighted music.

If you are in doubt as to what *is* "copyrighted music" we would point out that the United States Copyright Law requires that notice of copyright ownership, showing the name of the owner and the year of copyright, be printed on all copies of a copyrighted work. Therefore, when such notice appears, it is definite evidence that permission for copying must be secured from the copyright owner *before* it may be copied.

To avoid the hazard of infringement, check carefully the copyright ownership as shown in this notice, and first obtain the desired permission or *leave it alone!*

In the case of materials published outside the United States, the laws require no specific notice of copyright, and inquiry as to copyright status should therefore be made of the publisher or his American representative.

MARKET FOR ARRANGEMENTS

The so-called renaissance of choral music in this country in the past 25 years has opened a rich market for choral music. Never before have music publishers, both popular and standard, been so eager to obtain choral compositions and arrangements suitable for school, church, and amateur choirs. Many publishers are devoting the greater part of their efforts to the publication of appropriate choral music. Therefore, if an arranger can feel the pulse of the choral needs of these amateur choirs and can write music accordingly, there is a waiting market for his wares.

CONSIDERATION OF MANUSCRIPTS

The reluctance of many publishers to consider manuscripts of unknown arrangers and composers, especially in the popular field, has already been mentioned. Nevertheless, it is true that most publishers will consider manuscripts which seem to fill a style needed in their catalogues. (As mentioned before, arrangements and compositions for three-part treble voice groups are always in demand.)

It is probably best to submit the arrangement to a publisher's representative with whom he may be acquainted, preferably one in the education department. This representative may personally send it to the editorial department; or, he may give the arranger permission to use his name when submitting it himself to the publisher. This personal touch may or may not do any good (especially if it is a bad arrangement) but it can't hurt. If the number has had performances and has been included on printed programs, it is well to send these along with the manuscript. Naturally, publishers will show more interest in an arranger's manuscripts if the arranger is in a position to help exploit the music by obtaining performances of it or aranging for its use by school and amateur groups. Nevertheless, regardless of personal contact or professional prestige, the secret of securing consideration of one's manuscripts is the ability to turn out good material that is needed in the field.

SUBMITTING OF MANUSCRIPTS

In submitting manuscripts an arranger should be careful that they are neat and correct. If an author submitted a book to a publisher with words mispelled, grammatical mistakes, and wrong punctuation, the publisher could hardly be expected to review it in a favorable light. When a music publisher receives a manuscript written sloppily and filled with mistakes, he naturally assumes that the arranger doesn't know his business and gives it little consideration.

The manuscript should be written in ink on large, 12 stave, manuscript paper of individual four page sheets. A very clear pencil copy (Use a No. 1 pencil) is also acceptable. The writing should be spread evenly so as not to appear crowded or cramped. (Don't be stingy with manuscript paper.) The words should be printed clearly or typed in under each voice part.

The *tempo* and expression marks may be written in Italian or English. It is most logical to make it a practice to use *either* the Italian or the English terms consistently throughout the arrangement, never to mix the two. Except for *tempo* marks at the beginning, which should appear above the top voice part and piano part, all other expression marks should be written in each part as follows:

Ex. 91

CORRECT NOTATION

All arrangers should be acquainted with the established practices of music notation. Turning in correctly edited manuscripts is important.

116

General rules for the mechanics of notation:

1. Time signatures follow the key signatures on the staff.

   Time signatures are used only at the beginning of the music and at each change of meter.

   Key signatures are used on each staff throughout the piece.

Ex. 92

etc.

2. Stems turn up wnen note-head is below the third line.

Ex. 93

3. Stems turn down when note-head is above the third line.

Ex. 94

4. Stems turn up or down when note-head is on the third line.

   Many editors always turn the stem down; others follow the practice of keeping a symmetry with the general pattern.

Ex. 95

5. When several stems are joined together the stems turn up or down determined by the majority or general position of the note-heads.

Ex. 96

6. When more than one voice part appears on a staff, all stems turn up for the higher part and down for the lower part.

   When both parts sing the same note, stems turn both up and down.

Ex. 97

7. The indication for triplets is written near the note-heads, (not the stems).

Ex. 98

8. The dot after a note is always placed in a space, (not on a line).

Ex. 99

9. A dot after a note-head on a line is placed slightly above the line.

Ex. 100

10. Rests are placed in the middle of the staff when there is only one voice part, whole rests and half rests being written in the third space.

Ex. 101

11. The positions of rests vary when two or more voice parts are written on a staff. (A whole rest is used to indicate a full measure regardless of the number of beats.)

Ex. 102

12. The flags of eighth and sixteenth notes are always placed on the right side of the stem, unless stems are connected, then they are placed on the inside.

Ex. 103

13. The tie or slur is usually written near the note-heads. However, in engraving, the slur may be placed next to the flag of connected notes to save space.

Ex. 104

14. First and second endings are notated as follows:

In choral music it is best to write out repeats rather than indicate them when words are different for each repetition, unless the length of the number makes it prohibitive in terms of costs.

Ex. 105

15. No repeat marks are necessary to accompany the *Da Capo* (D.C.), (back to the beginning); or *Dal Segno* (D.S.), (back to the sign).

16. In notating syncopated rhythms extreme care must be taken that each beat of the measure is clear.

Ex. 106

17. In voice parts, stems are separated for each syllable but in piano parts they are connected. Stems are connected in voice parts when several notes are used with one syllable.

Ex. 107

TUTU MARAMBA★
Chorus for Mixed Voices A Cappella
S.A.T.B.B.

Translation by
H. R. W.

BRAZILIAN FOLK SONG
Arr. by H. R. W.

★Pronounced Too-Too Mah-rahm-bah

18. In octavo music when the piano part is a duplication of the voice parts, stems are separated in voice parts and connected in piano parts.

Ex. 108

AT PARTING
T.T.B.B.

FREDERIC PETERSON   HARRY R. WILSON

The fra-grance it ex - hales, ___ Ah! if you on - ly knew! ___

19. When one piano staff serves for both voices and piano, (as in hymn books and song books) the notes of each staff are written on the same stem, its direction depending upon the position of the note-heads, except in unisons, seconds, and cross rhythms.

Ex. 109

NOW THE DAY IS OVER

SABINE BARING GOULD   JOSEPH BARNBY

Now the day is o - ver, Night is draw-ing nigh; ___

Shad-ows of the eve - ning Steal a-cross the sky. A-men.

20. The direction of the stems in piano accompaniments are illustrated in the following two examples. Notice, that in Ex. 110, the stems of the melody turn up regardless of the position of the notes, while the stems of the afterbeats turn down, except when the melody is below the afterbeats as in Measure 4. In Ex. 111, the stems of the bass notes turn up while the stems of the afterbeats turn down.

Ex. 110

Ex. 111

122

21. When employing enharmonic changes of notation to avoid the use of double flats or double sharps, the shift of key should be made gracefully, usually at the beginning of a bar, rather than within the bar. The following example illustrates the use of enharmonic notation.

Ex. 112

THE SONG OF THE SWAMPS
BARITONE SOLO
(S.A.T.B.)

Lyric by
FLORENCE TARR

Music by
HARRY ROBERT WILSON

CONCLUSION

More details of the practices in editing music can be learned by studying representative publications. Of course, the editors and proof-readers are responsible for the correctness of the published copy. However, there is a better chance to have the published copy perfect if the composer or arranger turns in a carefully edited manuscript with as few mistakes as possible. This would obviate the necessity for making changes on engraved plates, which is a very costly operation.

As a parting paragraph, to give a word of encouragement to amateur arrangers who are endeavouring to break into the publication field. Don't ever give up. Don't submit a book full of manuscripts — rather select a few of the best and send them in, or, better yet, concentrate on one if it is something a little unusual. The first step is to have faith in your own work! Creative talent of professional calibre in the choral field is limited and there is always an opportunity for those who persevere! Good luck!

From Munich to Pearl H

FROM MUNICH
TO PEARL HARBOR

*Roosevelt's America and the
Origins of the Second World War*

David Reynolds

The American Ways Series

IVAN R. DEE   *Chicago*

Library of Congress Cataloging-in-Publication Data:
Reynolds, David, 1952–
     From Munich to Pearl Harbor : Roosevelt's America and the origins of the Second World War / David Reynolds.
          p. cm. — (The American ways series)
     Includes bibliographical references (p.) and index.
     ISBN 1-56663-389-3 (alk. paper)
     1. United States—Foreign relations—1933–1945. 2. United States—Politics and government—1933–1945. 3. Roosevelt, Franklin D. (Franklin Delano), 1882–1945—Political and social views. 4. World War, 1939–1945—Diplomatic history. 5. World War, 1939–1945—Causes. 6. World War, 1939–1945—United States. 7. World politics—1933–1945. 8. National security—United States—History—20th century. I. Title. II. Series.

E806 .R45 2001
973.917—dc21   2001023480

For John, Alan, Roger—and Martin at Midway

Contents

Acknowledgments

MY AGENDA for this book is summarized at the beginning of Chapter One; my "answers" are set out in the conclusion. Here I simply wish to thank those who made this project possible. First and foremost Ivan Dee and John Braeman, respectively the publisher and editor of the American Ways series. John's invitation to revisit terrain I had partly traversed years before as a graduate student came out of the blue. But it arrived at an opportune moment, when I was in need of relief from a nightmare administrative job. Moreover, in the intervening quarter-century the literature on the subject had developed significantly, and my own perspective had enlarged through teaching and writing on World War II, the cold war, and indeed the whole twentieth century. The task was therefore a great pleasure. Throughout Ivan and John have been highly supportive, the latter in particular through his incisive editorial comments. For also reading the manuscript, I am grateful to Warren F. Kimball, an old friend and trusted colleague. The book also owes much to conversations about U.S. foreign policy over many years with John Thompson. My debts to the staff at the Roosevelt Library stretch back to the days of William R. Emerson, whom I remember with great affection. The pleasure of renewing my acquaintance with Hyde Park has been enhanced by the energetic presence of Cynthia Koch as the director of the Roosevelt Library and of David Woolner as executive director of the Franklin and Eleanor Roosevelt Institute. To all of them, my warm thanks.

On a personal level, I am immensely grateful to Margaret for her tolerance of yet another book. This one is dedicated to older members of her family: to four brothers of the generation of 1941—two from West Point, two from Annapolis—for whom Pearl Harbor began the most momentous years of their lives and, in the case of one of them, his last.

D. J. R.

The Original Cambridge
April 2001

From Munich to Pearl Harbor

1

On Histories and Historians

ON DECEMBER 7, 1941, Japanese bombers surprised the U.S. Pacific fleet at its Hawaiian base at Pearl Harbor. Six of the eight battleships were sunk or damaged. More than 2,400 service personnel and civilians were killed. The day that "will live in infamy," as President Franklin D. Roosevelt called it, was a turning point in American history. Four years before, at the beginning of 1938, the United States was a country still mired in the Great Depression, with nearly a fifth of its workforce unemployed and investment at less than half the level of 1929. Congress had passed Neutrality Acts to prevent entanglement in another European war. Four years after Pearl Harbor, at the end of 1945, the United States accounted for half the world's manufacturing output and boasted the largest navy and air force in the world. It enjoyed a monopoly of atomic weapons, and U.S. troops occupied the ruined homelands of its vanquished enemies, Germany and Japan. The world's leading "superpower"—a word coined in 1944—was a far cry from the anxious, introverted America of 1938.

This book has three main objectives. First, to provide a succinct narrative of the twisting road from Munich to Pearl Harbor, drawing on my own research and on recent scholarship. The chapters unfold chronologically, with an introductory section prefiguring the themes of each one, and the overall account is summarized in the first part of the conclusion. The story is partly about the transformation of American politics. By 1938 a loose but effective coalition of congressional conservatives had halted Roosevelt's New Deal. In 1939–1941 this coalition fractured over foreign policy. Slowly Roosevelt created a new political consensus, built around aid to Britain and its allies. This replaced the policy of hemisphere defense that in the mid-1930s had held sway. But domestic politics are only one side of the story. Roosevelt, Congress, and the American people were responding to some of the most dramatic changes in twentieth-century world history. U.S. foreign policy was revolutionized by Hitler's surprise victories in Europe in the spring of 1940, by his attack on the Soviet Union in June 1941, and by the devastating Japanese strikes across the Pacific and Southeast Asia in the following December. Together these campaigns transformed the European conflict that broke out in September 1939 into a truly global war.

In retrospect that transformation is obvious. But at the time the interconnection of events seemed obscure, particularly to Americans accustomed to focus on what was called "the Western Hemisphere." Moreover, as we now know, the ties among the Axis powers—Germany, Italy, and Japan—were very tenuous. A second objective of the book is therefore to analyze how Roosevelt led Americans into a new global perspective on international relations. This involved both geopolitics (an expanded geography of U.S. security) and ideology (the assertion of U.S. principles of liberal, capitalist democracy). Against "hemispherism," FDR insisted with growing fervor that, in the age of airborne warfare, the world could and did threaten America, and that American values could and should transform the world. The two themes were interconnected, for the president argued that only in a world in which American values reigned supreme could the United States feel secure. This global perspective on international events was distinctively Rooseveltian. In the 1930s Americans (and Germans, though not the British) were used to talking about 1914–1918 as "the world war." But it was Franklin Roosevelt in 1941 who popularized the term "the second world war."

Roosevelt's globalism proved to be a worldview of lasting significance. That brings me to the third main aim of the book, which is to spotlight developments in the period 1938–1941 that were later important for U.S. foreign and defense policy in the cold war era. Along with globalism, major themes included the articulation of the bipolar ideologies of "totalitarianism" and Americanism; the emergence of a military-industrial complex and the strategy of technowar; the origins of the "imperial presidency"; the precedent of a peacetime draft; a durable commitment to the security of Europe and the "Atlantic Area"; and, in contrast with the timidity of the depression, a growing belief in American omnipotence. In many general histories of American foreign policy, the origins of the cold war bulk so large as almost to obscure the origins of World War II. That seems to me unfortunate. By the end of 1941 many features of what would emerge as the "national security state" were already apparent in embryo, albeit applied to a very different enemy. Tracing the construction of America's second world war may help us understand the relative alacrity with which the United States after 1945 took on the role of a global superpower in a bipolar confrontation with the Soviet Union.

The early historiography of the approach to war was rooted in the great debate of 1940–1941 between those advocating aid to Britain and those who argued that this would turn the United States into a belligerent. The former stigmatized their opponents as "isolationists" while the latter, in turn, insisted that they were combating the "interventionists." More exactly, the two sides differed about where to draw the geographical line in U.S. security—around the Western Hemisphere, as noninterventionists generally argued, or on the other side of the Atlantic, according

to the Roosevelt administration and its allies. By contrast, there
was relatively little discussion or controversy about the increasingly firm U.S. policy toward Japanese expansion in Asia. Attention was concentrated on the European war, and traditional
American stereotypes of the Old World and of European entanglements still exerted a powerful influence.

The Pearl Harbor attack ended this political debate almost
overnight. Although privately unrepentant, Roosevelt's opponents rallied around their commander-in-chief. After the war,
however, the battle was rejoined. Authors of the major postwar
revisionist critiques of Roosevelt's policies, such as the historians
Charles A. Beard and Charles C. Tansill, had been open opponents before Pearl Harbor. On the other side were those whom
Tansill called the "Court Historians"—writers who had been
closely linked to the Roosevelt administration during and before
the war. Among them were Robert E. Sherwood, one of FDR's
speechwriters, who wrote the 1948 Pulitzer Prize–winning study
of the president and his confidant, Harry Hopkins; Herbert Feis,
a State Department official who published *The Road to Pearl
Harbor* in 1950; and William L. Langer and S. Everett Gleason,
whose massive two-volume study of 1937 to 1941, *The World Crisis and American Foreign Policy,* appeared in 1952–1953. Langer
and Gleason were professional historians who had both served in
the State Department and in U.S. intelligence during the war.
Their works, based on privileged access to official documents
and on interviews with the leading policymakers, constituted a
semi-official refutation of revisionism.

The essentials of the revisionist case were twofold. First, Roosevelt had deceived the American people about the belligerent
implications of his policies, often acting behind the back of Congress. According to some extreme accounts, he had even allowed
the Pearl Harbor attack to happen, using it (in Tansill's title) as
the *Back Door to War.* Second, this had been an unnecessary war.
Revisionists claimed that throughout the period up to December

1941 there had been no serious and immediate threat to U.S. interests or security. In their view, hemisphere defense, backed by prudent rearmament, remained an adequate policy.

In general, public debate in the United States has run against the revisionists. Pearl Harbor ended the political argument; Auschwitz settled the moral argument. After 1945 most Americans were convinced that they had fought a just and necessary war. By the 1970s many looked back on it, in Studs Terkel's phrase, as the "good war," in contrast to the moral uncertainties and popular divisions that poisoned the conflict in Vietnam. In the 1990s it became the heroic war, its participants celebrated in movies such as *Saving Private Ryan* and consecrated by TV anchorman Tom Brokaw as "the greatest generation any society has produced." Underpinning this consensus was the overwhelming reality of the cold war—understood as a global struggle of power and ideology against the forces of international communism, spearheaded by the Soviet Union. The war had turned the United States into a "superpower," into the self-styled guardian of the "Free World." While grumbling about the cost, most Americans accepted these roles as axiomatic. And the collapse of the Soviet bloc and the Soviet Union itself in 1989–1991 served to vindicate those assumptions. The Good War and the Cold War made the No War debate of 1940–1941 seem like a stupid irrelevance.

From this perspective, assuming the essential rightness of U.S. belligerency against Germany and Japan, the debate shifted to means rather than ends, to the appropriateness of Roosevelt's actions in 1940–1941. There were two related strands—policies and politics. On policies, Robert Divine and Arnold Offner were among several historians who portrayed FDR as a 1930s isolationist, inclined to appeasement, who painfully metamorphosed into an interventionist between Munich and Pearl Harbor. According to Divine in 1969, "Roosevelt pursued an isolationist policy out of genuine conviction," and in 1941 his "deep-seated aversion to war still paralyzed" his conduct of affairs. Historians have also examined Roosevelt's political tactics, his conception of presidential leadership. Biographer James MacGregor Burns wrote that the president "seemed beguiled by public opinion," preferring to "wait on events" rather than give a clear lead. Divine detected a pattern of "two steps forward, one step back" whenever the president made a major move. By contrast, Robert Dallek, in his comprehensive study of FDR's foreign policy from 1932 to 1945, depicted a fairly consistent internationalist who was obliged by the strength of public opinion to conform to the nationalist and isolationist mood of the 1930s. According to Dallek, writing in 1979, FDR's "appreciation that effective action abroad required a reliable consensus at home and his use of dramatic events overseas to win national backing from a divided country were among the great presidential achievements of this century."

The debate about FDR's policies and politics enlarged in the 1980s in two ways. One was by moving away from the president himself to look at key advisers such as Sumner Welles, at parts of the government bureaucracy, as in Jonathan Utley's study of the State Department and Japan, or at the plasticity of political opinion—the theme of Thomas Guinsburg's study of isolationism in the Senate. This body of work suggested that the main barriers to a coherent and decisive foreign policy lay within the administration as much as outside it. A second development was the opening of key foreign archives, particularly in Britain. Several major studies of Anglo-American relations in this period shed light from new sources on this opaque president. They showed the extent of secret U.S. entanglement with Britain long before Pearl Harbor, but also the president's ambivalence about his covert ally. This British material informed more general accounts written during the 1980s. To Frederick W. Marks it helped show that the president was parochial in outlook and indecisive in style, ever prone "to substitute words for action." By contrast, Waldo Heinrich's interpretation of FDR's global policy during 1941 presented Roosevelt as "an active and purposeful maker of foreign policy, the only figure with all the threads in his hands." Warren Kimball, in a collection of essays on FDR's diplomacy, acknowledged wishful thinking, devious tactics, and a "debonair administrative style" but found a "broader consistency that shaped his policies" at the level of "assumptions."

To a large extent, therefore, the presidential paradigm holds sway. The debate keeps returning to Roosevelt, usually within the terms set by the orthodox consensus that this was a good war that the United States entered for justifiable ends, albeit by slightly dubious means.

On the other hand, the two main streams of revisionism remain a continuing undercurrent. Pearl Harbor still attracts conspiracy theorists. During the 1990s, after the end of the cold war, the opening of U.S. and British intelligence archives prompted a new round of charges and rebuttals about the foreknowledge of Roosevelt (and Churchill) concerning the Japanese attack. Meanwhile the extensive research of Wayne Cole, Justus Doenecke, and others has given a clearer sense of the noninterventionists. Earlier work in this area had concentrated on the ethnic or regional basis for "isolationism"—implicitly the problem was to explain deviation from a mainstream internationalist consensus. These more recent studies looked at the intellectual arguments used by noninterventionists, seeking to show both their complexity and plausibility. The proponents of hemisphere defense, who included two future U.S. presidents, John F. Kennedy and Gerald R. Ford, cannot simply be dismissed as obscurantists or closet Nazis.

Some scholars, such as Bruce Russett, Melvin Small, and John A. Thompson, have moved this discussion of noninterventionism onto a more general plane. In the title of Russett's interpretive essay, published in 1972, they argue that there was *No Clear and Present Danger* in security terms to justify Roosevelt's increasingly belligerent policies. Russett was an erstwhile supporter of

FDR who found that his growing doubts about U.S. intervention in Vietnam knocked over "a row of intellectual dominoes" running right back to Pearl Harbor. Vietnam also strengthened the "New Left" critique of U.S. internationalism and prompted several studies of Roosevelt's policy from this angle. Rather than a defensive concern with security, they emphasized an ideology of economic expansion. Lloyd Gardner's pioneering *Economic Aspects of New Deal Diplomacy* (1964) highlighted the concern of the depression generation for the survival of capitalism at home and abroad. This became an all-embracing interpretation of U.S. policy from 1937 to 1941 in Patrick Hearden's *Roosevelt Confronts Hitler* (1987).

Like all historians, I stand on the shoulders of others. This book takes seriously both the domestic and the international pressures on U.S. foreign policy, focusing on Roosevelt but also trying to set him in bureaucratic and political context. Equally, like any historian, I am influenced by my time and place. If the omnipresence of the cold war led most scholars to accept U.S. globalism as axiomatic, so the end of the cold war enables us to recognize the novelty of this worldwide superpower role. And the recent intellectual anatomy of noninterventionism reminds us that alternatives to Roosevelt's emerging worldview were well entrenched and prods us to ask why and how they were displaced.

International events in 1940 and 1941 undoubtedly shook the foundations of contemporary thinking. In many ways this period was the "fulcrum" of the twentieth century, the turning point in the endgame of the old Europe-centered order. But an awareness of global crisis was not the same as a recognition of world war. Roosevelt's carefully crafted speeches joined up the dots of disparate events into an interconnected pattern, which he popularized in 1941 as "the second world war." And his distinctive responses to global crisis—undeclared war in the Atlantic and undesired war in the Pacific, the origins of the "imperial presi-

dency" and the foundations of the military-industrial complex—
shaped U.S. foreign policy during the conflict of 1941–1945 and
long after. In short, it is time for World War II to reemerge from
its cold war eclipse. America's approach to the Soviet Union after
1945 owed much to the attitudes and practices established as
Roosevelt moved his country from "neutrality" to "world war"
between 1938 and 1941.

2

Roosevelt's America and an Alien World

AS ALLIED TROOPS spread out across Nazi Germany in 1945, revealing the horrors of Auschwitz and Bergen-Belsen, the origins of the war seemed fairly simple. It still does to later generations. "In the end the war was Hitler's war," wrote British historian D. C. Watt in 1989. "Hitler willed, wanted, craved war and the destruction wrought by war." But, added Watt, "he did not want the war he got." It takes two sides to start a fight: remember that it was Britain and France who declared war on Germany in 1939, rather than the other way round. Moreover, their declarations began what we now call the Second World War. "Second" implies some connection with the issues that provoked the First World War of 1914–1918. "World" reminds us that 1939–1945 involved a global conflict. Italy and Japan became Germany's "Axis" partners in June 1940 and December 1941, respectively, while the Soviet Union and the United States entered the conflict in June and December 1941 as Britain's allies. Any account of the causes of this war must take a broad view, both in time and space.

Germany's immediate aim was dominance on the continent of Europe; Italy sought a new Roman empire around the Mediterranean; Japan envisaged a "New Order" in East and Southeast Asia. As the events of 1940–1945 showed, there was little connection between the German and Japanese wars, while the link between Berlin and Rome entailed a diversion from German objectives, forced on Hitler because the Italian war effort was so inept. The fusion of these three regional conflicts owed much to Hitler's victories in 1940 and 1941, which emboldened Italy and Japan to mount their own bids for power and drove Hitler on into Russia. But the fusion was also due, in part, to Franklin Roosevelt. His responses to these regional crises in 1940–1941 helped connect them in a global conflict. And, at the level of rhetoric, months before Pearl Harbor he established the idea that this was already "the second world war." So the Allies mattered as well as the Axis. Just as it took Britain and France to start a European war in 1939, it took the United States to make a world war in 1941.

For all their contrasts, however, these regional conflicts also had some common roots, which were apparent to contemporaries in the 1930s. In shorthand the salient issues were empire, ideology, and economics—the dynamics of great-power territorial rivalry and nationalist self-assertion; the challenges to political liberalism from national fascism and international communism; and the debate between economic liberalism and autarkic planning at a time when the global economy had collapsed. These issues preoccupied much of Europe and Asia. The United States lay on the periphery of world affairs for most of the thirties, absorbed by its debilitating depression. Yet its potential, fleetingly asserted in 1917–1918, was enormous. And, led by Roosevelt, it started to voice distinctive answers to the three big challenges of the decade. In 1937–1938 FDR began taking a greater initiative in foreign affairs, albeit cautiously and still from the sidelines.

EMPIRE, IDEOLOGY, AND ECONOMICS

In 1910 much of the world was structured around great empires. By 1960 it was largely a world of nation-states. The era of World War II was a turning point in that transformation. One fundamental issue in the 1930s was therefore empire—the rivalry between the major powers to create, defend, or enlarge empires, and the countervailing pressures on large, multinational empires from nationalist politics.

In the late nineteenth century the scramble for empire had been global in scope, with a carving up of Africa by the European powers and their comparable bid to partition China. Before, during, and after World War I, a similar struggle occurred as the Ottoman Turkish Empire was broken up to the benefit of new Balkan states and also by Britain and France in the Middle East. Germany, a belated nation-state created only in 1871, was a latecomer to empire. Its challenges to France's position in North Africa and Britain's supremacy at sea helped push these two imperial rivals into an unlikely alliance. Increasingly, however, German policy focused on Europe: fears of being squeezed on two sides by France and its main ally, Russia, encouraged Germany to risk war in August 1914. In March 1918, when Germany had knocked Russia out of the war, its forces were lodged deep in Eastern Europe and Eurasia, covering most of what is now Poland, the Ukraine, and the Caucasus. This massive German Empire was short-lived, lasting only until Germany collapsed in the autumn of 1918, but it prefigured Hitler's bids in 1939–1942 for *Lebensraum* (living space) in the East. Most Germans were never reconciled to their humiliating status after 1918—stripped of an empire and a fleet, denied an army, air force, and general staff. The reassertion of Germany as a major European power was a common aspiration. It helped, in particular, to reconcile the German officer corps to the demagogic Hitler after he became chancellor in 1933.

Italy was another new nation-state, established in 1861. Mussolini, who had seized power in 1922, trumpeted his goal of a modern Roman Empire, playing on popular demands for territory in the Adriatic and Africa. This placed him on a collision course with Britain and France, the predominant powers in northern Africa, especially after his 1935 invasion of Abyssinia. His grander aspirations for dominance in the Mediterranean challenged those of France, particularly when Mussolini came to the aid of the Nationalists in the Spanish Civil War of 1936–1939. This posed for France the threat of war on two fronts.

In Asia, Japan constituted the third newcomer nation-state seeking an empire of its own. Through victories in 1895 and 1905 over the waning empires of Qing China and Romanov Russia, Japan secured Taiwan and most of Korea. By 1920 it had the third-largest navy in the world. At the height of the Russian civil war its troops controlled vast tracts of Siberia. In the 1930s Japanese empire-building in East Asia resumed with the occupation of Manchuria in 1931–1932 and eastern China in 1937–1938. In 1938–1939 Japan fought a large-scale border war against the Soviet Union. To the south lay the rich European empires of France in Indochina, Britain in Malaya and Burma, and the Dutch in the East Indies (present-day Indonesia). They controlled vast reserves of oil, rubber, tin, and other vital raw materials.

From this perspective, what we call World War II was the climax of a long struggle for empire among most of the world's leading powers. This pitted the "haves," notably Britain and France, against the "have-nots" (or "have much less"), particularly Germany and Italy in Europe, and Japan in Asia. Of course these various empires were not monochromatic. The British, for instance, had already conceded self-government to "white dominions" such as Canada and Australia; in the 1930s they were also engaged in a long and difficult process of establishing representative institutions in India, a vast subcontinent fractured by divisions of caste, religion, and princely power. That said, Britain's leaders had no intention of surrendering the essentials of global power. As Admiral Sir Ernle Chatfield put it in 1934: "We are in the remarkable position of not wanting to quarrel with anybody because we have got most of the world already, or the best parts of it, and we only want to keep what we have got and prevent others from taking it away from us." What, from the perspective of London, was a philosophy of peace seemed in Tokyo, and other revisionist capitals, to be a policy of intransigent and sanctimonious imperialism. If Britain said, in effect, "What we have, we hold," then the revisionist cry was "What you hold, we will take."

The 1930s was therefore an age of imperialism. But a waning imperialism. For the other side of the coin was the challenge to large multinational empires from those seeking to establish separate national states. Again Europe epitomizes the process. In 1914 Germany shared a border with Russia; the two were also neighbors of Austria-Hungary. These three great dynastic empires—the Hohenzollerns, the Romanovs, and the Habsburgs—all collapsed in the endgame of war in 1917–1918. From the rubble of empires new states were constructed, the most fragile being Poland, created at the expense of Germany and Russia, which never accepted the loss of their territory. Most of the borders of the new Eastern Europe were contested. Moreover these new states were usually multinational states rather than the political embodiment of a single national group. Thus Poland was barely two-thirds Polish. In its southern neighbor, Czechoslovakia, only half of the population was Czech while 22 percent was German, 16 percent Slovak, 5 percent Hungarian, and 4 percent Ukrainian. The German question was particularly significant. After 1918 more than twelve million Germans lived outside the new Germany—equivalent to one-fifth of the country's population. The creation of an inclusive German nation was one of Hitler's more plausible aims: in 1938 he used it to justify the annexation of Austria and then the Germans of Czechoslovakia (the *Sudetendeutsch*). The other contentious ethnic minority in Eastern Europe was the Jews—victims of pervasive anti-Semitism but also resented as the prosperous commercial class in many urban areas. In Hitler's Germany, where the "people" were defined in racial terms, the Jews were persecuted with increasing fervor as an alien, non-Aryan infection in the body politic.

Across the world, in China, the 1920s and 1930s witnessed another attempt to build a modern nation-state on the debris of empire, both domestic and foreign. The Qing (or Manchu) dynasty had been hollowed out by decades of outside commercial penetration as the Europeans powers, Russia, Japan, and the United States vied for trading privileges, military bases, and railroad concessions. The dynasty finally collapsed in 1911, and China was engulfed by civil war waged by regional warlords. In the late 1920s, General Chiang Kai-shek and his National People's party (*Guomindang*) established their military authority over much of the country. The new government sought to reform the administration, develop urban areas, and reduce foreign control over the Chinese economy. The Communist party, led by Mao Zedong, offered a rival vision of modernization, based on rural revolution, from enclaves in the interior. But neither the Nationalists nor the Communists could pursue their goals for China once the Japanese took control of much of the eastern portion of the country during the 1930s. National state-building took second place to a renewed struggle against foreign imperialism.

China's contest between Nationalists and Communists exemplifies a second major theme of the 1930s, namely the ideological controversy about how to run a modern state in an age of mass politics. Across Europe and Asia the collapse of dynastic empires usually resulted in the creation of democratic franchises, giving all adults (or at least adult males) the vote. Even where there were no revolutions, democratic politics marked a major change. In Britain, for instance, the electorate in 1918, under a new democratic franchise, was three times that of 1910—21.4 million instead of 7.7 million, despite the loss of 750,000 men during the war. In this new era of mass voting, the business of politics and the task of effective government were far more complex. One response was to graft democracy onto older structures of nineteenth-century political liberalism. This was the pattern in Britain and France. They were classic "liberal" polities in which the populace enjoyed substantial civil rights guaranteed by law and parliamentary constitutions, and the executive was accountable to representative assemblies. Here the democratization of politics therefore meant enlarging the definition of "the people." But Italy and Germany were new nation-states, with bitterly contested governments. In Germany, like imperial Japan, the liberal doctrines of individualism and equality ran up against deeper traditions of authoritarian rule. These three countries tried parliamentary government on democratic franchises after 1918, only to abandon it in a backlash against party corruption and governmental ineptitude. Instead Mussolini's Italy pioneered what became known as the fascist model.

"Fascism" is a notoriously slippery concept. Historians even debate whether it can be applied to Germany as well as Italy. They note the ways in which, particularly in the economic order, both regimes fell short of fascist ideals. It is certainly doubtful that the term can be applied to Japan, where there was no single charismatic leader and where traditional elites in the military and bureaucracy remained in control. In many respects Japanese society throughout World War II remained less regimented than that of the Soviet Union and Guomindang China, which both fought on the side of "the democracies."

But in the 1930s many onlookers were struck by similarities, not differences. Fascists preached the politics of national renewal, seeking to mobilize mass movements by an often mystical vision of national greatness rooted in historical myths and directed toward imperialist expansion. "Preached" is an apt word, for Mussolini in Italy and Hitler in Germany were messianic politicians who propagated new civic religions of national devotion. Against the traditions of the Enlightenment, fascists also prized willpower, not reason. They argued that violence and war were the dynamos of history and the rejuvenators of national character. They appealed to those for whom political liberalism and aristocratic conservatism both seemed outdated and decadent philosophies, irrelevant to the modern age. A core constituency of the fascists was veterans bonded together by the horrific experience of total war and then, as they saw it, betrayed by civilian politicians. But the attacks by fascists on the corruption and ineptitude of established political parties won them far wider support among the middle classes and workers during the crisis of the Great Depression. In a loose sense, these features of nationalism, militarism, and imperial expansion could also be applied to the opponents of parliamentary government in Japan.

Hitler did not call himself fascist. And "Nazi" was a shorthand first used by opponents of his National Socialist German Workers party. Its full name reminds us of the other great ideological challenge in the age of mass politics, namely international communism led by the Soviet Union. Hitler appealed to the working masses, but he was trying to mobilize *German* workers in the name of *national* socialism. In both Italy and Germany, the danger of Communist revolution was one of the major rallying cries of the regimes. Hitler, for instance, used the burning of the parliament building (the Reichstag) in February 1933 to justify suspending civil liberties to save Germany from a supposed Communist takeover.

Soviet leaders, too, exploited the foreign ideological threat to consolidate support. After the Bolshevik Revolution of 1917, the Russian Empire fell apart. It took four years of brutal civil war

before Lenin's government emerged victorious, albeit over do-
mains much reduced from those of the tsars. The civil war also
drew in various foreign forces, including Britain, France,
Poland, the United States, and especially Japan—initially to
maintain an eastern front against Germany but increasingly to
topple a regime whose avowed goal was international revolution.
Foreign intervention in the civil war was never forgotten by Soviet leaders. In the late 1920s Joseph Stalin, Lenin's successor,
played up the danger of imperialist attack to justify the conver-
sion of agriculture from peasant plots to collective farms and his
drive to establish heavy industry, especially for armaments. "We
are fifty or a hundred years behind the advanced countries," he
warned industrial managers in 1931. "We must make good this
distance in ten years. Either we do it or they crush us."

Although Stalin had committed himself to building up "socialism in one country," the project of international revolution
was still advanced in the 1920s through the Comintern (the
Communist International) in Moscow, which coordinated political and subversive activity abroad. In the mid-1930s, however,
the party line shifted to a call for "popular fronts" with non-
Communist political groups in the overarching struggle against
fascism. Communist propaganda helped to create the image of
fascism as a distinctive, unitary ideology, depicting it as the last
gasp of financial capitalism. This helped strengthen the sense of
general threat to the Soviet Union and distracted attention from
the potentially embarrassing concept of National Socialism proclaimed by Hitler.

For politically active contemporaries, the Spanish Civil War of
1936–1939 constituted a microcosm of Europe's ideological bat-
tlelines. The Republican government received support from the
Soviet Union and many leftist groups. General Francisco
Franco's Nationalist rebels were backed by Italy and Germany,
as well as by rightist and Catholic opinion. Anxious to prevent
the conflict from escalating, Britain and France tried to impose a

nonintervention policy on the other powers. Its transparent failure seemed to symbolize the democracies' loss of will. By contrast, entanglement in Spain drew Hitler and Mussolini closer together, heightening the sense of fascism on the march, while Soviet involvement strengthened the impression that communism was the only real competitor to fascism. In short, the Spanish Civil War was widely taken as testimony to the weakness of liberal parliamentary democracy in the 1930s. Meanwhile, in Eastern Europe, the new democracies established in the wake of World War I collapsed into military-backed authoritarian regimes in every country except Czechoslovakia.

Part of the appeal of both German Nazism and Soviet communism in the 1930s derived from their evident economic success. Here lies a third general theme of the decade, paralleling the travails of political liberalism, namely the failure of liberal capitalism in confronting the Great Depression. In this the United States was centrally implicated. After the boom of the 1920s, the Wall Street crash of October 1929 was followed by the collapse of the U.S. banking system and a severe contraction of investment at home and abroad. This undermined the big banks of Central Europe in 1931 and helped force Britain—the region's other big foreign lender—off the gold standard because its reserves were exhausted. Most major countries followed Britain over the next few years, including the United States. Their currencies were no longer fixed against a set amount of gold but fluctuated against those of other countries. As a protective measure, financial groupings began to emerge, in which smaller states pegged their currencies to that of a leading economy with which they already had close relations. Examples were the zones formed around the French franc, the German Reichsmark, the U.S. dollar (particularly in the Americas), and the "sterling area" covering parts of the British Empire but also Scandinavia. In Asia, Japan's reliance on imports made it less self-sufficient. But expansionists in Tokyo used terms such as

"Greater East Asian Co-Prosperity Sphere" as euphemisms to mask their own aspirations for a regional bloc.

This drift from global to regional trade was reinforced by protective tariffs. In the early 1930s tariff rates were raised substantially by major capitalist economies, led by the United States, to defend their domestic industries in an era of depression and also to benefit their trading partners. In 1930, for instance, 83 percent of Britain's imports entered the country duty-free; in 1932 the proportion was only 25 percent. But countries of the British Empire, such as Australia or South Africa, were allowed either lower or no tariffs on their goods. This "Empire Preference System" was extended by trade agreements during the 1930s to more than twenty other countries in Europe, Scandinavia, and Latin America. The British presented Imperial Preference as a reaction to U.S. tariffs and a way to start reflating world trade in conditions of economic depression and global dislocation.

There is no question that the credibility of liberal capitalism was severely damaged by the depression. Low investment and stagnant output, reduced trade and high unemployment—these were hardly good advertisements for the classical liberal doctrines of a free market of individual entrepreneurs operating under limited government regulation and trading freely across the world. During the 1930s more interventionist theories of capitalism were emerging. Most famously, John Maynard Keynes, the English economist, argued that governments could safely foster demand by increased spending if they abandoned the liberal shibboleths of low taxes and a balanced budget. But Keynesian ideas did not enter mainstream economics or government policy until the 1940s. For much of the depression decade capitalism seemed to be intellectually as well as financially bankrupt. By contrast, Hitler's heavy spending on public works and armaments helped pull Germany out of its depression. Unemployment fell from a peak of 30 percent in 1932 to 2 percent in 1938.

Nazi economic advisers developed ambitious plans for self-sufficiency within an economic bloc in Central and Southeast Europe. Autarky and government direction seemed more successful than economic liberalism.

More striking still was the success of Stalinism in industrializing a backward agrarian and craft economy through rigorous state planning. Three five-year plans, starting in 1928, built a modern industrial base in heavy industries such as iron, steel, and above all armaments—reflecting Stalin's conviction that the Soviet Union would soon have to fight for survival. Symbols of the "Great Leap Forward" such as Magnitogorsk (the Magic Mountain), a new metallurgical complex created in the wilderness beyond the Ural mountains, caught the imagination of many intellectuals and left-wingers in the West. In 1935 Sidney and Beatrice Webb, the celebrated British socialists, published a massive book entitled *Soviet Communism: A New Civilisation?* In later editions the question mark disappeared. Such enthusiasm for Soviet planning was vehemently contested on the right of the political spectrum, where critics pointed to the huge human losses from farm collectivization and the political purges. But no one could deny the dynamism of the Soviet experiment. In the 1930s it contrasted strikingly with the evident failures and stagnation of capitalism.

Thus the spread of regional trading blocs and the apparent success of planned economies cast doubt on the efficacy of liberal capitalism based on the minimal state. This development paralleled the defensiveness of political liberalism against the dynamism of fascism and communism. In general, European liberalism seemed to many a nineteenth-century ideal whose time had passed. And its exemplars were nineteenth-century empires who, by the 1930s, were struggling to hold their own against the revisionist powers. Such was the international crisis of the 1930s.

AMERICAN DISTINCTIVENESS

What in shorthand I have called the issues of empire, ideology, and economics were the source of enormous tension and conflict in Europe and parts of Asia during the 1930s. The United States itself was not completely immune. America's severe depression cast doubt on the efficacy of liberal capitalism. In 1933, 25 percent of the American workforce was unemployed; in 1938 the proportion was still 19 percent. Was liberal democracy also outmoded? In the dark days of 1934–1935 some commentators saw Huey Long, the demagogic governor of Louisiana, or Father Charles E. Coughlin, the "radio priest," as possible candidates for the role of an "American Mussolini."

The battle cries of imperialism and nationalism also had American echoes. The United States had its own, albeit small, colonial empire, mostly acquired in 1898–1900 during the war with Spain. Its Pacific outposts of Hawaii and the Philippines were to prove hostages to fortune in the face of Japanese ambitions. The country was also wracked by its own ethnic tensions. Agitation on the West Coast had resulted in total bans on immigrants from China and then Japan. In the East and Midwest, the largely British and Protestant politico-cultural elites were alarmed by the mass waves of immigration from Southern and Eastern Europe in the years before World War I. After the Red Scare of 1919–1920, "Anglo-Saxon" American nationalists succeeded in imposing tight quotas on immigration from Europe.

Imperialism and nationalism had been central to the creation of the United States itself, for there was no necessary reason why this vast country should extend from the Atlantic to the Pacific. It had been established by war at the expense of the European powers such as Britain, France, and Spain, and also by seizing territory from Mexico and from the Native American Indians. In that sense the United States was a product of imperialism. It had also defeated a major nationalist movement—the bid to establish the Confederate States of America in 1861–1865. This victory was achieved at the staggering cost of 620,000 lives, making the war to preserve the Union truly America's "Great War."

But if one might see the United States as an empire, it was, in Thomas Jefferson's phrase, an "empire of liberty" (at least for whites). Unlike most of Europe, the country was not ruled by a monarchy that operated with little constitutional restraint. Nor did it have an entrenched national landed aristocracy or a wealthy state church that controlled education. And by the 1830s most states had given the vote to white adult males. In short, the United States was a democracy long before it industrialized, became a world power, or established the institutions of a strong central government. These were profound contrasts to Europe, where democracy usually had to be grafted onto vigorous governments that were already industrial powers and vast empires.

The survival of the United States as a country the size of a continent owed much to the system of federalism established by the Constitution of 1787. Although the balance between the states and the Union shifted significantly over the next century and a half, federalism remained the basic principle on which the empire of liberty rested. The Founding Fathers had pondered whether it was possible to operate republican government on such a vast scale—republics, based on a large measure of citizen participation, being traditionally confined to city-states. But the essence of American liberal democracy was local self-government. This worked because, in the historian Robert Wiebe's phrase, America was a "segmented society," one in which power, wealth, and natural resources were geographically dispersed. Federalism was therefore the appropriate political expression. Even at the end of the 1930s Uncle Sam accounted for only 40 percent of total government taxation in the United States.

Equally unusual, compared with Europe, was the lack of ideological diversity. Because liberal democracy was securely established, because the ownership of land was widespread among white males, the United States did not experience the ferocious struggles between the old order and the new mass politics so familiar across the Atlantic. Whatever the fears about Long and Coughlin, no serious American fascist movement took shape. Even more significant, the United States strikingly lacked a substantial Communist or even Socialist party. The whole left-of-center half of the European political spectrum simply did not exist as mainstream politics in the United States. Nor was economic planning ever a serious prospect, even in the 1930s. Roosevelt's New Deal adopted halfhearted expedients such as business self-regulation rather than systematic economic planning.

At a deeper level still, the United States was distinct from most of Europe and Asia in its degree of security. This mattered because a sense of external threat was frequently the spur to the establishment of strong states, planned economies, and autocratic ideologies. By the early twentieth century, Americans lived on a continent in which no great power contested their predominance. And, in an era of sea power, vast oceans gave them a sense of security from turbulence elsewhere. Despite their spectacular economic development of the late nineteenth century, thanks to which the United States produced nearly one-third of world manufacturing output by 1913, less than 5 percent of gross domestic product derived from foreign trade. Growth depended mainly on the vast internal market, undivided by tariff barriers and increasingly integrated by the railroads.

American entry into the European war in 1917, therefore, did not stem from dire necessity. There was no threat to American security, and, though the boom of 1915–1916 was largely attributable to war orders, President Woodrow Wilson's refusal to limit trade, travel, and loans to belligerent countries owed as much to his sense of right as to narrow American self-interest.

Wilson believed that by affirming the freedoms of trade and travel he was standing up for the rights of all peace-loving nations against the tyranny of war. What Wilson, like many world leaders, failed to appreciate was that, because of the surprise stalemate that resulted on land after 1914, the conflict became an economic war of attrition. His refusal to limit market forces, given the close commercial links with Britain, meant that America's economic power was increasingly mobilized by the Allies, not by Germany and the Central Powers. By the fall of 1916, 40 percent of the money Britain needed to pay for the war was being raised in the United States, mostly by private loans. When the Germans unleashed their U-boats against American shipping in January 1917, in an attempt to cut Britain's economic artery, Wilson had little choice but to ask Congress to declare war.

Yet the president justified his decision in high moral terms. His stated goal was not freedom of shipping in the Atlantic, nor even the defeat of German militarism; it was nothing less than "to make the world safe for democracy." Entry into a European conflict was explained as a global crusade. With victory achieved, in 1919 Wilson devoted himself to establishing a League of Nations to ensure global peace and order. His principal Republican critic, Senator Henry Cabot Lodge, wished to concentrate on the overriding problem of Europe by offering an American guarantee of French security against renewed German aggression. But Wilson believed that, in the era of modern technology, nothing less than world peace was needed to prevent another world war. Convinced that the president should exercise prime authority in foreign affairs, he hoped to force his plans through the Senate by appealing to public opinion. He embarked on an arduous national speaking tour, but this precipitated a major stroke in October 1919. Incapacitated yet intransigent, Wilson could not coerce the Senate, yet he would not compromise his ideals. The Covenant of the League of Nations, tied to the peace treaty, failed to win the necessary two-thirds majority in the Senate.

Not only did the United States renounce the League, Wilson's failure prompted a backlash against international entanglements and against his activist style of leadership. The backlash would have a profound effect on Franklin Roosevelt.

The United States never joined the League of Nations. In this sense the country remained true to the hallowed advice of George Washington in his Farewell Address of 1796, "to steer clear of permanent alliances with any portion of the foreign world."* But this did not imply a posture of isolation, which, as many commentators observed, had never been the pattern of U.S. policy and was certainly not practical in the modern era. In particular, America's international economic relationships had been transformed by the conflict of 1914–1918, what was now being called "the World War." The Federal Reserve Act of 1913 had created a loose regional banking structure to provide some degree of coordination. This had been totally lacking since the demise of the Second Bank of the United States in the Jacksonian era. The act also made it easy for American banks to establish foreign branches: before, most U.S. traders had handled their foreign transactions through London. Then came the huge wartime Allied demand for loans, for which major Wall Street banks, notably J. P. Morgan, organized American consortia. By 1919 the United States was a net creditor nation in the amount of $3.7 billion; in 1914 it had been a net international debtor on almost exactly the same scale.

In the 1920s the new American money power was used for diplomatic ends. Republican administrations encouraged private bankers to cooperate in the public interest to finance European financial stabilization, as in the 1924 Dawes plan and the 1929 Young plan. Foreign loans also helped lubricate U.S. trade. In 1929 the United States accounted for an eighth of world imports

---

*Less frequently quoted was Washington's rider that "we may safely trust to temporary alliances for extraordinary emergencies."

and nearly a sixth of world exports, displacing Britain as the world's leading exporter. By 1930 the United States had also replaced Britain as the largest foreign investor. The U.S. economy was now vital to the prosperity of the rest of the world, yet the domestic market remained far and away the major focus of American production and investment. The United States did not have the same stake in world trade as Britain, still the world's leading importer, for whom imports accounted for about 25 percent of national income (in the United States the figure was still about 5 percent). In short, America mattered to the world economy far more than the world economy mattered to the United States. This structural imbalance lay at the root of the worldwide depression that followed the American stock market crash of 1929.

The years 1922–1929 had seen one of the longest booms in American history to date. During that period, per capita gross domestic product rose by 24 percent and manufacturing output by nearly 30 percent. Yet growth was uneven, with much of the boom stemming from demand for new consumer goods such as automobiles and electrical equipment. Farm prices lagged behind, and older industries such as textiles were in trouble because of foreign competition. The stock market became particularly fevered, with share values in New York rising from a total of $4 billion in 1923 to $67 billion by the beginning of 1929. Another $20 billion were added in the last nine months of that year, until prices collapsed in the crash of October. In 1928 and 1929 agricultural prices also fell sharply, and many farmers could not maintain payments on their debts.

Some kind of cyclical downturn was inevitable. What helped turn recession into depression was the inadequacy of American financial institutions to deal with a modern industrial economy. The Federal Reserve System was a far cry from a national central bank. In so far as it did intervene in the economy, its anti-inflationary policies served to exacerbate the depression. Moreover, America's local banks were atomistic. In the 1920s there were some thirty thousand separate, unitary banks, most entirely reliant on their own resources. When local farmers defaulted on their mortgage payments as incomes fell, many banks collapsed—four thousand of them in 1933 alone. (There was a marked contrast here with Britain, where a central national bank and an integrated local banking system run by five major nationwide companies prevented the "slump" from becoming an American-style financial collapse.) The stock market also suffered from inadequate regulation. Although stock trading involved only a fraction of the population, the indices had become a benchmark of confidence for both businessmen and consumers. The crisis coincided with a period of major structural change in the U.S. and global economies, in which old staple industries such as textiles and footwear were being displaced by new technologies such as motor vehicles and electrical goods, and in which services were becoming as important as manufactures. Profound problems of readjustment complicated the task of recovery.

And so the crash became the depression. In 1933 investment stood at less than 10 percent of the 1929 figure; the surge in consumer goods had dried up. Automobile sales in 1932 were a quarter of the 1929 figure of 4.5 million. With new industries starved of demand, old ones still in decline, and labor markets largely rigid, unemployment soared from 3 percent of the workforce in 1929 to 25 percent in 1933. Millions lost their jobs and their savings. After dreaming of wealth in the 1920s, Americans woke up to a nation of poverty. Research in 1930 suggested that more than half of farm families lived on $1,000 a year, or half the notional poverty line. The depression was also long-lasting: after a renewed recession in 1937, unemployment in 1938 was still 19 percent, and investment languished at 40 percent of 1929 levels. The collapse was psychological as much as economic. "What we have lost," said the literary critic Edmund Wilson in 1931, was "not merely our way in the economic labyrinth but our conviction of the value of what we are doing."

President Roosevelt focused on this psychological malaise in his inaugural address of March 1933, insisting that "the only thing we have to fear is fear itself." He also recognized that nineteenth-century institutions had to be adapted to twentieth-century conditions. Structural reforms of the banking system and the stock market were major priorities when he took office. But FDR's New Deal did not end the depression. Rearmament, European war orders, and the draft in 1940–1941 constituted the real turning points. As the historian Anthony Badger has put it, the New Deal acted as "a holding operation for American society: a series of measures that enabled the people to survive until World War II opened up new opportunities."

Appreciating the gravity of the depression is essential if we wish to understand the conduct of U.S. diplomacy in the 1930s. This was a country that had turned in on itself—preoccupied with its great economic and social crisis, unsure that past values offered signposts to the future. Not a society in revolutionary upheaval—unlike Nazi Germany or Stalinist Russia—but one that had lost its nerve.

This can be seen starkly in the changed attitude to foreign economic policy. With Wall Street and big business already scapegoats for the depression, attention turned in 1934 to their roles in foreign policy. Best-sellers such as *The Merchants of Death* and the 1934–1936 Senate inquiry into the munitions industry encouraged the belief that bankers and arms manufacturers had inveigled America into the World War for their own financial gain. Lobbied intensively by various peace groups, Congress in August 1935 passed a Neutrality Act. This radically changed America's historic policy of freely trading with belligerent countries in time of war—the policy that Wilson had gone to war to preserve. Instead, in the event of a war, the president would be obliged to impose an embargo on the sale of munitions to all bel-

ligerents. A new act in February 1936 added a mandatory ban on
the provision of loans, and a third Neutrality Act, in May 1937,
included prohibitions against U.S. citizens traveling on belligerent passenger vessels and against American vessels carrying arms
to belligerents. As critics remarked, the neutrality legislation was
like a belated attempt to avoid American entry into the war of
1914–1918. The commercial and financial wealth that in the
mid-1920s had seemed a mark of international power was now
viewed as a source of vulnerability. The Neutrality Acts were
emblematic of a nation that had lost confidence in itself.

Yet the neutrality legislation was a hybrid. While the 1937 act
included mandatory bans on arms, loans, travel, and shipping, it
also gave the president discretionary power to place all non-arms
trade with belligerents on a "cash-and-carry" basis if he believed
this necessary for American peace and security. "Cash and carry"
was a phrase popularized by Bernard Baruch, the former chairman of Wilson's War Industries Board, in an influential article in
1936. "We will sell to any belligerent anything except lethal
weapons, but the terms are '*cash on the barrel-head and come and
get it.*'" Baruch offered an ingenious way to preserve the profits
of neutral commerce while minimizing the danger of economic
or emotional entanglements in a future war through vested interests or loss of American life. And, as the State Department
recognized, cash and carry in a future war would benefit Britain,
with financial reserves and a large merchant fleet, and operate
against Germany and Japan. A recipe for biased neutrality, it accorded with the instincts of Roosevelt himself.

ROOSEVELT: "PINPRICKS AND RIGHTEOUS PROTESTS"

Even to his closest associates, Roosevelt remained an
enigma. "You are one of the most difficult men to work with that
I have ever known," Interior Secretary Harold Ickes once told
him. "You keep your cards close up against your belly. You never

put them on the table." This was a deliberate policy. Treasury Secretary Henry Morgenthau, who, like Ickes, served for the entire Roosevelt presidency, recorded these words from the president in 1942: "You know I am a juggler, and I never let my right hand know what my left hand does." Historian Warren F. Kimball took this as the epigraph for his 1991 study of FDR's foreign policy, *The Juggler.* General Douglas MacArthur, another wartime associate but no friend, put it more bluntly. In 1945 he referred to FDR as "a man who would never tell the truth when a lie would serve him just as well."

Roosevelt's secretive handling of foreign policy has been a fertile source of conspiracy theories, particularly about Pearl Harbor. Less melodramatically, it poses acute problems for the historian, since the president put so little on paper. The secrecy was ingrained: the only son of a wealthy Hudson Valley landowner, Franklin was by nature a loner, especially close to his mother. But self-reliance was also learned the hard way. In his youth FDR was athletic and gregarious—a natural politician who relished his years as Wilson's assistant secretary of the navy. Then in 1921, aged thirty-nine, he was struck down with polio, which left him paralyzed from the waist down. For years, with the help of family and friends, he fought to regain his mobility. Although he returned to politics in 1929 as governor of New York and then president in 1933, he would never again walk unaided. Henceforth life was lived in a wheelchair. If he wished to stand, ten pounds of metal braces locked his useless legs in place. Every night he had to be undressed by a valet and heaved into bed.

Few Americans knew the extent of their president's infirmity. Observing an unwritten code, the media virtually never used photographs or film that showed him in a wheelchair or being lifted out of his automobile. But Roosevelt's handicap cannot be ignored if we wish to understand his foreign policy. For one thing, it probably strengthened his secretive nature. After this

"trial by fire," as his wife Eleanor called it, he became even more
self-reliant. On the other hand, in foreign affairs he became more
dependent. Lacking his own legs, he used close associates such as
Sumner Welles and Harry Hopkins as his eyes and ears. More
than was true of other leaders, he drew heavily on the formative
experiences of his twenties and thirties—on the intellectual legacies of his kinsman Theodore Roosevelt and his former boss
Woodrow Wilson.

The Roosevelts of Hyde Park were traditionally Democrats,
and FDR did not change that allegiance. But in his youth he was
much influenced by Teddy Roosevelt, a distant relative, and cast
his first vote in a presidential election for "Cousin Theodore."
When he married TR's niece, Eleanor, in 1905, the president
gave away the bride. FDR's progressive politics owed a lasting
debt to Teddy Roosevelt's "New Nationalism"—the belief in
strong governmental regulatory powers. Although serving in the
Wilson administration and supporting the League of Nations
project loyally, FDR later parted company with Wilson in three
crucial respects.

First, he believed that Wilson had adopted too autocratic a
foreign policy, failing to build a domestic consensus behind the
League. As he observed to an aide in 1937: "It's a terrible thing to
look over your shoulder when you are trying to lead—and to
find no one there." Wilson had led from the front and got too far
ahead of political opinion. FDR learned from those mistakes: as
speechwriter Robert Sherwood wrote in 1948, "the tragedy of
Wilson was always somewhere within the rim of his conscious-
ness." Second, FDR came to believe that Wilson's League was
the wrong approach to peacekeeping. Like TR, he placed more
emphasis on the role of power in international affairs. With regard to the Neutrality Acts, Roosevelt sought greater presidential discretion to apply the legislation in a way that discriminated
against aggressor states. Discriminatory neutrality implied,
third, that the great powers would take a leading role in peace-

keeping rather than leaving it to the League of Nations. Roosevelt therefore placed great stock on cooperation with Britain. He shared with TR the turn-of-the-century conceptions of an "Anglo-Saxon race" with distinct responsibilities for ordering and civilizing the world. In this task a big fleet and Anglo-American naval cooperation were deemed especially important: both Roosevelts were disciples of Admiral Alfred T. Mahan's theories of sea power. They also considered German militarism as a grave and persistent threat to peace.

In all these respects Franklin owed much to Cousin Theodore. Yet in the 1930s he continued to insist on his loyalty to essential Wilsonian ideals. In 1932, for instance, he told a critic of his apostasy on the League that he was looking for "the best modern vehicle" to reach these ideals, more suited to contemporary realities. And his attitude to Britain reflected Wilson's own deep ambivalence. Although often referring privately to the British as "cousins," he had no intention, as he said in 1937, of tying U.S. policy "as a tail to the British kite." He was scathing about the British upper class, ascribing many failings in British policy to "too much Eton and Oxford." Like many New Dealers he suspected that a pernicious Wall Street–City of London axis lay at the root of many of America's economic problems. Above all, he was a relentless critic of the British Empire—proud of his family's Revolutionary heritage, confirmed by his reading of Jefferson in the 1920s as to the jaded and corrupt nature of the Old World. Roosevelt's conviction that the United States was a noncolonial and indeed anti-colonial great power—with, in consequence, a special virtue and responsibility—was fundamental to his thinking. Like Wilson, FDR's worldview reflected many of the values of mid-nineteenth-century English liberals and radicals about the iniquities of empire, the danger of large armaments, and the desirability of free trade. Even more than Wilson, he was passionately convinced that democratic America was the supreme exemplar of such values. Roosevelt's "Americanism" constituted a fundamental, if still inchoate, reassertion of democracy and liberal capitalism against the belligerent imperialism, political authoritarianism, and economic nationalism that were so much in the ascendancy in Europe and Asia.

During his first term and much of his second, Franklin Roosevelt took few foreign policy initiatives. In large part this is explained by the gravity of the depression at home and the intense political battles over New Deal programs. The latter reached a peak of intensity in 1937 over the president's plans to reform the Supreme Court. Many critics cited this as proof of FDR's dictatorial tendencies—a charge that he had no desire to strengthen by activist diplomacy. This remained a lasting concern. Yet the passivity of his foreign policy was born of conviction as well as circumstance. U.S. interests were not significantly touched by events in Europe or Asia. More important was Latin America, where Roosevelt sought to advance his country's economic and political goals in forms that did not smack of overt colonialism. The administration portrayed its "Good Neighbor" policy in the Western Hemisphere as an example to great powers in other parts of the world.

The leading foreign policy theme of the administration for its first few years was Secretary of State Cordell Hull's drive for Reciprocal Trade Agreements (RTA). The RTA Act of 1934 gave the president authority to reduce U.S. tariffs by up to 50 percent where others would do the same—these cuts then being extended to all other nations with which the United States had signed agreements. The act was largely a response to the depression. It wrested the initiative in tariff policy from Congress to the president in an effort to find outlets for the South's agricultural surplus (Hull was formerly a Tennessee congressman). But the secretary of state made this an issue of principle as well—animated, in the historian Arthur Schlesinger's phrase, by "a peculiar combination of evangelism and vindictiveness." Hull was an unreconstructed exponent of the ideals of one of Wilson's heroes, the nineteenth-century British radical Richard Cobden. Like Cobden, he saw prosperity as the key to peace, trade barriers as the cause of war. With Germany largely outside the U.S. trading orbit, Hull concentrated on securing a deal with Britain, both as an example to the rest of the world and as a wedge into the British and Canadian markets.

FDR gave Hull his head in the mid-1930s, partly because the president sympathized with the basic approach but mainly because he had few other policies to offer. From 1936 FDR also toyed with various proposals by Hull's undersecretary and bitter rival, Sumner Welles, for America to convene a new international conference. This would establish basic Wilsonian principles of freer trade and international disarmament. Like Wilson, the Roosevelt administration was offering global answers to regional problems. On the other hand, drawing on his intellectual heritage from TR, the president mused repeatedly about ways to control aggression through trade embargoes and naval blockades. Hence his concern for the right kind of neutrality act, including cash-and-carry clauses and presidential discretionary powers.

Controlling aggression seemed more urgent in 1937 with the escalating conflict in Spain (the Basque town of Guernica was obliterated by German bombers in April) and Japan's renewed attack on China in July (which led to a brutal battle for Shanghai). Having initially connived at nonintervention in Spain and the accommodation of Japan in China, FDR concluded that both wars were embryonic regional conflicts. In October 1937 he spoke publicly in Chicago about the need to "quarantine the aggressors," likening international lawlessness to a global epidemic of a contagious disease. As he told reporters afterward, he was expressing "an attitude" and did not have "a program" to implement it. But when a U.S. gunboat was sunk by the Japanese in China's Yangtse River in December 1937, he told his cabinet and the British ambassador privately that he hoped to control Japan by means short of formal war, such as an Anglo-American naval blockade and economic sanctions. He added, "We don't call them economic sanctions; we call them quarantines. We want to develop a technique which will not lead to war." These ideas for the "containment" of Japan, to use cold war parlance, were to guide his policy in the Pacific right through 1941. In 1937, however, they were simply Rooseveltian musings—what the British ambassador called the president "in his worst 'inspirational' mood."

In January 1938 FDR lurched back into Wilsonian mode, picking up Welles's idea of a series of steps toward an international peace conference but trying the idea first on the British. Prime Minister Neville Chamberlain was just about to embark on bilateral talks with Italy and Germany; his approach was therefore fundamentally at odds with FDR's internationalism. Explaining this, he asked the president to postpone his initiative "for a short while." A week later, persuaded by the Foreign Office that this might seem to rebuff Roosevelt, he invited the president to go ahead, perhaps by presenting his proposals as a complementary effort to establish general international principles while the British addressed specific problems. Thereafter the ball was in FDR's court, but he let it drop. Some historians have judged that the president was upset by Chamberlain's response. More likely, as with quarantine, he had no real program and, once informed of British plans, he was ready to let them go ahead.

Roosevelt was wary of Chamberlain: "We must recognize that fundamentally he thoroughly dislikes Americans," FDR remarked in 1936. (Chamberlain's maxim was that "it is always best and safest to count on *nothing* from the Americans except words.") The president stayed on the sidelines in 1938 as the British intensified their efforts to reach agreements with Mussolini over his conquest of Ethiopia and with Hitler over his demands to incorporate the Germans of Czechoslovakia (the

Sudetendeutsch) in the Reich. The British line was essentially that, given the arbitrariness of European and African borders in an era when old empires were collapsing and new states were being formed, great-power agreements were better than another international war, even at the expense of some local resentment and suffering. The administration's instinct, on the other hand, was to assert the basic Wilsonian principle of national self-determination. FDR wrote of Chamberlain in March 1938 (using characteristic language about international policing): "As some-one remarked to me—'If a Chief of Police makes a deal with the leading gangsters and the deal results in no more hold-ups, that Chief of Police will be called a great man—but if the gangsters do not live up to their word the Chief of Police will go to jail.' Some people are, I think, taking very long chances." As to whether Chamberlain would succeed, FDR told his ambassador in Spain, it was "impossible to guess. But fundamentally you and I hate compromise with principle."

Chamberlain's efforts to resolve the Sudeten crisis came to a head in September 1938. He had hoped to arrange an orderly cession of people and territory to Germany. But by September 27 Hitler's demands for an immediate transfer without interna-tional supervision brought Britain and France to the point of war. At that point Hitler blinked first, warned by his command-ers that the army was unready for a major war and sobered by mobilization of the Royal Navy and other signs of British re-solve. Mussolini also made clear that he would not enter a war and urged Hitler to keep talking. Briefly losing his nerve, the German leader proposed a further meeting in Munich on Sep-tember 29. There Chamberlain gave him almost all he wanted on a slightly longer timetable, but coupled with an Anglo-German agreement, signed by the two leaders, pledging to re-solve their differences by peaceful means. Chamberlain placed great stock on this pledge, talking of "peace with honor." He re-turned home to a hero's welcome.

Throughout the crisis the Roosevelt administration insisted publicly that the United States was in no way involved, even as an intermediary. The State Department dignified this as a "policy of non-action." Privately FDR continued to question the sacrifice of principle, even talking in mid-September of Britain and France washing "the blood from their Judas Iscariot hands." But when news came that Chamberlain was flying to Munich, the president sent what he later called the shortest telegram of his life. It contained just two words: "Good Man."

The ambiguities of Roosevelt's policy are most evident in a September 19 meeting he had with the British ambassador, Sir Ronald Lindsay. This was shrouded in secrecy: the president told the ambassador that if his remarks leaked out he would probably be impeached. According to Lindsay, FDR said that "if the policy now embarked on [by Chamberlain] proved successful he would be the first to cheer." There might be scope for an international conference to resolve problematic frontiers on rational lines. But if peace could not be preserved, as then seemed likely, Roosevelt urged the Allies to fight a defensive war, based on naval blockade. He hoped to find ways to amend or manipulate the Neutrality Act so that the United States could assist the blockading powers.

The meeting had no effect on British policy or on the crisis itself. But it shows again FDR's mix of Rooseveltian and Wilsonian ideas, and the tensions between them. Its secrecy also reflects his fears of domestic opinion. In 1937–1938, as his biographer James MacGregor Burns observed, "the President was still confined to a policy of pinpricks and righteous protests." Yet the pinpricks mapped out patterns for the future, and the protests laid down distinctive moral markers. The world was still a long way from global war, the United States a far cry from belligerency. But, as international circumstances changed in 1939, 1940, and 1941, so Roosevelt's foreign policy would evolve from an attitude toward a program.

3

Revising Neutrality and Ideology
(October 1938 to November 1939)

THE MUNICH AGREEMENTS had averted war. Neville
Chamberlain hoped that they would permit a new bid for a European settlement. But other world leaders saw Munich as a
turning point. Hitler, cheated of a military triumph by his own
loss of nerve and by Chamberlain's diplomacy, was now bent on
subjugating the rest of Czechoslovakia and destroying Poland.
The way the Sudeten crisis had been resolved convinced him
that the British and French—those "little worms"—would not
stand in his path. Stalin drew similar lessons. Hitler's annexation
of the Czech lands, and with this the neutralization of one of the
strongest armies in Eastern Europe, threatened Soviet security.
Clearly Britain and France would not intervene to stop German
expansion eastward. Stalin judged that a deal with Hitler was
the wisest course, at least for the short term. These policy shifts
by Hitler and Stalin would result in the Nazi-Soviet Pact of August 23, 1939, to divide Poland between them.

For Roosevelt, too, Munich was a turning point. On October
5, 1938, he cabled Chamberlain: "I fully share your hope and belief that there exists today the greatest opportunity in years for
the establishment of a new order based on justice and law." Privately, however, he too was reflecting on the recent crisis. One re-

sult was his attempt to revise the Neutrality Act, to help Britain and France resist Germany. Because of congressional opposition, this strategy could not be realized in the summer of 1939. Nevertheless, the events of 1938–1939, interpreted by FDR, helped reshape public perceptions about international affairs. Especially after the Nazi-Soviet Pact, most Americans discerned a stark moral divide between democracy and "totalitarianism." Fascism and communism were both subsumed under the totalitarian umbrella.

The pact had other international consequences. It forced Japan to end its border conflict with the Soviet Union, thereby reducing American concern about Asia for the moment. It also facilitated the German invasion of Poland on September 1, 1939, and that triggered declarations of war by Britain and France two days later. The start of a European war, and the diminution of the Asian conflict, enabled Roosevelt to secure revision of the Neutrality Act on his own terms in November 1939.

Toward Armed Unneutrality

During October 1938 Roosevelt spent time mulling over the lessons of the Czech crisis. His ambassadors in Europe sent their appraisals; one of them, William C. Bullitt, came back from Paris to brief the president in person on October 13. Bullitt conveyed the drama of Munich, drawing on the French leaders' accounts of Hitler's ranting monologues to offer a much sharper impression than FDR formerly had of the secretive German leader. Roosevelt seems to have concluded that meaningful negotiation with Hitler was totally impossible. (That was not his view, then or later, about talking to the other "dictators," Mussolini and Stalin, or to the military regime in Tokyo.) In January 1939 he told senators that some people said this "wild man" was motivated by "paranoia," others that he had a "Joan of Arc" complex. One tirade, the president added, showed that Hitler believed himself "to be a reincarnation of Julius Caesar and Jesus Christ." The only word for such a personality, said Roosevelt, was a "nut."

Bullitt also helped the president understand the fear of massive airborne destruction that had gripped Paris and London during the crisis. Today, in the atomic age, it is hard to evoke the 1930s terror of the bomber. Yet Harold Macmillan, a British politician who was prime minister during the Cuban missile crisis of 1962, wrote in his memoirs in 1966 that "we thought of air warfare in 1938 rather as people think of nuclear warfare today." The reports from Bullitt and from Joseph Kennedy, U.S. ambassador in London, persuaded Roosevelt that Hitler had achieved a real psychological dominance over the French and British. In Roosevelt's view, only the German supremacy in the air could explain the extent of Hitler's victory against Europe's premier powers. Helping them redress the air balance, in the long-term interests of American security, became his preoccupation during the winter of 1938–1939.

In Roosevelt's mind, the air age called into question the concept of a separate Western Hemisphere. The administration was already concerned about signs of German penetration of Latin America. Although the United States remained the region's largest trading partner, during the 1930s Germany's share of Latin America's imports came to exceed Britain's. German political influence seemed to be on the increase, particularly in Argentina and Brazil. In private, Roosevelt spoke excitedly in January 1939 of a possible insurgency by the 1.5 million Germans in southern Brazil, which might then create a base for Nazi forces. Since 1919 the main U.S. fleet had been based on the West Coast, at San Diego, against a possible Pacific challenge from Japan, with only an antiquated training force in the Atlantic. But in the autumn of 1938 Roosevelt created an operational Atlantic squadron, and the annual fleet maneuvers the following February took place for the first time off the East Coast. The practice

exercise was designed to stop a German fleet from aiding a
fascist-led revolt in Brazil. But that did not address the air threat.
In April 1939 FDR told newspaper editors that the Axis had fifteen hundred planes capable of crossing the Atlantic to Brazil in
a day (refueling in, say, the Cape Verde Islands). From bases in
countries like Brazil or Mexico they could threaten New Orleans
in a couple of hours. Said Roosevelt: "It is a very small world."

There were, of course, some big "ifs" in Roosevelt's analysis.
Axis long-range air capability was nothing like what he claimed.
His fears about Latin American stability were exaggerated. But
the air age did have significant implications for America's *sense*
of security. And the administration's concern about Latin America reflects the pervasive 1930s belief that fascism was on the
march and democracy was in danger. Behind both anxieties was
the growing post-Munich fear that Britain and France were in
retreat. "What the British need today," wrote Roosevelt in February 1939, "is a good stiff grog, inducing not only the desire to
save civilization but the continued belief that they can do it. In
such an event they will have a lot more support from their
American cousins." During the spring of 1939 FDR spoke of
British chances in a war against Germany as only fifty-fifty. If
they were defeated, he feared the seizure or neutralization of the
British fleet, thereby opening up the Atlantic to Nazi expansion,
followed by increased economic and political penetration of
Latin America. "At the end of a very short time," he told adviser
Adolf A. Berle, "we should find ourselves surrounded by hostile
states in this hemisphere." FDR admitted that this was currently
only a possibility, but it was one, he said, that no farsighted
statesman could afford to permit.

The president therefore argued that, in the air age, defense of
the Western Hemisphere against a possible Nazi threat required
bolstering the airpower of Britain and France. A month of meetings culminated in a major conference with the military and
senior administration officials in the White House on the after-

noon of November 14, 1938. On this occasion the president was unusually forthright. According to his best information, FDR said, France had fewer than 600 planes it could put in the air, Britain had 1,500 to 2,200 such planes, and Germany 5,500 to 6,500 first-line planes and about 2,000 second-line planes. This gave Germany, on the most conservative estimate, at least a two-to-one air superiority.* Roosevelt went on to argue that

> the recrudescence of German power at Munich had completely reoriented our own international relations; that for the first time since the Holy Alliance in 1818 [the coalition of European monarchies that prompted the Monroe Doctrine] the United States now faced the possibility of an attack on the Atlantic side in both the Northern and Southern Hemispheres. He said that this demanded our providing immediately a huge air force so that we do not need to have a huge army to follow that air force. He considered that sending a large army abroad was undesirable and politically out of the question.

Roosevelt then made two points about the urgency of rearmament. First, that in 1917 it took the United States thirteen months after declaring war to put the first plane on the battlefront in Europe. This time such a delay would be disastrous. His second reason was diplomatic:

> I am not sure now that I am proud of what I wrote to Hitler in urging that he sit down around the table and make peace. That may have saved many, many lives now, but that may ultimately result in the loss of many times that number of lives later. When I write to foreign countries I must have something to back up my words. Had we had this summer 5,000

---

*It should be noted that FDR, along with the British and French governments, swallowed Nazi propaganda and seriously overestimated German air strength. In fact Britain and France had more first-line aircraft than Germany and considerably larger reserves. The serviceable first-line strength of Britain alone was equal to that of Germany.

planes with the capacity immediately to produce 10,000 per year, even though I might have had to ask Congress for authority to sell or lend them to the countries in Europe, Hitler would not have dared to take the stand he did.

Roosevelt therefore wanted authorization from Congress to build ten thousand planes immediately, plus a capacity to produce twenty thousand a year. Since the output of America's large airplane plants was only twelve hundred planes a year, he wanted seven government-owned plants built, mostly on War Department property. Although the estimated cost would be about $70 million, the work could be done by the Works Progress Administration—the New Deal relief agency run by his close aide, Harry Hopkins. Roosevelt claimed that "Hopkins could build these plants without cost to the Treasury because it would be work relief which otherwise would have to be provided in any case."

Several points should be made about Roosevelt's statement. First, it shows his new anxieties about the effects of airpower on U.S. security and about Hitler's supposed superiority. Although exaggerated, these anxieties were to be a feature of the next few years. FDR also made clear his aversion to the idea of sending another American Expeditionary Force to Europe. Instead he insisted that a large air force would be a real alternative in war as well as adding weight to his diplomatic leverage in peacetime. Then there was the pregnant phrase about asking Congress for authority "to sell or lend" planes to the Europeans. Here was the embryo of what would become lend-lease in 1941. Yet the comments about government-owned plants did not prove a signpost for the future. The military-industrial complex of World War II would be based largely on cooperation with private industry.

That last point excepted, the president's secret statement of November 14, 1938, provides a clear insight into his goals for un-neutral rearmament, short of war. Yet his plans came to very little in the next few months, for several reasons. The international situation remained ambiguous, Washington politics were unpropitious, and Roosevelt and his congressional backers mismanaged business on Capitol Hill.

The president set out his broad objectives in major speeches to Congress at the beginning of 1939. He asked for $500 million in appropriations for rearmament and urged revision of the neutrality laws because, in their present form, they "may actually give aid to the aggressor and deny it to the victim." Particularly in his mind was their effect on the civil war in Spain. In 1937 FDR had encouraged the extension of the arms embargo to cover civil wars, but this had served to help the fascist-backed forces of General Francisco Franco against the Republican government. By 1939 Roosevelt regretted his action. But on both fronts—rearmament and legislation—FDR had to trim his sails in the face of unfavorable political winds. The War Department strenuously opposed his plans for air rearmament: it wanted a balanced program to build up the army and navy as well as the army air corps, and FDR's grandiose figures of November 14 were soon trimmed back to around three thousand new planes. A French purchasing mission arrived in December with authority to buy one thousand planes in the United States, but the army air corps was reluctant to reveal any of its newest prototypes, especially the Douglas DB-7 bomber, until commanded to do so by an angry president. When one of the planes crashed in California on January 23, with a French official on board, news of the mission became public and prompted an outcry from congressional critics.

To limit the damage, FDR privately briefed the Senate Military Affairs Committee on January 31 with what he called "unusual candor and forthrightness." To the senators, as to his advisers in November, he set out his assessment of the Nazi threat to the Western Hemisphere, the new challenge of airpower, and the need to recognize that "the first line of defense in

the United States" was "the continued independent existence" of
key nations in Europe, particularly Britain and France. He
warned that, if it came to a European war in the present circumstances, there was "a fifty-fifty bet" that Hitler and Mussolini
would win. He was frank about his determination to build
planes and to get them to Britain and France, cash "on the bar-
relhead," while denying munitions to Germany, Italy, or Japan.
He admitted that this policy might be called unneutral but insisted that it was a matter of "self-protection" and that it would
reduce, not increase, the chances of U.S. entry into another European war. This was not, however, the impression that senators
derived from the meeting. Many found Roosevelt's candor
alarming. When leaks appeared in the press that he had said
America's frontiers were on the Rhine (not his precise words but
a reasonable paraphrase), the president made matters worse by
denouncing the leak in a press conference as a "deliberate lie" by
"some boob" in the Senate.

It is clear that, in the weeks after Munich, Roosevelt embarked
on a major bureaucratic and political effort to establish a policy
of unneutral rearmament. In doing so he took considerable political risks and was, for such a cautious leader, unusually forthright. But it is also clear that the domestic situation was very
difficult. The midterm elections in November 1938 saw the return of a significant bloc of Republicans to the House for the first
time since 1932. The Seventy-sixth Congress, which convened in
January 1939, had 261 Democrats and 164 Republicans. When
the latter combined with the substantial number of conservative
Democrats who were disaffected with the New Deal and suspicious of FDR's "dictatorial" tendencies, the result was legislative
deadlock. For this reason the president did not give a strong lead
on neutrality revision, leaving it to Democratic managers on
Capitol Hill, who held back after the furor about the French military mission. Not until March 15, 1939, when Hitler broke the

Munich agreement and took over the rest of Czechoslovakia, did the logjam begin to break. As FDR told the press, Hitler could no longer say that he was simply bringing neighboring Germans into the Reich. And the British and French decision finally to draw a line and to guarantee the political independence and territorial integrity of Poland increased the likelihood of European war and therefore of applying the existing neutrality legislation. Moreover, the cash-and-carry provisions of the 1937 act expired May 1. For all these reasons, something had to be done.

On March 20, Key Pittman of Nevada, chairman of the Senate Foreign Relations Committee, introduced his carefully named "Peace Bill" into the Senate. Pittman's neutrality legislation reflected the administration line—repeal the arms embargo and put all trade with belligerents on a cash-and-carry basis while retaining the 1937 bans on loans and travel to prevent economic and emotional entanglements from drawing America into another war. Subsequent hearings revealed strong opposition to these reforms, but also a lack of clear administration leadership. This was partly the fault of Pittman, a congenital alcoholic who was now seriously ill, but also of the president, who judged that a strong lead from the White House would be counterproductive. He left Hull and the State Department to resolve the mess that Pittman's indecisive management had created. Although an amended bill squeezed through the House at the end of June, it was tied to a limited arms embargo. In the Senate Foreign Relations Committee, Pittman's opponents demanded a postponement until the 1940 session. Even a personal conference with the president at the White House on July 18 proved unavailing. Senator William E. Borah, the veteran isolationist from Idaho, rejected FDR's assertion that a European war was imminent. When invited to look at the incoming State Department cables, Borah claimed that his own sources of information were more reliable. Unable to persuade a majority of the committee, Roo-

sevelt had to acknowledge defeat. "You haven't got the votes,"
Vice President John Nance Garner told him bluntly, "and that's
all there is to it."

For a president determined to send a clear message to Hitler,
this was a humiliating rebuff. Lack of White House leadership
was partly to blame, but it was clear that the anti-Roosevelt backlash on the Hill in 1938–1939 meant that any legislation giving
the president greater powers would be viewed with suspicion.
Congressmen were unsure of their constituents and waited for a
clear lead before deciding how to jump.* The Gallup polls
showed the volatility of American public opinion. On July 8, for
instance, 60 percent favored the sale of arms to Britain and
France in a European war. A month later 51 percent of those
questioned said they thought Congress was right to retain the
arms embargo, while 37 percent disagreed and 12 percent expressed no opinion. This ambivalence was a lasting feature of
American opinion about a European war. Consistently Americans opposed renewed belligerency by the United States. Yet
their sympathies were clearly on the side of Britain and France.
The solidification of those ideological sympathies was, in part,
the result of events in the winter of 1938–1939.

DEMOCRACY AND TOTALITARIANISM

Five weeks after Munich, on the night of November 9,
1938, a wave of Nazi-inspired violence against Jews and Jewish
property swept across Germany. Nearly one hundred Jews died,
some thirty thousand were arrested, and thousands of homes and

---

*Secretary of State Hull told the story of a math teacher who asked one of
her class: "Tommy, if there are sixteen sheep in a pen and one jumps the
fence, how many are left?" "None," said Tommy. "Well," said the teacher,
"you don't know anything about arithmetic." Tommy replied, "You don't
know anything about sheep."

hundreds of synagogues were destroyed. Pictures of storm troopers, armed with axes and crowbars, smashing shops and looting property were featured on the front pages of newspapers around the world. In retrospect, the night of broken glass (*Kristallnacht*) seems part of a remorseless and inevitable persecution of Jews by a dictator bent on their destruction. But while Hitler wanted a "final solution" (*Endlösung*) of the "Jewish problem," he had not come to power with a clear blueprint. After initial violence against Jews and political opponents in 1933, the Nazis concentrated on pressuring Jews to emigrate. But party radicals led by Joseph Goebbels, the propaganda minister, wanted tougher measures. In early November 1938 a German diplomat in Paris was shot dead by a Polish Jew. Goebbels seized on this pretext, and his speech on November 9 unleashed the Kristallnacht. Even the party was surprised at the extent of the destruction. Many Germans were genuinely shocked, and Hitler ensured—until late 1941—that there would be no more public attacks against Jews. But the international reaction was even more important. Despite deep anti-Semitism across Europe and the United States, the German pogroms evoked international outrage. Nazi race policy had now been clearly and publicly defined.

Roosevelt said he could "scarcely believe that such things could happen in a twentieth-century civilization." He summoned home the U.S. ambassador to Berlin for consultation. A Gallup poll showed nearly three-quarters of respondents in favor of "temporary withdrawal" of the ambassador "as a protest." ("Temporary" became indefinite after the German entry into Prague in March 1939.) Roosevelt's efforts to amend the 1924 Immigration Act to permit the entry of German refugee children into the United States proved unavailing because of nativist pressure groups. So were his efforts, through intermediaries, to bribe Hitler to allow 150,000 Jews to emigrate through a massive international loan. But Kristallnacht sharpened the moral divide between Nazi Germany and American values.

Roosevelt sought to make that divide explicit. His State of the Union Address on January 4, 1939, not only developed his security themes about the need for rearmament and the impossibility of hemisphere isolation. It also highlighted the ideological issues: "Storms from abroad directly challenge three institutions indispensable to Americans. The first is religion. It is the source of the other two—democracy and international good faith." Religion, said FDR, imbued a sense of personal dignity and mutual respect. "Democracy, the practice of self-government, is a covenant among free men to respect the rights and liberties of their fellows," while international good faith was the transposition of that mutual respect to the level of relations between nations. "Where freedom of religion has been attacked, the attack has come from sources opposed to democracy." And "where religion and democracy have vanished, good faith and reason in international affairs have given way to strident ambition and brute force." No names were mentioned. But to an American audience mindful of the Sudetenland and Kristallnacht, FDR's meaning was clear. Just as he was arguing that American security was not divisible from that of the world, so he insisted that American values could not flourish in an alien ideological environment. "We have learned that God-fearing democracies of the world which observe the sanctity of treaties and good faith in their dealings with other nations cannot safely be indifferent to international lawlessness anywhere. They cannot forever let pass, without effective protest, acts of aggression against sister nations—acts which automatically undermine all of us."*

On January 30 Hitler also spoke out about religion. On the sixth anniversary of his becoming chancellor, he gave a two-hour

*Compare the language of the Truman Doctrine speech of March 1947: "Totalitarian regimes imposed upon free peoples, by direct or indirect aggression, undermine the foundations of international peace and hence the security of the United States."

speech to the Reichstag about the Nazi party "saga." At the end he warned: "Europe cannot find peace until the Jewish question has been solved." He suggested that agreement could still be reached on emigration. But he also made a lurid "prophecy" that "if the international Jewish financiers in and outside Europe should succeed in plunging the nations once more into a world war, then the result will not be the Bolshevizing of the earth, and thus the victory of Jewry, but the annihilation of the Jewish race in Europe!" As yet, Hitler had no clear conception of how that annihilation would take place. But the devastating effect of the pogroms on the Jews encouraged the Nazi regime into more violent measures. And Roosevelt's private and public intervention in the Jewish question may well have strengthened Hitler's paranoid linkage of the United States and Jewish money power. In retrospect, his "prophecy" takes on sinister significance. "World War" (*Weltkrieg*) was the term used by Germans to distinguish the 1914–1918 conflict with Britain and America from earlier "European" wars. Nazi plans for a "final solution" of the Jewish question would take shape at the end of 1941 as British defiance, Soviet resistance, and American intervention made another "world war" a reality.

Roosevelt already saw the issue in global terms. The day after Hitler's Reichstag speech, on January 31, he gave his ill-fated briefing to senators about the international situation. He told them that "about three years ago we got the pretty definite information that there was in the making a policy of world domination between Germany, Italy and Japan. That was when the first anti-Comintern pact was signed." Since then, he went on, "that pact has been strengthened almost every month," and "there exists today, without any question whatsoever—if I were asked to prove it I could not prove it, of course—what amounts to an offensive and defensive alliance." Roosevelt added: "What Hitler said yesterday would come as a shock to a good many people." But really "there isn't anything new in what he said that we

haven't known for a year or two." The president did not necessarily believe that the Axis pact would hold. He told the senators:
"We always felt that if Mussolini found his bread was not but-
tered on the Hitler side, he would throw him over." (Hence the
scope for negotiation with Italy and, by extension, Japan.) But
FDR's assumption that Hitler's "ultimate objective" was "world
domination" did not change. And his fears of a tight "offensive
and defensive alliance" among Germany, Italy, and Japan were
to intensify over the next two years.

In the early months of 1939, Roosevelt continued his efforts to
"educate" American opinion. In an address on April 14, after the
Germans had taken over Czechoslovakia and the Italians had invaded Albania, he asked why nations could "find no better
methods of realizing their destinies than those which were used
by the Huns and the Vandals fifteen hundred years ago?" Next
day he invited Hitler and Mussolini to guarantee the integrity of
thirty-one specified countries in Europe and the Middle East for
at least ten years. These messages, broadcast worldwide, were
mocked in Germany and Italy,* but FDR had rated the chances
of a positive response at no more than one in five. As he told the
Canadian prime minister: "If we are turned down the issue becomes clearer and public opinion in your country and mine will
he helped." Another publicity ploy was the visit in June by King
George VI and Queen Elizabeth to the United States—the first
by a reigning British monarch. Roosevelt saw the visit as a safe
but effective way to dramatize Anglo-American amity, and as a
chance to show off the British monarchy, past symbol of transatlantic differences, in a favorable light. To this end he minimized
official functions in Washington and made much of the royal
couple's informal visit to his family home at Hyde Park, complete with an outdoor lunch of hot dogs and beer. He was sure
"the simplicity and naturalness of such a visit would produce a

*"A result of infantile paralysis," sneered Mussolini.

most excellent effect," enhancing "the essential democracy" of
the British king.

The most significant of these ideological benchmarks was the
Nazi-Soviet Pact of August 1939. The United States had been
the last great power to acknowledge officially the Bolshevik Revolution of 1917. Formal diplomatic recognition was extended by
the new Roosevelt administration only in November 1933. Relations soon soured over Soviet repudiation of the tsarist government's war debts, but in 1936 Roosevelt made a big effort to
improve the atmosphere by sending Joseph E. Davies as ambassador. Davies was a wealthy lawyer, with no diplomatic experience. FDR hoped to bypass the skepticism of Soviet specialists in
the State Department toward the chances of significant cooperation with Stalin.

But Moscow was playing a watching game. Berlin and Tokyo
had signed an anti-Communist pact in November 1936, and it
was in Stalin's interests to open links with their opponents. He
therefore acquiesced in the efforts of Maxim Litvinov, his foreign
minister, to develop a network of "collective security" with the
Western democracies. Then Munich exposed the hollowness of
that policy as a protection for Soviet security. In early 1939 Stalin
put out feelers to Berlin, and in May he replaced Litvinov with
Vyacheslav Molotov, a loyal henchman. During the summer
Stalin played with Germany and with Britain and France, seeking to discern what each side had to offer. He became convinced
that Britain and France had no intention of fighting for Poland,
and that Hitler was ready to gobble it up. In that case, the Soviet
Union would become the front line. On August 23 Molotov and
his German counterpart, Joachim Ribbentrop, signed a treaty of
nonaggression and a secret protocol dividing up Eastern Europe.

The Nazi-Soviet Pact was a stunning turnaround. For most of
the 1930s the fundamental ideological battle line in Europe had
been Nazism versus bolshevism. When the Soviet authorities
had to decorate Moscow airport for Ribbentrop's arrival, the only

swastika flags they could find came from a film studio that was making anti-Nazi propaganda movies. Then suddenly Stalin was toasting Hitler. The secret protocol to the pact divided Poland between the two powers. Of the other spoils, Stalin would get Latvia and Estonia; Lithuania was added in a separate agreement in September. Hitler was now free to invade Poland, and he did so after a trumped-up incident on September 1.

To his surprise, however, Britain and France honored their guarantees: the Munich "worms" had turned. Persuaded now that Hitler's aims threatened the whole European balance of power, on September 3 they reluctantly declared war. But they were neither ready nor willing to intervene in Eastern Europe. Within weeks, German and Soviet troops had carved up Poland. On September 28 the two powers signed a treaty of friendship, under which vast quantities of Soviet food and raw materials would flow to Germany. Over the next two weeks Moscow concluded "mutual assistance" pacts with the Baltic states of Estonia, Latvia, and Lithuania. This permitted the Soviet Union to station troops on their soil and to establish naval and air bases. When similar negotiations with the Finns broke down, the Red Army invaded Finland on November 30, beginning what became known as the "Winter War."

Once again the United States stood on the sidelines. In early August Roosevelt sent a message to Stalin that "if his Government joined up with Hitler, it was as certain as night followed day that as soon as Hitler had conquered France, he would turn on Russia." But Roosevelt kept well clear of the British and French negotiations. The main significance of the Nazi-Soviet Pact for the United States was ideological. It consolidated the American image of "totalitarianism."

The word originated in fascist Italy in 1923, initially as a pejorative term, to denote the "totalitarian spirit" that sought to take control of all areas of politics, religion, and morals. The idea of a "total state" was applied to Germany in the early 1930s by critics of Nazism. The term was then popularized in the United States from the mid-1930s to German emigrés, particularly Herbert Marcuse and others of the "Frankfurt School." On May 7, 1939, the cover story in the *New York Times Magazine* featured the "titanic struggle" of totalitarianism versus religion and democracy. Two vast figures were poised for battle above the caption: "The totalitarian church-state, presenting a species of man-god, presumes to offer a substitute for both religion and democracy." Although FDR did not make much explicit use of the term "totalitarian," the reference to religion and democracy perhaps owed something to his State of the Union Address.

Some American commentators, such as William Henry Chamberlin and John Dewey, wanted to apply the term "totalitarianism" to the Soviet Union as well. In the mid-1930s this was a matter of intense debate, especially during the Spanish Civil War of 1936–1939 when Hitler and Stalin were pitted against each other in a proxy war. But the Nazi-Soviet Pact and the partition of Eastern Europe ended all discussion, except for a minority on the extreme left. Stalin's Soviet Union—the country of atheistic communism and brutal purges, of the leadership cult and the one-party state—had revealed itself as the true partner of the Nazi führer, persecutor of the Jews and conqueror of Czechoslovakia and Poland. To most commentators the Soviet Union and Nazi Germany now seemed indistinguishable in methods and character. References to Hitler's "Brown Bolshevism" and Stalin's "Red Fascism" became commonplace in the U.S. press. Over the next couple of years, countless editorials and articles, seminars and lectures, established "totalitarianism" as a staple concept of American political thought.

STALEMATE IN ASIA

The Nazi-Soviet Pact also had a profound impact on East Asia. Here a major regional war had been going on since July 1937, when Japanese and Chinese forces clashed near Beijing. By the autumn of 1938 Japan controlled most of northeastern China, down to Shanghai and Wuhan. Added to its 1931–1932 conquest of Manchuria (renamed Manchukuo by Japan), this gave the Japanese a rich area of raw materials as a base for its industrial development as a major power. The problem for the leadership in Tokyo, where civilian politicians were increasingly under the control of the army and navy, was that they could not bring the "China Incident" to a successful conclusion. A third of the army was bogged down in Japan's "China Quagmire."

The Sino-Japanese War provoked an international outcry. China's great cities were home to thousands of Western missionaries and traders. Japanese atrocities therefore attracted the attention of the international media. The summer 1937 battle for Shanghai—the world's fourth most populous city—and the notorious "Rape of Nanjing" in December, when thousands of civilians were attacked and murdered, left an enduring image of Japanese brutality. In the twenty-first century, inured as we are to television violence, it is hard to recapture the shock felt by millions as they viewed newsreels of the aerial bombing of Chinese cities and the savage destruction of people and property. Japanese brutality also served to consolidate Americans' positive image of China as a society moving toward Western ways under a Westernized leader and his glamorous, American-educated wife, while Japan slipped from fragile democracy into military dictatorship. China's historic openness to Western influences, particularly religious, in contrast with Japan's proud insularity also made the Chinese seem "more like us." Christian missionaries and their offspring played a disproportionate role in the powerful "China lobby" that promulgated the idea of a special relationship between the United States and China.

The Sino-Japanese War therefore sharpened the Japan-China polarity in American political debate. Its brutality also provoked a keen sense of engagement in Asia. Opinion polls in 1938–1939 indicated that the public consistently espoused a tougher line in Asia than in Europe, partly because of the sense of moral outrage. In addition, there was apparently less fear of the consequences of a tough line than in the case of antagonism to Germany. That in turn reflected traditional American suspicions of Old World machinations; by contrast one detects an underlying, racially motivated complacency that the Japanese, however barbaric, were not formidable foes. Although the Chinese were subject to similar racial stereotypes (and immigration walls) if they came near the United States, "at home" they were regarded with patronizing favor. For a variety of reasons, therefore, Americans were less wary of entanglement in Asia than in Europe. This divergence in attitudes was to be a significant theme over the next couple of years.

Not that the United States was spoiling for a fight with Japan. The official State Department line, expressed in repeated legalistic statements by Hull, was neither to confront Tokyo nor to approve its actions. Not everyone in the administration was happy about this, particularly Henry Morgenthau, the treasury secretary. Roosevelt, too, chafed at State Department passivity: his Quarantine Speech of October 1937, which included a vehement denunciation of Japanese atrocities, was an expression of his frustration. The outcome of these tensions was not so much a clear policy as a series of impulsive reactions at times of particular tension with Japan when the activists were able to win the bureaucratic battle. In November 1938, for instance, Japan outlined its plans for a "New Order" in East Asia at the expense of Western economic interests. The following month Morgenthau secured a

$25 million oil credit for China. Yet this was just another of the Roosevelt administration's pinpricks. What entangled the United States deeper in Asia during 1939 was not popular indignation, nor the agitation of administration activists, but concern about the deteriorating balance in Europe. This was also to prove a recurrent pattern over the next two years.

In mid-March 1939, after Hitler's takeover of Czechoslovakia and Mussolini's invasion of Albania, British policymakers feared an imminent European war. In those circumstances they would have little to offer in Asia. British strategy in the event of war with Japan was to send the Mediterranean Fleet, based at the Egyptian port of Alexandria, out to Singapore, Britain's vast new naval base in Southeast Asia. But this would not be possible if Britain was fighting Italy as well. On March 19 the British therefore urged FDR that if war broke out in Europe, the main U.S. fleet should be sent to Hawaii and that secret naval conversations should take place to update those held in January 1938.

Roosevelt responded to both requests. The main fleet had been in the Atlantic that spring, for Caribbean maneuvers intended to signify U.S. concerns about hemisphere defense. But at the end of April, amid much deliberate publicity, it moved back through the Panama Canal to its main bases around San Diego. Then, in June, a senior British naval officer arrived in Washington to share contingency plans in the event of war. These talks took place in the home of the chief of naval operations, Admiral William Leahy—a sign of how wary the administration was of press leaks—but they confirmed that in the event of a European war, the United States intended to concentrate the main fleet at Pearl Harbor to deter Japan. These were noncommittal talks, for information. The administration was anxious to avoid explicit entanglement with the British, and most naval officers, Leahy excepted, opposed sending the fleet farther west to Singapore because that would imply "pulling Britain's chestnuts out of the fire." But the parallelism of policy was clear: as Britain became committed in Europe, America would do more in Asia.

A similar pattern can be observed during the Tianjin crisis in the summer of 1939. Tianjin, southeast of Beijing, was one of China's major ports. Here, as elsewhere, foreign powers had their own self-governing settlements in which Chinese law did not apply and that the warring armies usually respected as neutral territory. In consequence the settlements became home to many Chinese Nationalist guerrillas. When the British refused to hand over four of these men in Tianjin to the local Japanese army commander, he blockaded the settlement. Quickly a minor incident escalated into a trial of strength between Japan's New Order and the old order of Western extraterritoriality in Asia. With war looming in Europe, the British were in no position to provoke conflict in the Far East. An agreement signed in Tokyo on July 24 between the British ambassador, Sir Robert Craigie, and the Japanese foreign minister, Arita Hachirō, explicitly acknowledged Japan's "special requirements" for security in China.

Hull had privately followed a similar policy, but he had never conceded the principle. U.S. policymakers regarded the Craigie-Arita agreement as a damaging precedent. Coming just days after Congress had rejected the revised neutrality bill, it suggested that both America and Britain were indifferent to events in Asia. Roosevelt therefore announced on July 26 that Japan was being given six months' notice of the abrogation of the 1911 commercial treaty. In January 1940 the United States would be in a position, if it wished, to impose trade sanctions on Japan. The idea of abrogation had been touted by Morgenthau for some time, and there was considerable public support. A bill to that effect had recently been introduced by Republican Senator Arthur A. Vandenberg of Michigan. (Vandenberg was a leading proponent of strict neutrality in the case of Europe.) The administration took up the idea in late July because of the perceived need to do something to offset the Craigie-Arita agreement. Adolf Berle of the State Department confided to his diary: "It is a curious fact that the United States, which bolts like a frightened rabbit even from remote contact with Europe, will enthusiastically take a step which might very well be a material day's march on the road to a Far Eastern war" because the American people apparently felt that "getting into trouble is quite all right if the trouble is in the Western Pacific; but very, very bad if in Europe."

In the summer of 1939 a general Asian war seemed possible. For months there had been incidents along the disputed border of Japanese Manchukuo and Outer Mongolia, a Soviet protectorate. At this time Germany and Japan were engaged in conversations for a full alliance, and Japanese commanders in Manchukuo were confident that the Soviets would not intervene. They were wrong. On August 20 Soviet forces under the command of General Georgi Zhukov launched a massive preemptive assault, with devastating success. The Soviet victory at Nomonhan (or Khalkin-Gol as it is known in Mongolia) was a severe blow to the prestige of the Japanese army. Even more devastating was news of the Nazi-Soviet Pact on August 23, which totally undermined Japan's pro-German policy. Prime Minister Hiranuma Kiichirō resigned five days later.

The diplomatic revolution of August 1939 paved the way for war in Europe. In Asia, however, it prevented the China war from escalating. Rebuffed by the United States, defeated by the Soviet Union, and deserted by Germany, Japan was forced to rethink the fundamentals of its foreign policy. Throughout the winter of 1939–1940 it remained quiescent, until new opportunities arose in the summer of 1940 thanks to events in Europe. China also reviewed its diplomacy after the shock of the Nazi-Soviet Pact. Instead of cultivating the Soviet Union as its main potential ally against Japan, Chiang Kai-shek's government turned increasingly to the United States.

UNNEUTRALITY IN THOUGHT AND DEED

Just before 3 a.m. on the morning of September 1, 1939, Roosevelt was awakened by a phone call from William Bullitt in Paris. The ambassador announced that Germany had invaded Poland. Over the next two hours the president arranged for messages to be sent to the governments of Germany, Italy, Britain, France, and Poland urging them not to embark on the aerial bombing of civilians and unfortified cities. Roosevelt's fears of airborne disaster were shared in Europe. In the first few days of September, three million people fled London for the countryside. Yet the panic was unfounded. Until the spring of 1940, most of Europe hung between war and peace—what many British called the "bore war," or the "phony war" as it became known across the Atlantic. Of course it was neither boring nor phony for the Poles, brutally partitioned between Hitler and Stalin, or for the Finns, invaded by the Soviet Union at the end of November. But these were localized and relatively brief conflicts. Despite clashes at sea, there was no unrestricted submarine warfare. Nor did either side begin air bombing or major land offensives. In Europe, Italy did not join Germany; in Asia, Japan remained neutral. The all-out, three-front global conflict that British planners had dreaded did not materialize.

In his radio fireside chat to the nation on September 3, the president did not even hint at aid to Britain and France. He did state "a simple but unalterable fact of relations between nations. When peace has been broken anywhere, the peace of all countries everywhere is in danger." Unlike Woodrow Wilson in August 1914, FDR did not call for neutrality in thought and deed. "This nation will remain a neutral nation, but I cannot ask that every American remain neutral in thought as well. . . . Even a neutral cannot be asked to close his mind or his conscience." The existing Neutrality Act would be implemented, he said, but added: "I trust that in the days to come our neutrality can be made a true neutrality." He ended with an unequivocal statement of nonbelligerency:

> I have said not once, but many times, that I have seen war and that I hate war. I say that again and again. I hope the United States will keep out of this war. I believe that it will. And I give you assurance and reassurance that every effort of your Government will be directed toward that end. As long as it remains within my power to prevent, there will be no black-out of peace in the United States.

The neutrality legislation imposed on September 5 was a mixed bag. Bans on arms and loans to belligerents remained, while the cash-and-carry clauses for non-munitions had expired on May 1. But the war gave Roosevelt justification for calling back Congress (not due to reconvene until January) in a special session to review the Neutrality Act. He now had a clear strategy for revision, substituting cash and carry for the mandatory arms embargo. And he had learned from the fiasco on Capitol Hill in the summer. As his fireside chat indicated, the emphasis would now be on peace, not security—keeping America out of war rather than aiding Britain and France in the interests of American defense. Although he continued to work through Democratic leaders on the Hill, the administration campaign was better orchestrated. Great efforts were made to present revision as a bipartisan measure. Alf Landon and Frank Knox, the Republican presidential and vice presidential candidates in 1936, were enlisted to rebut isolationists such as Borah and Vandenberg.

The president himself took the issue to Congress, in contrast with his reticence in the spring. He told a joint session of Congress on September 21 that he wanted to return to a neutrality based on the fundamentals of international law. He argued that this had been the American position except for two disastrous periods, those of Jefferson's Embargo and Non-Intercourse Acts and again under the Neutrality Acts of 1935 and 1937. The first, he said, had brought America close to economic ruin and was a major cause of the War of 1812, during which the White House and Capitol were burned. As for the second period: "I regret that Congress passed that Act. I regret equally that I signed that Act." The parallel between the 1800s and the 1930s was powerfully made. The president went on to argue that by returning to "real and traditional neutrality" the United States would stop aiding aggressors, enhance its trade, and preserve its peace. Indeed, he asserted that by repeal "the United States will more probably re-main at peace than if the law remains as it stands today. I say this because with the repeal of the embargo, this Government clearly and definitely will insist that American citizens and American ships keep away from the immediate perils of the actual zones of conflict."

Four days later Senator Pittman presented a draft bill to the Senate Foreign Relations Committee. Hearings and debates in both houses of Congress attracted intense press and radio inter-est. They also became the foci of massive propaganda campaigns. In the last two weeks of September a deluge of letters, postcards, and telegrams opposing repeal of the arms embargo poured into Capitol Hill. Some senators were receiving four thousand a day, and in one three-day period a million pieces of mail arrived. Much of it seemed spontaneous rather than form letters, with the heaviest concentration from the Midwest. By October, however, the administration had mobilized a counterattack. A "Non-Partisan Committee for Peace through Revision of the Neutral-ity Act" was formed under the leadership of William Allen White, the respected Republican newspaper editor from Kansas. Its publicity drive centered on endorsements and addresses from opinion-makers in religion, education, journalism, and business. Meanwhile opinion polls indicated an emerging majority for re-peal and overwhelming support for cash and carry.

Although some congressional supporters of the bill made no secret of their desire to aid Britain and France, the administration sedulously avoided all such implications. Its critics insisted that this would be the consequence: "In the long run," declared Senator Vandenberg, "I do not believe we can become an arsenal for one belligerent without becoming a target for another." Privately he wrote in his diary: "My quarrel is with this notion that America can be half in and half out of this war." He went on, "I hate Hitlerism and Nazism and Communism as completely as any person living. But I decline to embrace the opportunist idea—so convenient and so popular at the moment—that *we* can stop these things in *Europe* without entering the conflict with everything at our command, including men and money. There is no middle ground. We are either *all the way in* or *all the way out*." It was a prescient comment, and one that exactly delineated Vandenberg's difference with Roosevelt. FDR wanted to have his cake and eat it too.

The administration's firm but discreet leadership, coupled with its insistence that this was a "peace" measure, gradually carried the day. The bill won a two-thirds majority in the Senate on October 27 and passed the House a few days later by 243 votes to 181. After a Senate-House conference committee had resolved minor differences, on November 4 the president signed the 1939 Neutrality Act into law. Thereafter all trade with belligerent countries, munitions or not, would be placed on a cash-and-carry basis. U.S. vessels were still prohibited from carrying any passengers or goods to belligerent countries, and there could be no legal export of goods until all "right, title, and interest" had been transferred. It remained illegal for Americans to travel on belligerent vessels, to arm U.S. merchant ships, and to provide loans to belligerent powers. As in earlier acts, Congress was still trying to avoid the economic and emotional entanglements that had drawn America into the World War. These were mandatory provisions, over which the president had no discretion. But he would have flexibility on one point: whether and how to define a "combat area," applicable to surface vessels and/or aircraft, from which citizens and vessels were barred. Roosevelt immediately issued a proclamation applying this to North Atlantic waters, despite vigorous opposition from American shippers. The president reckoned that banning U.S. vessels from a larger war zone around Europe would help avoid incidents. In October he also persuaded the Latin American republics to declare a Western Hemisphere Neutrality Zone three hundred miles into the Atlantic. Enforced by U.S. naval patrols, this was intended to keep belligerent ships away from the Americas.

The 1939 Neutrality Act was presented as a peace measure, and there is little doubt that Roosevelt genuinely believed it would not bring America into the European war. But there is also no doubt that he intended it as an unneutral act. Cash and carry was intended to benefit Britain and France—countries with substantial foreign exchange reserves and large merchant fleets. Roosevelt's determination to bolster the Allies is demonstrated by his secret messages to Chamberlain and to Winston Churchill, the vehement critic of appeasement whom Chamberlain had now brought into his cabinet as first lord of the admiralty (equivalent of the U.S. secretary of the navy). In cordial letters dated September 11, FDR urged both men to write personally and outside diplomatic channels whenever they wished. He assured Chamberlain: "I hope and believe that we shall repeal the arms embargo within the next month and this is definitely a part of Administration policy." Chamberlain immediately sent a warm note of appreciation for FDR's "sympathetic and encouraging" words, followed on November 8 by "a private line of thanks and congratulation" on repeal of the arms embargo. It was, said the prime minister, both an assurance of material help and a "profound moral encouragement." Meanwhile Churchill kept the president informed about naval matters, particularly where these impinged on the Western Hemisphere Neutrality Zone.

By November 1939, Franklin Roosevelt had established the basic framework for U.S. policy that he had been seeking, albeit erratically, for more than a year. The new neutrality legislation minimized the dangers of America being entangled unwillingly in another European war. Within that framework, however, it opened up the vast material resources of the United States to Britain and France. It was now up to the Allies to make use of the American arsenal. But, as Senator Vandenberg had noted, keeping America "half in and half out of this war" was a difficult posture to sustain. Much depended on events, and in the summer of 1940 Roosevelt was to be forced off the fence by a revolution in the European balance of power. Moreover, the great set-piece debate over neutrality in September and October 1939 had circumscribed Roosevelt's public position. "Because of our battle," wrote Vandenberg in his diary, "it is going to be much more difficult for F.D.R. to lead the country into war. We have forced him and his Senate group to become vehement in their peace devotions—and we have aroused the country to a peace vigilance which is powerful." Unneutrality in thought and deed—but not in word. Roosevelt's effort to wage proxy war under the guise of nonbelligerency would open up a momentous gulf between actions and rhetoric in the months ahead.

4

Redefining Politics and Geopolitics
(December 1939 to November 1940)

DURING 1940 the international situation was transformed. In the spring, Hitler knocked Norway, Denmark, the
Low Countries, and France out of the war. The Austrian corpo-
ral had gained far more in three months than the kaiser's best
generals had achieved in four years. Moreover Germany's success
emboldened the other two revisionist powers. In June, Italy entered the war, opening up new fronts in the Balkans and North
Africa, while Japan's leaders moved into the northern part of
French Indochina and intensified their pressure on China.

These dramatic shifts in the international balance changed the
agenda of America's domestic politics. At the start of the year,
the country had no idea whether FDR would challenge the tradition opposing third terms and run again for the presidency.
Probably Roosevelt himself was undecided. By November he
had been elected for another four years. Events also accelerated
his expansive redefinition of American security. To deter Japan,
the Pacific Fleet was moved to Pearl Harbor in the Hawaiian Islands. In Europe FDR now defined Britain as America's first
line of defense. This policy was symbolized by the agreement in
September 1940 to give Britain fifty old U.S. destroyers.

TWILIGHT OF PEACE

In December 1939 the winter dinner of the Washington press corps, the Gridiron Club, featured an eight-foot papier-mâché model of a sphinx. Or rather the form was that of a sphinx, but the grinning visage was unmistakably FDR, complete with spectacles and cigarette holder. For months the pressmen had been probing the president about his third-term intentions, but FDR had been sphinxlike in his evasions. The journalist John Gunther later summed up Roosevelt's probable reasons. If he declared he was not a candidate, he would become a lame-duck president. If he said he was a candidate, this would damage his prestige. In any case, he probably hadn't made up his own mind. So he carried on quietly encouraging various potential candidates while doing nothing to damage his own chances of reelection.

Deep down, Roosevelt probably yearned to retire. His new library and museum at Hyde Park were almost complete. (The papier-mâché sphinx would later become a prime exhibit.) Wearied by the battles of his second term and unable to shrug off a bad bout of the flu in the New Year, FDR talked to close associates about the attractions of retreating to Hyde Park and writing his memoirs. On January 24, 1940, he told Henry Morgenthau, his treasury secretary and Hudson Valley neighbor: "I do not want to run unless between now and the convention [in July] things get very, very much worse in Europe." On the 27th he actually signed a three-year contract with *Collier's,* the weekly magazine, to write twenty-six articles each year in 1941, 1942, and 1943. The annual salary would be $75,000. *Collier's* offered more, but FDR felt it would be improper to receive a larger income as a contributing editor than he did when president of the United States.

Whatever his private preferences, Roosevelt remained evasive in public. As he implied to Morgenthau, only a disaster in Europe would justify the Democratic party drafting him for a third term. Otherwise the "no third term" tradition, established by George Washington, would be too strong. But Europe, too, remained sphinxlike in early 1940, with threats of intensified war mingling with talk of compromise peace. Characteristically Roosevelt kept his diplomatic options open in both of these directions.

The Neutrality Act of November 1939 had unlocked the door to Anglo-French arms purchases. In order to avoid the notorious nexus with Wall Street that had characterized Allied purchasing in World War I, Roosevelt encouraged the British and French to establish a joint purchasing commission and to channel their orders through Morgenthau and the U.S. Treasury. This would ensure harmonization with the needs of American rearmament. The Allies also took Treasury advice and opened a special account with the Federal Reserve Bank of New York, available for inspection by Morgenthau. To New Dealers, acutely suspicious of Wall Street and the City of London, these were important conditions for transatlantic cooperation. In principle, all was now in place for the United States to act as the arsenal of the Allies. Anglo-French orders would bolster their resistance to Hitler and also stimulate U.S. industry to convert to rearmament, now that it was clear (contrary to FDR's hopes in the weeks after Munich) that Congress would not sanction any government-sponsored program of rearmament. There were also political benefits. As FDR told aides, "Foreign orders mean prosperity in this country, and we can't elect the Democratic party unless we get prosperity."

Big orders were slow to materialize, however. The British in particular were budgeting for the possibility of a long war, perhaps of three years duration. Unlike World War I, they were now prohibited under American law from raising any private or governmental loans in the United States. Yet, as the British

Treasury privately admitted, "Unless, when the time comes, the United States are prepared either to lend or to give us the money as required, the prospects for a long war are exceedingly grim." The estimate of three years was "very likely much too optimistic." In these circumstances the British decided to husband their gold and dollar reserves and to treat the United States as a marginal source of war supplies. The British Treasury expected to spend about $720 million in the United States during the first year of war, of which 17 percent would be on machine tools, a particular bottleneck. Aircraft orders, on which FDR and Morgenthau were pinning their hopes, would amount to only 11 percent of the total.

Moreover the British were determined to conserve foreign exchange for absolute essentials. They cut back sharply on agricultural purchases from the United States, such as cotton, fruit, and tobacco—much to the fury of the State Department and especially Hull, who was always sensitive to Southern agricultural interests. What made State even angrier was that at the same time the British were increasing purchases of tobacco and fruit from Greece, Turkey, and Italy to keep those countries out of the German orbit. Discouraging Mussolini from joining the war on Hitler's side was a major British objective in early 1940, even at a cost to Anglo-American relations. Chamberlain told his cabinet that "at this stage of the war, the goodwill of Italy was so important to us that we should do whatever might be necessary to secure it."

Knowing, as we now do, what happened in May and June 1940, such policies may seem ridiculous. But those events still lay in the future for policymakers during the time of the phony war. Balancing the fear of a long war was the hope that Germany's economy was overstretched. Chamberlain in particular hoped for an internal collapse, leading to the overthrow of Hitler and a new non-Nazi regime with which negotiations would be possible. This was a further justification for conserving Britain's economic resources. Given the moralizing noninterventionism across the Atlantic, there was also considerable resentment at the United States. Lord Chatfield, minister for the coordination of defense, remarked privately that Americans would "fight the battle for freedom to the last Briton, but save their own skins!" And memories were still vivid of Wilsonian "meddling" in 1918–1919. Edward R. Murrow, the London-based head of Columbia Broadcasting System operations in Europe, recalled that "In the opening months of the war, one often heard the comment, 'God protect us from a German victory and an American peace. Britain and her Allies propose to win this one alone.' "

Signs of American peacemaking could indeed be discerned across the Atlantic. At the beginning of 1940 the administration asked Congress to extend the Reciprocal Trade Agreements Act for another three years. By this time more than twenty agreements had been negotiated, of which the most important was signed with Britain in November 1938. Outside the South, most farmers remained unconvinced of the benefits, and British trade diversion to the European neutrals could not have come at a more sensitive moment. But Hull and Roosevelt shifted the argument from prosperity to peace, claiming that the U.S. economy was now recovering but that the act was still needed for international reasons. FDR told Congress on January 3 that the United States "must use its influence to open up the trade channels of the world, in all nations." The act "should be extended as an indispensable part of the foundation of any stable and enduring peace."

The votes in Congress were far closer than in 1934 or 1937: 218 to 168 in the House on February 23, and 42 to 37 in the Senate on April 5. Senator Key Pittman of Nevada, who had led the administration's campaign to revise the Neutrality Act, was an ardent opponent of the RTA program. The closeness of the victory was a reminder of the president's difficulties in leading Congress. Yet the fact of the victory was an indication that the administration was looking beyond the war to the peace. Freer trade was no longer an emergency response to the depression; it was becoming a major plank of U.S. foreign policy.

For a time it seemed that "an American peace" might be close at hand. Or at least an American peace effort, in the form of the visit by Undersecretary Sumner Welles to European capitals in the first half of March 1940. This was a recurrence of earlier initiatives, notably FDR's offer, prompted by Welles, in January 1938 to convene an international conference. Welles and Berle in the State Department were both clear that Hitler must be contained in Europe. But they wanted to avoid U.S. entanglement and feared that the British were using the war to strengthen their own economic position. A State Department committee had been formed in December to outline the bases of a future peace, with a reformed League of Nations, large-scale disarmament, and the elimination of economic blocs as central ideas. Berle, like Harry Dexter White in the U.S. Treasury, was musing about the reconstruction of the international monetary system on the basis of a gold-backed U.S. dollar—a concept that would triumph at Bretton Woods in 1944. As with earlier proposals by Welles, the idea was that neutrals (led by the United States) would have a key role in future peacemaking. Welles thought that Mussolini might prove particularly useful, as he had apparently been in averting war in September 1938.

In March 1940, as in January 1938, Roosevelt endorsed Welles's proposals with modifications. Privately he advanced two reasons for allowing the undersecretary to visit the main European leaders. One was that the trip might delay or even prevent the German spring offensive, thereby giving Britain and France more time to rearm and prepare. The second was to get the "lowdown on Hitler and get Mussolini's point of view." As usual, FDR wanted direct insight into the minds of his international counterparts, but the wheelchair president needed others to be his eyes and ears. Another unspoken reason was election politics. A bid for peace, however utopian, would help counter Republican charges of Democratic warmongering. Yet there are signs that Roosevelt, too, had a future peace in mind. After a long talk with him in mid-December, the British ambassador, Lord Lothian, wrote that the president evidently hoped he might "intervene as a kind of umpire" at some point in 1940. FDR also ruminated about the need for disarmament and outlined to Lothian the Four Freedoms that he announced publicly in January 1941.

By the time Welles visited Europe, however, the time for talking had passed. On March 28 the Anglo-French War Council agreed to place an order for 4,600 aircraft in the United States in the year from October 1, 1940. This would play havoc with the British Treasury's policy of financial conservation. On the same day the council decided to lay mines in Norwegian territorial waters to impede the flow of Scandinavian raw materials to Germany. As with the aircraft orders, this decision was the result of pressure from the British service ministries, especially Churchill at the Admiralty, and from the French—all of whom were unhappy with Chamberlain's readiness to wait for a German collapse. In Paris the government of Edouard Daladier had fallen in mid-March because of dissatisfaction with Allied inactivity.

These two decisions on March 28 were signs that Britain and France would prosecute the war with greater urgency. But so would Hitler. The mining operation prompted him to accelerate his own plans to intervene in Scandinavia. By the time the first mines were in place, the German invasion of Norway had begun. The phony war was over, and with it FDR's long equivocation between peace and war, between retirement and a third term.

THE FALL OF FRANCE

The German invasions of Norway and Denmark on April 9, 1940, were devastating successes. Serious resistance was eliminated on the first day, and the British and French efforts to

dislodge the Germans from Norway only exposed the incompetence of their forces. Parliamentary criticism of the fiasco helped
bring down Chamberlain's government, and on May 10
Churchill became Britain's prime minister. That same day Germany's oft-delayed offensive on the Western Front finally began.

For Hitler the delay had proved beneficial. On paper the two
sides were evenly matched, with 141 German divisions facing
144 Allied divisions (of which 104 were French and only 10
British). But the Germans were superior in the air, and they had
concentrated their tanks in mobile armored (*Panzer*) divisions for
maximum effect. During the winter German planners had
shifted the main thrust of their attack from Belgium southward
to the Ardennes Forest and the Meuse River, a weakly defended
sector of the Allied front. While the bulk of France's armored
and motorized forces drove into Belgium, the Germans concentrated their armored divisions in the crossing of the Meuse. Supported by dive bombers, they cut through the French forces,
whose generals back in Paris were dumbfounded at the speed
and savagery of this new mobile warfare. Despite the caution of
some German commanders and at times of Hitler himself, General Heinz Guderian's armored units were able to push on without waiting for the infantry. They reached the Channel coast
near Dunkirk on May 24, having covered two hundred miles in
two weeks. The Netherlands and Belgium had already been
overrun. Most of the British Expeditionary Force (BEF) was
trapped on the beaches around Dunkirk.

The next week was of decisive importance. Hitler halted his
armored divisions, expecting that the German air force would
finish off the BEF. The Panzers desperately needed time to rest
and repair before the main battle for France began, and Hitler
did not imagine that the Allied troops could be saved by sea. Nor,
initially, did Churchill's government. Although an evacuation
program was hastily mounted, it was assumed at first that no

more than fifty thousand could be saved. In fact, blessed by cloudy skies and calm seas, a third of a million British and French troops were evacuated to Britain by June 4, though without most of their equipment and weapons.

In late May—before the full success of the Dunkirk operation was clear—some members of Churchill's war cabinet had favored finding out what might be Hitler's peace terms. This argument was silenced by Churchill's own pugnacity and by the successful evacuation from Dunkirk. The cabinet rallied around Churchill's public rhetoric about "victory at all costs" and his promise that Britain would fight on the beaches and the landing grounds, in the fields, the streets, and the hills; "we shall never surrender." After the peace-loving Chamberlain, with his clipped speech and cautious manner, Churchill's bellicose, patriotic rhetoric was a tonic at home and abroad.

In early June the French army still seemed a strong fighting force, with some sixty-five divisions intact under a new command. But the troops were demoralized, the best units had been lost in Belgium, and the *Luftwaffe* enjoyed mastery of the skies. Resuming their offensive along the River Somme on June 5, the Germans broke through without difficulty. On June 10 Mussolini entered the war: the German victories had silenced his cautious army commanders, and Italians wanted a share of the spoils. By the 14th Paris itself had fallen, and on June 21 an armistice was signed at Compiègne in the historic railway carriage in which the French had accepted the German surrender in 1918. While most Germans had not exulted in Hitler's war, this carefully staged reversal of their recent humiliation struck a profoundly popular chord. Even critics of the Nazi regime found it hard to stand aside. For the moment, at least, the führer could do no wrong. His once-skeptical generals bowed before his strategic genius. Secretly plans were set in train for an invasion of Russia in 1941. Meanwhile German opinion eagerly awaited the settling of scores with the other victor of 1918. When Hitler's "final" peace offer on July 19 was rejected by London, Germans expected the early invasion and defeat of Britain.

For Britain the United States was now its only potential source of help. This was axiomatic for half-American Churchill who, unlike Chamberlain, was a long-standing exponent of transatlantic cooperation. His correspondence with Roosevelt, intensified now that both men were heads of government, became the main axis of transatlantic communication, and he badgered FDR for all kinds of supplies, from destroyers to aircraft, from foodstuffs to ammunition. Britain's policy of conserving foreign exchange—already modified in March—was thrown to the winds. Churchill told Roosevelt on May 15: "We shall go on paying dollars for as long as we can, but I should like to feel reasonably sure that, when we can pay no more, you will give us the stuff all the same." Roosevelt made no response to that inquiry. He also deflected Churchill's request in mid-June for a U.S. declaration of war, if only to keep the French from surrendering. Privately FDR had reservations about Churchill. Reflecting the general tendency in Washington (and Whitehall) at this time to question the new prime minister's sobriety and balance, Roosevelt said (according to Interior Secretary Harold Ickes) "that he supposed Churchill was the best man England had, even if he was drunk half of his time."

Despite these doubts, Roosevelt used the German onslaught in the West to intensify his dual policy of American rearmament and material aid to Britain and France. But the events of May 1940 highlighted the tension within that policy. The strength of America's regular army was only 245,000. That put it twentieth in the world, with the Dutch in nineteenth place. In an immediate crisis only 5 fully equipped divisions could have been deployed in combat: Germany, as we have seen, committed 141 on the Western Front alone. Most of the army's equipment, such as Springfield rifles and 75mm guns, dated back to the World War.

It took FDR and Morgenthau three weeks, against stubborn War Department opposition, to secure the release of 500,000 rifles, 129 million rounds of ammunition, and 80,000 machine guns for sale to the British army. To get round the Neutrality Act, the hardware was sold to private corporations which then sold it to Britain.

This transaction was invaluable to the British: the rifles and ammunition helped rearm the troops who came back from Dunkirk. Yet War Department concern was understandable. The ammunition, for instance, constituted more than one-fifth of total U.S. stocks, and current production was a mere four million rounds per months. During the summer substantial appropriations bills were rushed through Congress for planes, tanks, munitions, and, in July, a "two-ocean" navy. But as Bernard Baruch, mobilization director in 1917–1918, put it, "You cannot just order a Navy as you would a pound of coffee, or vegetables and meat, and say, we will have that for dinner. It takes time. It takes organization." In 1940 organization was minimal and time seemed desperately shortly. The challenge was therefore to decide whether the existing scarce resources should be used for defense of the Western Hemisphere or for aid to the Allies. Roosevelt, characteristically, insisted that you could do both. His speech at Charlottesville, Virginia, on June 10, when he denounced Italy's "stab in the back" of France, was his most explicit statement to date of the dual policy. But many of his advisers believed that it would now be best to concentrate on defense of the Western Hemisphere.

To strengthen his position the president reshuffled his administration. On June 20 he announced that Henry L. Stimson would head the War Department and that Frank Knox would become secretary of the navy. Stimson, aged seventy-three, had been William Howard Taft's secretary of war and Herbert Hoover's secretary of state, while Knox, publisher of the *Chicago Daily News,* had been the Republican vice presidential candidate in 1936. Both men were outspoken supporters of aid to the Allies, and they quickly developed good working relationships with the leading cabinet hawks, Morgenthau and Ickes. By reaching out to the Republicans in this way, Roosevelt gave his cabinet a coalition character and strengthened its support for his foreign policy. Stimson's predecessor, Henry Woodring, had stubbornly opposed the sale of equipment to Britain and France. Knox (like Ickes) even favored U.S. entry into the war.

Roosevelt was also able to move on rearmament. On May 16, in a restatement of his scenario of the air threat, FDR set a production goal of at least fifty thousand warplanes a year. Like his target of ten thousand in November 1938, the figure was plucked from the air for propaganda effect. On May 26 he announced that the federal government would provide credits for firms converting their plant to armanents. By early July, Congress had passed legislation allowing both the Navy and War departments to negotiate directly with aircraft firms and to sign cost-plus-fixed-fee contracts, guaranteeing assured profits. This was a marked change from the 1930s when congressmen, anxious to avoid a military-industrial cartel, insisted on competitive bidding and even denied companies ownership of their designs for military aircraft. In 1940 these restrictions seemed counterproductive, with business still gripped by the "depression psychosis" and fearful of overinvestment. As Stimson observed later, if you are preparing for war in a capitalist country, "you have got to let business make money out of the process or business won't work." Behind the scenes, big businessmen were beginning to move into Washington as "dollar-a-year men" to assist with rearmament. One of them, the Wall Street banker Robert A. Lovett, toured aircraft plants that summer. His report depicted an industry still making customized products instead of applying assembly-line techniques from the auto industry. "This is a quantitative war," Lovett warned. "The airplane industry has, so far, been qualitative." By the end of 1940, Stimson had appointed Lovett as assistant secretary of war for air, with the goal of building up U.S. airpower on mass-production lines.

The appointment of Republicans to the cabinet, the influx of big businessmen into Washington, and the new attitude toward military contracts were all signs that the administration was burying the hatchet with (and not in) business. To the alarm of left-wing Democrats, including Eleanor Roosevelt, they symbolized the endgame of the New Deal.

By the time Stimson and Knox joined the administration in mid-June, however, France had fallen and Britain stood alone. Over the next six weeks the British received little assistance from the United States. This was due in part to Roosevelt's own doubts. In early July, according to Democratic politico Jim Farley, Roosevelt told him that Britain's chances were one in three. Of particular concern, given Churchill's persistent request for U.S. destroyers, was the possibility that the British fleet might fall into German hands. When the British shelled and neutralized the French fleet in North African ports on July 3–4, to avert just such a contingency in the case of France, that relieved some of the administration's fears. But it did not dispel them completely. During July and August the U.S. military held secret staff talks with its Canadian opposite numbers. Their object was to obtain U.S. bases in Canada and concert strategy in case the Royal Navy lost control of the North Atlantic.

Aside from administration doubts, which FDR probably shared to some extent, the president faced strong bureaucratic and political resistance to aiding Britain. On June 22 General George C. Marshall and Admiral Harold R. Stark, respectively the army chief of staff and the chief of naval operations, asked Roosevelt for a virtual ban on further arms sales to Britain. The president refused to be pinned down, but on July 2 he was obliged to sign into law an amendment pushed through the Senate by leading isolationists. This prohibited the sale of U.S. equipment unless Marshall or Stark could certify that it was "not essential for U.S. defense." Given the parlous state of U.S. rearmament, hardly anything could be considered nonessential. During maneuvers in Louisiana, commented *Time* magazine, "the U.S. Army looked like a few nice boys with BB guns" compared with "Europe's total war."

An even more serious constraint was the election campaign. In July 1940 events abroad took a backseat to FDR's political gymnastics as he finally climbed off the fence.

During the spring, plans had quietly continued for the president's move back to Hyde Park. On every visit FDR would bring with him documents and memorabilia to be sorted for the new library. But the fall of France constituted the crisis of which Roosevelt had spoken to Morgenthau in January—an event of sufficient moment to justify the country not changing horses in midstream. Yet Roosevelt still refused to campaign for the nomination: to justify breaching hallowed political tradition, he must appear a reluctant draftee. He therefore did not attend the Democratic convention in Chicago and refused to allow his emissaries to give delegates any clear hint. On the second night, July 16, a message from the president was read to the convention announcing that Roosevelt did not have "any desire or purpose" to be a candidate, and that all delegates were free to vote for whomever they chose. There was a stunned silence. Then from the loudspeakers came a voice: "We want Roosevelt." A few delegates took up the cry, waving their state standards. "Everybody wants Roosevelt," boomed the voice. More delegates shouted and paraded down the aisles. "The world wants Roosevelt." The voice echoed round the hall amid pandemonium as ecstatic delegates shouted the president's name.

The disembodied voice was later identified as Chicago's superintendent of sewers, who had instructions from the city's Democratic boss, Mayor Ed Kelly, to begin the shouts as soon as the president's statement had been read. But the stampede was largely spontaneous. Although the president's disingenuous tactics left many with an unpleasant taste in the mouth, he had secured what he wanted. On the first ballot, next day, Roosevelt gained 946 votes. All the other candidates received 150 between them. After another messy battle to secure the nomination of his preferred running mate, Henry A. Wallace of Iowa, the president went on national radio early on July 19 to announce his acceptance of the nomination. He spoke of lying awake at nights asking himself whether, as commander-in-chief, he had the right to ask others to serve or prepare to serve their country and then decline that call himself. His own private plans for retirement, "like so many other plans, had been made in a world which now seems as distant as another planet. Today all private plans, all private lives, have been in a sense repealed by an overriding public danger."

One reporter called the speech "painful humbuggery." But the Chicago charade satisfied essential political appearances. Roosevelt could represent his bid for a third term as duty, not desire. Furthermore, though nomination was not election, he was now a little freer to address Britain's deepening crisis.

DESTROYERS FOR BRITAIN, DETERRENCE FOR JAPAN

At the top of Churchill's essential "shopping list" were U.S. destroyers. He raised the matter in his first message as prime minister, on May 15, and returned to it with increasing urgency during the summer. Roosevelt ignored him, however. Indeed, after France fell in mid-June there was only one message between the two leaders during the next six weeks. Churchill tried again at the end of July, advised by the British ambassador in Washington, Lord Lothian, that this was a good time now that the Democratic convention was over. On July 30 the prime minister reiterated his request for "fifty or sixty of your oldest destroyers" to protect Britain's western approaches from submarine attack on vital supply convoys from the Western and Southern

Hemispheres. He told Roosevelt that "the whole fate of the war may be decided by this minor and easily remediable factor." Lothian had also advised the British government to take a generous attitude to Anglo-American cooperation. He favored offering the United States aircraft landing rights on three of Britain's Caribbean colonies. Despite the rivalry in civil aviation between the two countries, on July 29 the British cabinet agreed in principle. Even though there was to be no formal linkage, Lothian and the Foreign Office viewed this offer as an inducement to get the destroyers.

Roosevelt began shifting his ground. At a (rare) cabinet meeting on August 2 it was generally agreed that the destroyers were essential for British survival. But FDR had no doubt that congressional approval would be required and that this was unlikely given the amendment on surplus equipment passed on July 2. He expected substantial Republican opposition and observed that in the Senate, where there was no mechanism for closing debates, fifteen or twenty determined isolationists could filibuster indefinitely. The cabinet discussion therefore centered on "molasses" to sweeten the pill. One was the possibility of acquiring air and naval bases on British territory in the Americas to enhance the defense of the United States. The other was a public assurance that the Royal Navy would never be allowed to fall into German hands and would, if necessary, fight on from North America and the British Empire. These concessions would enable the administration to say that the overall deal strengthened the defense of the Western Hemisphere. Over the next ten days the administration sounded out the British and the Republican leadership. On August 13 FDR and his advisers prepared a proposal which was then cabled to Churchill. "For the first time that I discussed the destroyers with the President," Morgenthau noted, "he seemed to have made up his mind."

There were several reasons for Roosevelt's change of heart. One was the growing confidence in Washington that Britain would survive. The British had publicly dismissed Hitler's peace offers, and by August U.S. intelligence was skeptical that the Luftwaffe could gain the air supremacy necessary to mount an invasion. An upbeat report from Colonel William Donovan, whom FDR had sent on a special mission to London in July, was particularly influential for the president. At the same time Roosevelt was reflecting the changed balance of opinion in his cabinet. The cabinet "hawks" pushed the matter energetically, with Knox in the lead in advocating a package deal. The new navy secretary was in close touch with Lothian, and both also liaised with a newly formed pressure group of ardent interventionists known as the "Century Group," after the club in Manhattan where they often met. This was a bipartisan organization of Eastern Establishment figures, including Henry R. Luce, the publisher of *Time*, *Life*, and *Fortune* magazines; the journalist Joseph Alsop; the attorney Dean Acheson—who had served in Roosevelt's administration in 1933; and another lawyer, Allen W. Dulles, who would later become director of Eisenhower's CIA. By their pressure, publicity, and networking, Century Group members helped Roosevelt feel that a deal was both necessary and possible. Just as the politics of neutrality revision in the summer of 1939 had turned on the attitude of a few obdurate senators, so the destroyers deal a year later owed much to the efforts of a few determined and well-connected private citizens.

Dean Acheson, in particular, played a signal service by his long letter in the August 15 issue of the *New York Times*. In this he argued that congressional approval was not necessary because the destroyers could be transferred by executive agreement. Acheson's argument is worth a moment's attention, partly because it had an immediate effect on Roosevelt but also because it had long-term implications for presidential conduct of foreign policy. Acheson's advice was confirmed by an opinion from the attorney general, Robert H. Jackson, who cited the Supreme Court's 1936 opinion in the *Curtiss-Wright* case. At a time when the "Nine Old Men" were cutting back the New Deal presidency, this important but neglected judgment drew a "fundamental" distinction between the president's powers in domestic and foreign affairs. In the latter, the president was deemed by the Court "the sole organ of the federal government" and had an inherent and independent power that did not require legislation as authority for its exercise. Like most Supreme Court decisions, the central judgment was limited, being confined to foreign trade. But the Court's general comments had vast implications, which cold war presidents would exploit. Already in 1940 Attorney General Jackson used the *Curtiss-Wright* case in partial justification of his advice regarding the destroyers.

The decision to bypass Congress helped Roosevelt enormously. Through Century Group contacts he also obtained an informal promise from the Republican presidential candidate, Wendell Willkie, that the GOP would not make the deal an election issue. In the end the British were more sticky. Although willing to offer some civil aviation landing rights on British colonies, they had not envisaged what FDR proposed, namely ninety-nine-year leases to build air and naval bases on eight of their Western Atlantic possessions from Newfoundland to British Guiana. Nor was Churchill keen to make a public declaration about the fate of the fleet if Britain fell: hardly a point to dwell on when he was trying to bolster domestic and international confidence. But the balance of the Anglo-American relationship had shifted dramatically over that summer. Britain was in no position to bargain. Eventually the agreement for bases on Newfoundland and Bermuda was represented as a British gift, while the rest were explicitly linked to the destroyers. Churchill duly reiterated his parliamentary assurances that the fleet would not be surrendered. These concessions enabled Marshall and Stark to take deep breaths, cross their fingers, and certify that the destroyers were "obsolete" and "useless."

Initially neither side gained much from the destroyers-for-bases agreement. It took months of argument to determine the sites for the U.S. bases, and by the end of 1940 only nine of the fifty aged destroyers were fit for service with the Royal Navy. But the deal was significant in several ways. Roosevelt had exploited legal opinion to bypass Congress, which had blocked most of his spasmodic forays into international affairs during the 1930s. As Churchill later said, the gift of destroyers was "a decidedly unneutral act by the United States"—affirmation by Roosevelt that, despite the fall of France, Britain alone constituted America's front line. And Hitler considered the bases to be a sign that the United States was moving into the Atlantic. Although insisting that U.S. rearmament would not be significant until 1945, by which time the war would be over, the führer gave the go-ahead for plans to occupy eastern Atlantic islands such as the Canaries and the Azores. The destroyers deal also had global implications. Hitler approved new talks for an alliance with Japan.

Japan's search for an alliance with Germany, spearheaded by the army, had come to an abrupt halt in August 1939 with the Nazi-Soviet Pact and the Soviet victory in Mongolia. During the winter of 1939–1940 two successive ministries tried vainly to improve relations with the United States. Japan's war in China remained unresolved, with 850,000 troops bogged down, and the country's supply position worsened as imports from Germany dried up with the onset of the European war. The United States, for its part, abrogated its commercial treaty with Japan in January 1940—as announced six months earlier. The general U.S. policy remained to avoid war with Japan, but without sacrificing fundamental principles.

Hitler's triumphs in Europe had a dramatic impact on Asia. Just as they emboldened Italy to enter the war, opening new fronts in the Balkans and North Africa, so they encouraged Japan to advance its "New Order" in Asia. Hoping to finish off the war in China, the Japanese pressed the European powers to stop supplying the Chinese Nationalists. In no position in July to contemplate a war with Japan, the British agreed to close the so-called Burma Road into China for three months, as a short-term tactical concession. Japan also put pressure on the Dutch to guarantee supplies of oil, rubber, and tin from the East Indies, in the hope of reducing Japan's economic dependence on the "Anglo-Americans." On July 16 the army withdrew its support for the cabinet of Admiral Yonai Mitsumasa. In his place, Prince Konoe Fumimaro returned to the premiership, but as symbolic head of a government animated by the army's determination to end British and American dominance in the Pacific. The new foreign minister, Matsuoka Yōsuke, was a leading revisionist. Konoe's cabinet revived the search for a German alliance and a neutrality pact with the Soviet Union as the basis from which to mount a southward advance. The emphasis remained on diplomacy (or threats) rather than belligerency, but there was a clear determination in Tokyo to seize this unprecedented opportunity to extend its Asian sphere of influence at the expense of the colonial powers.

U.S. policymakers recognized that a disturbing power vacuum was opening up in Southeast Asia. But opinions were divided about how far the United States could and should try to fill it. Proponents of both hemisphere defense and aid to Britain shared a common concern not to become embroiled in Asia. A crucial issue was the disposition of the main U.S. fleet. At the end of March 1940 it left its bases in southern California for war games in Hawaiian waters. FDR then delayed the fleet's return in the hope that its continued presence at Pearl Harbor would deter Japan from aggression against the Dutch East Indies. By late June, following the French collapse, both Marshall and Stark were very unhappy about this de facto shift in policy. Backed by Welles in the State Department, they urged that at least part of the fleet be moved to the East Coast in case Britain collapsed. The Royal Navy's neutralization of the French fleet and the German failure to invade Britain relieved these anxieties, and the fleet stayed at Pearl Harbor. But this was an improvised policy, opposed by the fleet's commanders, who lacked clear instructions about what to do if Japan went to war. Improvisation and confusion were to characterize U.S. strategy in the Pacific throughout 1940 and 1941.

The other instrument of deterrence that the United States could apply against the island nation of Japan was trade sanctions. With Washington's abrogation of the trade treaty, commerce between the two countries was no longer guaranteed by formal agreements. The National Defense Act, signed into law on July 2, gave the president authority to declare certain items vital to national defense and exportable only under government license. The act was intended to facilitate domestic rearmament, but it could be used to wage economic warfare. Aware of this, Hull had only agreed to it on the understanding that he would not apply it against the Japanese. But Hull did not control the bureaucracy of the new National Defense Advisory Commission (NDAC), especially its crucial Export Control Office. The new balance of the cabinet was also weighted against Hull's cautious policy. Knox and Stimson both supported the strongly anti-Japanese policy of Morgenthau and Ickes. This quartet saw the totalitarians as a global challenge. Mindful of the supposed lessons of Munich, they were also confident that tough measures would deter the Japanese rather than provoke them. For the next year the small print of export control regulations became the arcane but vital battleground between Washington "hawks" and "moderates" in the struggle over policy toward Japan.

In late July, Morgenthau took advantage of Hull's absence from Washington and tried to railroad through an embargo on all petroleum products, scrap metal, and steel to Japan. But this went too far for the president, let alone Hull when he returned. The embargo was restricted to aviation fuel, which the Japanese were feverishly buying up on the West Coast, and the definition of aviation fuel was eventually set at 87 octane or above. Since

U.S. planes burned 100-octane gasoline, this assured domestic supplies while still allowing the Japanese to buy 86-octane fuel that they could refine. Buy they duly did—in vast quantities over the next few months. They also intensified their pressure for guaranteed oil supplies from the Dutch East Indies, which, cabinet hawks such as Knox failed fully to note, was also a major supplier of Britain. The hawks returned to the issue in late September when Japanese troops moved into the north of French Indochina, giving them an important new base for waging the war in neighboring China. Although Hull now conceded a ban on all scrap metal, this was already in the works because of pressures from U.S. industry. For the moment the secretary of state was able to hold the line, but he was fighting a rearguard action. As the historian Jonathan Utley has observed, the problem was "not the absence of a foreign policy, but too many policies within one administration."

Meanwhile Japan had aligned itself formally with Germany and Italy, signing a Tripartite Pact on September 27 in Berlin. After the destroyers-for-bases deal and the limited economic sanctions, both Berlin and Tokyo had a common interest in deterring new forward moves by the United States. The third article of the pact committed all three signatories to mutual assistance if one were "attacked by a power at present not involved in the European war or in the Sino-Japanese conflict." Since article five explicitly excluded the Soviet Union, the pact, as Foreign Minister Matsuoka told the emperor, clearly envisaged "a military alliance aimed at the United States." Yet Japan's intentions were still deterrent, in the hope that a display of Axis unity would make the United States back off. Unknown to Washington, a secret exchange of letters confirmed that the question of whether there had been an attack within the scope of article three would be "determined through joint consultation" between the three governments. This satisfied opponents of the pact within the Japanese navy and preserved Japan's freedom of action. To a significant degree the Tripartite Pact was a hollow alliance.

But appearances mattered as much as realities in international diplomacy. Japanese leaders knew little of Washington's tangled bureaucratic debate about sanctions, and concerned themselves only with its outcome. The Roosevelt administration was struck by the public alliance between the Axis powers, remaining ignorant of its private hollowness. Both American and Japanese efforts at deterrence therefore proved counterproductive. Just as U.S. sanctions had helped push Tokyo closer to Berlin, so the Tripartite Pact confirmed the American image of a totalitarian threat and strengthened the administration's resolve not to back down.

In Washington, cabinet hawks returned to the charge in early October, pressing for a total oil embargo and for the movement of the U.S. fleet to Singapore. Eventually both ideas were shelved: the election campaign made new foreign initiatives impossible. But the lack of a precise policy in the Pacific could not be ignored, especially given the exposed position of the fleet at Pearl Harbor. During October the U.S. navy worked up its own secret contingency plan in the event of war. This was drafted personally by Admiral Stark, the chief of naval operations—an indication of both the importance and the sensitivity of the document. Stark's war plan was the first to link U.S. security explicitly with the European balance and the survival of the British Empire. If Britain fell, and with it her fleet and her colonies, Stark argued, the United States could not keep open the "profitable foreign trade" needed for its rearmament economy and would be left alone, "at war with the world." Ruling out three possible options (hemisphere defense, a Pacific-first strategy, and a two-ocean war), Stark advocated Plan D, or Dog, in naval terminology. This envisaged concentration on the Atlantic, including an eventual American Expeditionary Force to invade Hitler's Europe, and a "strict defensive" posture in the Pacific. The latter entailed avoiding war with Japan if possible, eschewing even an economic blockade, and no major commitment of forces west of Hawaii. This implied, if necessary, abandoning the Philippines. On November 11 Stark gave Plan Dog to Secretary Knox for transmission to the president. The CNO never received a reply; nor did he receive a rejection. In the Roosevelt administration, presidential silence often signified tacit consent. For the moment, Plan Dog defined strategy in the Pacific. It also testified to the impact of the international revolution of 1940 on U.S. strategy: an incipient globalism and the embryo of an Anglo-American alliance.

Public Opinion and the Election Campaign

During the spring and summer of 1940 the surge of events had been so rapid that American opinion struggled to keep up. The crucial policy moves were made in Washington by the administration or by influential networks around it, such as the Century Group. In the fall, however, the American public became more engaged. With summer vacations over and the election campaign under way, noninterventionists and supporters of the president's policy began to organize at the grass roots.

The Committee to Defend America by Aiding the Allies (CDAAA) was formed in mid-May 1940 because of the crisis in Europe. Headed by the Kansas editor William Allen White, it built on networks formed the previous autumn in the battle to revise the Neutrality Act. On July 1 there were 300 local chapters; by November the total was 750, in every state of the Union, with about 10,000 active members. The CDAAA had raised nearly a quarter of a million dollars. On the other side, the principal noninterventionist organization was not created until after the destroyers deal. The America First Committee (AFC) was the brainchild of R. Douglas Stuart, a student at Yale Law School, who started canvassing support in the spring of 1940.

Early backers included classmates Kingman Brewster, a future president of Yale, and Gerald R. Ford, a future president of the United States. Its chairman was Robert E. Wood, the head of the mail-order giant Sears, Roebuck. Initially America First concentrated on publicizing its arguments; a big organizational drive to establish local chapters came only after the November election. But the positions staked out by both sides in the fall of 1940 exposed the major issues in U.S. foreign policy.

As its name suggests, the Committee to Defend America by Aiding the Allies used the main intellectual arguments about an Axis threat that had been developed by the Roosevelt administration over the previous couple of years. One theme, featured in publicity for the destroyers deal, was the importance of control of the Atlantic. The CDAAA insisted that the Monroe Doctrine had been plausible only because a friendly fleet, the Royal Navy, had helped prevent hostile powers from dominating the Atlantic Ocean. Now British naval supremacy was in danger: hence the need to bolster Britain's defenses. William C. Bullitt, recently returned from the Paris embassy, claimed in August 1940 that "the destruction of the British Navy would be the turning of our Atlantic Maginot Line." A second CDAAA theme was the threat from "fifth columns." The success of Hitler in overrunning Norway, abetted by collaborators within, suggested that even apparently strong countries were vulnerable to subversion. The playwright Robert Sherwood produced a full-page advertisement for major metropolitan newspapers on June 10–11 entitled "STOP HITLER NOW!" This warned of the propaganda by Nazis, Communists, and fellow travelers against national defense and aid to the Allies. Fifth columns in weak Latin American countries were a particular concern because their success could enable the Axis to gain a foothold in the Western Hemisphere. This tied into a third theme of the administration and its CDAAA allies, namely the capacity of airpower to bridge America's oceanic barriers. In May 1940 Roosevelt had warned that "the width of these oceans is not what it was in the days of clipper ships. At one point between Africa and Brazil the distance is less than from Washington to Denver, Colorado." If Axis states established bases in Latin America or on European colonies in the Caribbean, much of the United States would come within bombing range.

The CDAAA's opponents considered these arguments exaggerated and alarmist. America First's central contention was that the traditional philosophy of hemisphere defense was still viable. Its inaugural press release on September 4, 1940, enunciated four basic principles:

1. The United States must build an impregnable defense for America.

2. No foreign power, nor group of powers, can successfully attack a *prepared* America.

3. American democracy can be preserved only by keeping out of the European war.

4. "Aid short of war" weakens national defense at home and threatens to involve America in war abroad.

In short, America Firsters claimed that if the United States built up its national defense and husbanded its resources, it could not be successfully attacked. As point three indicated, there were also fears, echoing those of the New Deal era, that the strengthening of government necessary for all-out war could undermine freedom and democracy at home.

Values as well as security were also at stake, as historians such as John A. Thompson have argued. America Firsters were less engaged emotionally by the conflict in Europe. They tended to see it as a continuing struggle between the "imperialists" and the "have-not" powers, with Britain fighting for its empire, not for democracy. Many reckoned that the best answer was a negotiated peace. By contrast, the administration and its allies portrayed the struggle as a battle between democracy and totalitarianism, and depicted the ideological differences between the United States and Great Britain as insignificant. Sherwood's

STOP HITLER NOW! advertisement warned that Hitler and his Axis partners were agreed on one primary objective: "Democracy must be wiped from the face of the earth." If Hitler wins, wrote Sherwood, "government of the people, by the people, for the people" would be "the discarded ideal of a decayed civilization." From this standpoint the Atlantic Ocean was a cultural bridge as well as a geopolitical barrier. In the summer of 1940 the *Chicago Daily News*—owned by Navy Secretary Frank Knox—was already editorializing about "Atlantic Civilization." This was its shorthand for a "tightly woven net of mutual exchanges, values and interests" that had developed over the previous century and now embraced every American.

The debate over U.S. foreign policy therefore involved ideology as much as geopolitics. Moreover the Luftwaffe's attacks on Britain that autumn helped the administration's cause by strengthening Americans' identification with the British people and their values.

Although Hitler's ambitions extended to Britain's overseas empire, his immediate concern was a free hand on the continent. He assumed that with France out of the war, the British would see sense and make peace. But they did not. The plan to invade Britain (codenamed Operation Sealion) was cobbled together belatedly and with reluctance from the middle of July. Hitler himself was skeptical, and his navy very unhappy. The essential precondition was air supremacy over the Channel. From August 13, therefore, the Luftwaffe began an intensive campaign against the fighter bases of the Royal Air Force. Despite heavy losses, the RAF's modern Spitfires and Hurricanes kept the Germans at bay, aided by early warning from the new system of radar stations along the English coast. On September 7 the Luftwaffe suddenly shifted tactics and began massive bombing raids on London and other cities. Caught off guard, the RAF was initially unable to save the London docklands from severe damage. But over the next two weeks Fighter Command inflicted heavy losses on the Luftwaffe's aerial armadas, and on September 17 Operation Sealion was postponed "until further notice." The Luftwaffe settled down for an autumn and winter of bombing raids on British cities, ostensibly to destroy industrial targets but in practice to terrorize the civilian population.

For Americans the Blitz was supremely a radio war. The major U.S. networks sent some of their best correspondents to London. The most celebrated was Edward R. Murrow of CBS, whose live broadcasts of air raids brought the sounds of modern war into American living rooms. Murrow's matter-of-fact, gravelly voice told its story against the wail of air-raid sirens, the crump-crump of exploding bombs, and the clatter of anti-aircraft guns. "You burned the city of London in our homes, and we felt the flames," wrote the poet Archibald MacLeish in tribute. The British Ministry of Information (MOI) gave Murrow and colleagues such as Eric Sevareid full cooperation, waiving their normally strict censorship requirements because of the evident effect in the United States. The MOI's documentary film about the Blitz, entitled *London Can Take It,* was also aimed at U.S. audiences. The MOI deliberately recruited an American commentator, the journalist Quentin Reynolds, who began his account of a night raid on the capital with the words: "These are not Hollywood sound effects. This is the music they play every night in London." The MOI kept its name off the credits and used Warner Brothers to distribute the film around the United States. Opening in early November 1940, by the next spring *London Can Take It* had been screened at twelve thousand cinemas to an estimated sixty million Americans.

Accompanying the human drama of the Blitz, U.S. media depicted a Britain doubly tied to American values. On the one hand there were reminders of the transatlantic cultural heritage—of language and literature, religion and law. After Britain had rejected Hitler's peace offer and prepared for invasion, the *New York Times* editorialized on July 24: "It is twelve o'clock in London. . . . Is the tongue of Chaucer, of Shakespeare, of Milton, of the King James translation of the Scriptures, of Keats and Shelley, to be hereafter, in the British Isles, the dialect of an enslaved race? . . . It is twelve o'clock in England. Not twelve o'clock for empire—there is no empire any more. . . . Twelve o'clock for the common people of England out of whom England's greatest souls have always come."

The "common people." If 1940 was High Noon for the values that the United States shared with Great Britain, it also seemed to many U.S. commentators as the dawn of a Brave New World. Their frequent talk of an incipient "social revolution" in Britain in 1940 suggested that the country was finally escaping from the shell of its class system and emerging as a full-fledged democracy. Total war blurred the distinctions between what one correspondent, Samuel Grafton, called "old-school-tie England" and "cap-in-hand England." The heroism of ordinary soldiers and sailors at Dunkirk had already caught the journalists' imagination. In the fall of 1940 it was the people of London, rich and poor, carrying on their daily business despite Hitler's bombs, in their row houses, their air-raid shelters, or asleep on the platforms of London subway stations. The journalist "Scotty" Reston declared in September: "The democratization of Great Britain goes on apace. What centuries of history have not done for this country, Chancellor Hitler is doing now. He is breaking down the class structure of England every time his bombers come over. . . . Why it has now got so that total strangers speak to each other on the streets, a completely un-English thing to do. Many people think they are seeing the start of a great social movement here at last."

One of those people was Roosevelt himself. It was common gossip in Washington that winter that the president anticipated a "social revolution" in Britain, with the Labour party in control after the war. That was why, when Joseph Kennedy, the ambassador in London, resigned in November, FDR appointed John

Gilbert Winant as his successor. Winant was a convinced New
Dealer and former director of the International Labor Office in
Geneva, who had excellent contacts with the British Labour
party and union leaders.

The moving accounts of the Blitz, the evocations of Britain
having a shared cultural past and a convergent democratic future
with the United States—these all had a profound effect in America. In 1940 this was still a country whose center of gravity lay on
the East Coast, and many of its political, business, and cultural
leaders felt a close (albeit love-hate) affinity with Europe. As
Roosevelt noted in September 1939, American opinion had never
been emotionally neutral between the Axis and its opponents.
But most Americans were not persuaded that their antipathy to
Nazism required more than hemisphere defense. In the summer
and fall of 1940 that changed. An overwhelming majority still
opposed U.S. entry into the war. But nuanced questions by
Gallup pollsters exposed a shift in opinion. On June 25, just after
the fall of France, 64 percent of those questioned believed it was
more important to keep out of the war than to help England. On
October 20 the balance was exactly fifty-fifty. By November 19,
60 percent felt it was more important to help England, even at
risk of the United States getting into the war. For whatever reasons—geopolitical calculation or ideological empathy—U.S.
public opinion was moving behind the president's policy of treat-
ing Britain as America's front line.

On September 16, 1940—two weeks after the destroyers deal
and at the height of the Battle of Britain—Roosevelt signed into
law the Selective Service Act. For the first time in its history the
United States had a peacetime draft. The initiative did not come
from the president himself. As with the destroyers deal, he
floated on a rising tide whipped up by well-connected lobbyists.
In this case the prime mover was Grenville Clark, a New York
lawyer and old friend of FDR who harked back to the Plattsburg
movement of World War I. This had lobbied for voluntary mili-

tary training camps before the United States entered the war in 1917. Alarmed at the German blitzkrieg of 1940, Clark organized a dinner of Plattsburg buddies, among them Henry Stimson, on May 22 at the Harvard Club of New York. Informally Clark sounded out the president, who told him that "the difficulty of proposing a concrete set of measures 'short of war' is largely a political one—what one can get from Congress." Thus encouraged, Clark and his group raised money, sponsored publicity, and lobbied Capitol Hill. By late June they had found bipartisan sponsors to introduce a bill. Once hearings on it had begun, the president extended cautious but public support.

Noninterventionists were split. Committed to national preparedness, as the "America First" manifesto showed, some of them accepted the bill. Others insisted that the necessary manpower could be generated through volunteers, and warned of the threat to freedom and democracy at home. Senator George Norris of Nebraska claimed that a peacetime draft "would change the very nature of most of our citizens. We would become warlike, and when we had become warlike, there would be no doubt that we would soon be fighting with somebody." Burton K. Wheeler, the veteran senator from Montana and, like Norris, an old-line Progressive, called the draft "the greatest step toward regimentation and militarism" that Congress had ever undertaken. He feared it would "slit the throat of the last Democracy still living."

These warnings went largely unheeded. The bill passed through each House with close to a two-to-one margin. Presidential warnings about national security had clearly exerted a marked effect. Equally important was the commitment that no troops would serve outside the Western Hemisphere, except in territories or possessions of the United States. At a deeper level, New Deal agencies such as the Civilian Conservation Corps had made the nation more accustomed to directed federal programs. And Selective Service carefully balanced the national and the local, as befitted America's democratic federalism. Although all male citizens aged twenty-one through thirty-six were now liable and had to register to obtain a draft number, not all would be called up. The numbers would be selected by national lottery but the final choice would be left to 6,400 local draft boards, predominantly lawyers and businessmen. They would decide whether those with the unlucky numbers fitted the criteria for physical and mental fitness or for deferment on specified grounds, such as fatherhood or civilian work. The draft therefore balanced national obligation and local implementation: a man's fate was ultimately in the hands of his neighbors. Selective Service Director Lewis B. Hershey called it "the very essence of democracy."

After registration was completed, the numbers were drawn by lottery on October 29, a week before the presidential election. Roosevelt, who pulled the first number (158), avoided the words "draft" or "conscription" and called it instead a "muster," thereby evoking images of Lexington Green and the bridge at Concord. In this qualified way the United States began the fateful precedent of a peacetime draft.

Wendell Willkie, FDR's Republican opponent, basically supported the president's foreign policy, so that the election campaign of 1940 had a slightly artificial air at first. Willkie declined to make either the destroyers deal or Selective Service a partisan issue. But as the campaign progressed and Willkie sagged in the polls, he was persuaded to outbid the president for the peace vote. He told an audience in Chicago in late October that if Roosevelt's promise "to keep our boys out of foreign wars is no better than his promise to balance the budget, they're almost on the transports!" In Baltimore on October 30 he again blasted the president for past dishonesty and predicted, "If you re-elect him you may expect war in April 1941."

For seven weeks Willkie had toured the nation, traveling more than seventeen thousand miles through thirty states on his campaign train. He had given more than five hundred speeches, wearing out himself (and his voice) in the process. Initially FDR had astutely played the role of commander-in-chief, refusing to leave the Washington area but making frequent ostensibly non-partisan tours of defense installations to hammer home his point about being the man for the hour. But Willkie's attacks, and his surge in the polls in late October, forced the president onto the campaign trail for the last two weeks. On the day of Willkie's Baltimore speech, Roosevelt delivered his baldest anti-war commitment in Boston, speaking to the "mothers and fathers" of America. "I have said this before, but I shall say it again and again and again. Your boys are not going to be sent into any foreign wars." After some thought, FDR had left out the qualifying phrase in the Democratic platform, "except in case of attack." When one of his speechwriters questioned the omission, FDR shrugged it off: "Of course we'll fight if we're attacked. If somebody attacks us, then it isn't a foreign war, is it?" For his part, Willkie was incensed. "That hypocritical son of a bitch," he exclaimed. "This is going to beat me!"

Despite his fears, Roosevelt won decisively. He carried 38 states with 449 electoral votes, compared with 10 states and 82 votes for Willkie. The margin on the popular vote was narrower, however, with only 55 percent for FDR. Willkie had not fought an effective campaign. His organization was poor, and he had not staked out clear differences with Roosevelt until too late. On the Democratic side, Roosevelt had held the tenuous New Deal coalition intact—the white South and urban workers, ethnic groups and the black vote. As with any election, therefore, many factors explained the outcome. But the war was of major importance. In all likelihood FDR would not have run for a third term but for Hitler's blitzkrieg in Europe. Moreover his election promises about not entering the war—like similar pledges during the neutrality debate in autumn 1939—would hang around his neck in the months to come.

5

Abandoning Cash and Carry (December 1940 to May 1941)

ROOSEVELT'S POLICY of aid to Britain short of war was predicated on the principles of cash and carry. In early 1941 both principles were undermined. First, Britain was running out of gold and dollar reserves. FDR's solution—the Lend-Lease Bill—created the framework for a major government-funded rearmament program, on lines that he had been contemplating since autumn 1938. In this period the foundations of the postwar military-industrial complex were laid. But boosting U.S. rearmament and covering Britain's dollar gap were not sufficient if the materiel was then destroyed by U-boats in the Atlantic. In the spring of 1941 FDR extended the operations of the U.S. navy in the Atlantic to protect British and Canadian convoys. He had solved the "cash" crisis by going to Congress, but he addressed the "carry" problem by exploiting his powers as commander-in-chief. This use of executive power was another precedent that would cast a long shadow.

THE ROOSEVELT DOCTRINE

For weeks British leaders had awaited the result of the U.S. presidential election. After November 5 they expected that the floodgates of aid would now open. Many, including Churchill himself, seem to have anticipated an early declaration of war now that Roosevelt had a new "mandate." Consciously or not, they cast U.S. politics in a British mold, assuming that the president would now have the political backing to do what he wanted—in the same way as a British prime minister takes office with (and indeed only because) he has a working majority in the House of Commons.

Of course FDR did have greater freedom of political maneuver after November 5. When the Seventy-seventh Congress convened in January 1941 he would enjoy increased "overall majorities" of 268 to 167 in the House and 66 to 30 in the Senate. But these statistics counted little in his congressional arithmetic. Many conservative Democrats remained intensely suspicious of the president, including senior Southerners on key committees, and FDR was forever fearful that a rump of determined opponents could obstruct administration policy and undermine national unity. The arms embargo debate of summer 1939 was a recent example, but Wilson's tragedy in 1919 still lurked in his memory.

British leaders were shaken in November 1940 when their urgent needs were not immediately addressed. On December 2 Churchill confessed himself "rather chilled" at the American attitude since the election. At this stage, contrary to later mythology, the prime minister was still somewhat uncertain about Roosevelt and inclined to a hard-bargaining approach when seeking aid. But Lord Lothian, the British ambassador in Washington, was an experienced observer of the American scene. He had not expected a transformation in U.S. policy after the election, telling the Foreign Office in September: "Public opinion here has not yet grasped that it will have to make far reaching decisions to finance and supply us and possibly still graver ones next Spring or Summer unless it is to take responsibility of forcing us to make a compromise peace. Yet owing to the size of the country and its constitution it is usually impossible to get important decisions taken without at least six months preparation." He saw the election mainly as a chance to renew Britain's efforts to "educate" the United States. While home on leave in November, he persuaded Churchill to send Roosevelt a comprehensive overview of Britain's needs from the United States in 1941.

The text went through many drafts, with Lothian and Churchill arguing about phrasing and emphasis. The eventual letter, sent on December 8, highlighted the three interrelated problems of production, finance, and shipping. The United States needed to expand its rearmament while also guaranteeing Britain an increasing output of aircraft, ships, and munitions. The larger Britain's orders, warned Churchill, "the sooner will our dollar credits be exhausted," adding that "the moment approaches when we shall no longer be able to pay cash for shipping and other supplies." And only if the U.S. navy provided protection for Allied convoys could the disastrous losses in the Atlantic be reversed. Throughout his four-thousand-word letter, Churchill emphasized the "solid identity of interest" between the two countries in "the defeat of the Nazi and Fascist tyranny." He ended by asking Roosevelt to regard the document "not as an appeal for aid, but as a statement of the minimum action necessary to the achievement of our common purpose."

Churchill's letter, with its threefold focus on production, finance, and shipping, set out the issues with cogent clarity. It was delivered to the president as he sailed the Caribbean on a ten-day fishing trip. According to Felix Frankfurter, the Supreme Court justice, FDR faced his third term not with elation but "in a deep Lincolnesque mood," conscious of the magnitude of the task ahead. Roosevelt was desperately tired after the campaign. Sun and conversation, fishing and card games in the Caribbean helped him to recharge his batteries. Harry Hopkins told Churchill later that Roosevelt read and reread the letter, brooding in his deck chair. For two days, said Hopkins, the president did not seem to have reached any clear conclusion, but then he laid out the whole plan for lend-lease.

This is probably to overstate the impact of Churchill's missive. Contrary to the prime minister's fears, Roosevelt had already been mulling over Britain's predicament during November, relating it to ideas that had been in his mind for two years. On November 8 the president told his cabinet and then the press that he favored a fifty-fifty division of war materials with Britain. Privately he reverted to the idea broached after Munich about selling or lending planes to Hitler's enemies. He told Harold Ickes that "the time would surely come when Great Britain would need loans or credits" and talked of leasing ships and other property that was "loanable, returnable, and insurable."

Clearly, then, Churchill's letter did not force Roosevelt to think new thoughts. The basic principle of lend-lease was already in his mind; indeed, it had been there for two years. But in November 1940 FDR still thought that the crunch point was well in the future. He told Ickes that the British still had $2.5 billion in credit and property in the United States that could be liquidated. And he saw the loan idea as relevant mainly to merchant ships, without needing congressional approval. Churchill's letter, and well-publicized press comments by Ambassador Lothian on his return to the United States, made FDR appreciate that the matter was now urgent. They forced him to draw up a comprehensive response to Britain's supply crisis, which would have to be taken to Congress. FDR returned to Washington on December 16—refreshed, in good humor, and ready for one of the most creative months of his twelve-year presidency.

Roosevelt called a press conference for the afternoon of December 17. He stressed that he was "talking selfishly, from the American point of view." The "one thing necessary for American national defense is additional productive facilities," he told reporters. British orders helped create those facilities, so they must be encouraged. But how to do this? The president ruled

out both straightforward loans and direct gifts. Instead he favored the United States taking over British orders and then leasing them to Britain. "What I am trying to do is eliminate the
dollar sign." Roosevelt then offered an inspired everyday analogy
(adapted from a suggestion by Harold Ickes in August). Imagine
my neighbor's house catches fire, he said, and he doesn't have a
hose. I don't haggle over a price in advance, while his house and
possibly mine go up in flames. I lend him my hose straight away.
He either returns it later, or pays for a replacement if it gets damaged. The point, said FDR, was to lease Britain essential munitions in the interests of U.S. defense, "with the understanding
that when the show was over, we would get repaid sometime in
kind."

In answering questions, the president made clear that these
proposals would require congressional legislation. But he insisted that he was not seeking repeal of the Neutrality Act. Instead he wanted to bypass its anti-loan provisions and also avoid
the war debts that had poisoned Anglo-American relations in the
1930s. Asked whether he thought this "takes us any more into
the war than we are?" the president replied breezily, "No, not a
bit." He was also evasive when tackled on U.S. preparedness—
"Mr. President, before you loan your hose to your neighbor you
have to have the hose." Roosevelt intended lend-lease to galvanize U.S. rearmament as well as aid Britain.

This carefully prepared "impromptu" press briefing was the
first of three major statements on foreign policy that FDR made
in three weeks at the turn of 1940–1941. At 9 p.m. on December
29 he gave his first radio "fireside chat" in months, in which he
set his leasing ideas into the context of broad policy. According to
the president, this was "not a fireside chat on war" but a talk on
"national security"—another term with a long history ahead of
it. He reiterated his familiar geopolitical themes—Britain as the
friendly neighbor guarding the Atlantic, the dangers to the
Western Hemisphere from airpower and from subversion. But

he spent as much time on the ideological challenge to "our American civilization." The Tripartite Pact, he said, set out "a program aimed at world control." He quoted Hitler's recent statement that "there are two worlds that stand opposed to each other," with no possibility of reconciliation between them. The Axis "new order" was simply "a revival of the oldest and the worst tyranny" in which there was "no liberty, no religion, no hope." When "American appeasers" talked of a "negotiated peace," they were deluding themselves. That, said FDR, would be a "dictated peace" with "a gang of outlaws" who had made it clear that "there can be no ultimate peace between their philosophy of government and our philosophy of government."

Having sketched this Manichean view of a bipolar world in which the Axis posed a fundamental threat to the United States, FDR then elaborated his plans for aiding Britain. He insisted that he had no intention of declaring war or sending troops to Europe. The "sole purpose" of national policy was "to keep war away from our country and our people." What the British needed were "the implements of war," and their needs must be integrated with those of the United States. Finishing with words suggested by Harry Hopkins, Roosevelt called on Americans to be "the great arsenal of democracy."

This phrase has passed into cliché. But as the historian Robert E. Osgood noted, it was "the most extreme statement of the American mission, in terms of a tangible commitment, ever suggested by anyone charged with the conduct of America's foreign affairs." Like FDR's State of the Union Address in January 1939, it anticipated elements of the Truman Doctrine of March 1947.* One might say that the December 29 fireside chat set out the "Roosevelt Doctrine" in prelude to the concrete measures of

---

*For instance, its stark bipolarity. "At the present moment in world history," said Truman, "nearly every nation must choose between alternative ways of life. The choice is too often not a free one."

lend-lease, just as the Truman Doctrine was the ideological precursor of the Marshall Plan.

The president was delighted with reaction to his speech. Seventy-five percent of those polled said they had heard or read his words—the highest proportion for any Roosevelt speech on which there are polls—and of these 61 percent agreed with his position. Mail and telegrams to the White House were running at 100 to 1 in favor. Buoyed by this support, the president gave the Treasury Department the green light to finish drafting the appropriate legislation. Meanwhile, on January 6, 1941, he went to Capitol Hill for his annual State of the Union Address.

Implying that the election victory, his recent messages, and the reaction to them had given him a clear public and bipartisan mandate, the president crystallized "our national policy" in three phrases—"all-inclusive national defense," full support of "all those resolute people, everywhere, who are resisting aggression," and a refusal "to acquiesce in a peace dictated by aggressors and sponsored by appeasers. We know that enduring peace cannot be bought at the cost of other people's freedom." He then defined the "four essential human freedoms" that must be basic to any future peace. These were:

1. "Freedom of speech and expression."

2. "Freedom of every person to worship God in his own way."

3. "Freedom from want" which meant "economic understandings which will secure to every nation a healthy peacetime life for its inhabitants."

4. "Freedom from fear" which meant "a world-wide reduction of armaments" to the point where "no nation will be in a position to commit an act of physical aggression against any neighbor."

Roosevelt insisted that these four freedoms must be global in extent. Each was to apply "everywhere in the world." Nor was this a "vision of a distant millennium. It is a definite basis for a kind of world attainable in our own time and generation."

Against the Axis "New Order," Roosevelt set out a globalist American ideology whose realization was now the goal of U.S. policy.

The concept of the "four freedoms" was not novel. The president had outlined it privately on several occasions in the winter of 1939–1940. In a press conference on July 5, 1940, he had aired it publicly (in slightly different form) as part of a post–Independence Day meditation on the meaning of American liberty. There he contrasted the "parliamentary system" of government, with separate executive, legislature, and judiciary, against "the corporate state" of Italy, Germany, and Russia, which had abolished "two of the three safeguards of democracy, the Legislature and the Courts" and had also eliminated the "four freedoms" in the interests of "efficient" government. His reasons for reiterating the Four Freedoms in January 1941 are not entirely clear. But it is likely that he had two audiences in mind—the America First critics who spoke of a negotiated peace, and the British government, which, as anti-interventionists argued, had not articulated clear peace aims. Roosevelt wanted to show how a peace acceptable to the United States could not be negotiated with the Axis. But even as he linked his country's security with that of the British Empire, he also showed that he was not fighting for British goals.

Like Woodrow Wilson, with his "Peace Without Victory" and "Fourteen Points" speeches of January 1917 and January 1918, Franklin Roosevelt wished to define the fundamentals of an *American* peace. Hopkins told the British Foreign Office a few weeks later that they should consult FDR before making any statement of war aims. The president was "rather touchy" on this matter because he "regarded the post-war settlement so to speak as being his particular preserve." Unlike Woodrow Wilson, however, FDR wanted peace *with* victory because he was sure that without victory in this bipolar struggle, there could be no lasting peace. Months before the United States entered World War II,

Roosevelt had established the framework of what would become America's cold war worldview.

THE GREAT DEBATE ON LEND-LEASE

Shortly after noon on January 10, 1941, Majority Leader John McCormack introduced on the floor of the House of Representatives "a bill further to promote the defense of the United States, and for other purposes." The neat title was suggested by Justice Felix Frankfurter. Equally neat was the number of the bill, House Resolution 1776—a sleight of hand by the House parliamentarian who knew that bill numbers had already reached the 1760s.

The House held two weeks of committee hearings and then a week of floor debates before voting on February 8. The Senate began its hearings at the end of January, but there, unlike the House, the real battle took place on the Senate floor as a series of amendments were proposed, debated, and eventually voted upon. Not until March 8 did the Senate pass an amended bill, which Roosevelt finally signed into law on March 11. Approving the necessary appropriations took another two weeks. Thus for the best part of three months—from the president's "Arsenal of Democracy" speech to the voting of funds—lend-lease was at the center of national attention. The House and Senate hearings were packed as cabinet members such as Hull and Stimson and celebrity opponents such as Joseph Kennedy and Charles Lindbergh gave testimony. The hearings and floor speeches were extensively reported on the radio and in metropolitan and local papers. In short, this was one of the great foreign policy debates of U.S. history.

The administration knew it had the votes to force the bill through the Congress. But Roosevelt wanted sufficient public discussion to generate mass support and to claim that he had a popular mandate. As with the destroyers deal, he encouraged the

Century Group and the Committee to Defend America by Aiding the Allies (CDAAA) to mobilize support. On the other hand, as the historian Warren F. Kimball has emphasized, the administration wished to confine the debate to immediate issues and avoid a general examination of the thrust and implications of current policy. Administration spokesmen therefore repeated the now-familiar themes about aggressive Axis intentions, the centrality of Britain and its fleet to U.S. security, and the threats from airpower and subversion, particularly via Latin America. By contrast, the administration deflected all attempts to turn the hearings into a larger debate about convoying, even though there was little point in producing what Churchill called "the tools" if these could not be delivered.

For the America First Committee, the lend-lease debate was its first and, as it proved, largest campaign. After the presidential election the AFC had started organizing itself into local chapters, on the lines of the CDAAA. By the end of February it had some 650 embryonic chapters; the AFC had distributed 1.5 million leaflets, 750,000 buttons, and 500,000 bumper stickers. Much of its money came from big manufacturers and agribusiness in the Chicago area, but there were also many smaller donors. The young John F. Kennedy sent $100, adding, "What you are all doing is vital."

The AFC leadership did not expect to defeat the Lend-Lease Bill, but it was determined to mobilize opposition to Roosevelt's foreign policy. Its attacks centered on two themes. One was that the powers granted to Roosevelt would make him a virtual dictator. According to AFC chairman Robert E. Wood, "the President is not asking for a blank check, he wants a blank check book with the power to write away your manpower, our laws and our liberties." The other main charge was that the bill would have the effect, and probably had the intention, of getting the United States into the war. In one of the most celebrated barbs, Senator Burton K. Wheeler of Montana called it "the New

Deal's triple A foreign policy; it will plow under every fourth American boy." Roosevelt shot back that he regarded this "as the most dastardly, unpatriotic thing . . . that has been said in public life in my generation."

Some of the most trenchant criticisms of the administration came from Charles Lindbergh. Testifying before the House Foreign Affairs Committee in January, the transatlantic aviator questioned Roosevelt's interpretation of airpower. Although "trans-oceanic bombing" was becoming a possibility, Lindbergh predicted that it would be costly to the attacker and have limited effect. He insisted that a full-scale "air invasion across the ocean" was "absolutely impossible" at any time in the "predictable future." Lindbergh's reading of the air age, unlike Roosevelt's, confirmed the verities of hemisphere defense and militated against any thoughts of invading Hitler's Europe. Basically airpower had "added to America's security against Europe, and to Europe's security against America." But the debate generated by Lindbergh was as much about the man as the message. His admission that he preferred "to see neither side win" and his stated preference for a negotiated peace enabled administration supporters to label him as an "appeaser" and even a crypto-fascist. By again framing the geopolitical debate in ideological terms, FDR was able to stigmatize opponents of his policies as de facto friends of Hitler.

Although critics of the Lend-Lease Bill could not defeat it, they did force the administration to accept certain amendments. Among these were a time limit (the act would expire on July 1, 1943), a requirement that the president must report to Congress every ninety days about its operations, and a statement that nothing in the bill authorized the use of the U.S. navy to escort Allied merchant convoys. In a move that could damage Britain in the short term, House leaders also accepted an amendment limiting the amount of previously ordered materiel that could be transferred to a total value of $1.3 billion. On the other hand, House leaders defeated an amendment setting the total cost of lend-lease at $7 billion. In both Houses the administration resisted all attempts to limit the list of nations to whom lend-lease could be extended. The explicit target for vehement anti-Communists, such as Republican Representative George Tinkham of Massachusetts, was the Soviet Union. Roosevelt's unstated reason for adamantly refusing to exclude the USSR was (as we shall see) his secret intelligence about Hitler's impending drive to the east.

Lend-Lease passed with comfortable majorities: 260 to 165 in the House and 60 to 31 in the Senate. In both, the vote followed largely partisan lines, though 15 percent of House Republicans and 30 percent of GOP senators sided with the administration, while 10 percent of Democrats in the House and 20 percent of those in the Senate voted against the president. The outcome and the process were both major administration triumphs. The international situation had changed dramatically since the humiliating deadlock over neutrality revision in the spring and summer of 1939. There were also two significant differences in congressional politics. First, the conservative coalition of Republicans and Southern Democrats, who in 1938–1939 had been able to block further New Deal measures, did not function in foreign affairs. The South was strongly Anglophile and after the fall of France had led the country as the section most supportive of administration aid to Britain. Senator Walter George, a conservative Southern Democrat whom FDR had tried and failed to purge in the 1938 election, was a staunch backer of lend-lease. Second, the Democrats had new and effective leaders in both Houses. In the Senate, George had replaced the inept Key Pittman as chairman of the Foreign Relations Committee, while in the House the new team of Speaker Sam Rayburn and Majority Leader John McCormack was already proving a formidable combination.

The act that Roosevelt signed into law on March 11, 1941, gave him authority to arrange for the manufacture or procurement of "any defense article for the government of any country whose defense the President deems vital to the defense of the United States." He was also authorized to "sell, transfer title to, exchange, lease, lend, or otherwise dispose of, to any such government any defense article." The definition of "defense article" was extremely broad: it ranged from weapons to machinery, from component parts to agricultural commodities. The act also granted these powers to the president "notwithstanding the provisions of any other law"—a reference particularly to the Neutrality Act, whose restrictions FDR, in a characteristic strategem, was seeking to bypass rather than repeal. As soon as the act became law, the administration came back to Congress for an initial $7 billion in appropriations. Appropriately the first list of lend-lease goods to be transferred to Britain included 900,000 feet of fire hose.

During 1941 lend-lease provided only 1 percent of the munitions used by Britain and its empire. A further 7 percent came from the United States under pre-lend-lease contracts for which Britain had paid cash. But in the longer term the act was enormously important. During the whole of World War II, lend-lease covered more than half of Britain's balance-of-payments deficit, enabling it to concentrate on war production without having to generate exports to cover import needs. By the time Japan surrendered in 1945, the U.S. Congress had appropriated more than $50 billion for lend-lease worldwide.

Roosevelt's advisers hoped that the president would now reorganize the U.S. defense economy, for instance by establishing a unified Department of Supply. But FDR did not wish to create a new bureaucratic empire. Instead he established a small Office of Production Management within the White House, with limited staff and powers. The president hoped that lend-lease would galvanize and channel the defense effort. To this end he appointed his confidant Harry Hopkins as lend-lease administrator. Hopkins's forte was getting things done, usually by telephone rather than through long memoranda. Having just visited London—

sent by Roosevelt to get the measure of Churchill—he came back passionately enthusiastic about Britain and its pugnacious leader. Yet not even his zeal, ruthlessness, and unrivaled access to the president were sufficient. During 1941 the United States produced one million *more* automobiles than it did in 1939. Without effective war powers the administration could not coerce business, now sensing a consumer boom after years of depression and also wary that the flow of war orders could dry up as quickly as it was turned on. Carmakers were reluctant to convert their plants to aircraft production; steel manufacturers gave priority to firm domestic orders for automobile components and consumer durables. Many of the big businessmen who funded America First believed that war would lead to higher taxes and greater unionization. The new role for Hopkins, a tax-and-spend Democrat, strengthened their fears that lend-lease was a continuation of the New Deal by other means.

Nor was Hopkins successful in coordinating army and navy programs. Both services continued to place orders without regard to each other, exacerbating shortages of plants, labor, and materials. They were certainly unwilling to put aid to Britain before their own essential modernization. Even the latter had to proceed slowly, given congressional suspicions that the administration was preparing for war. The army air force set a production target for 1941 of only nine thousand parachutes. Although planners foresaw the vital importance of amphibious warfare, the production of landing craft was taboo—a policy that contributed to the delays in mounting a "second front" in 1942–1944.

Yet lend-lease did have profound consequences for U.S. rearmament. In 1941 federal spending was four times the mid-1930s figure, and most of the increase was generated by defense. In real terms, military spending constituted 11.2 percent of gross national product in 1941, compared with 1.4 percent in 1939, most of it funded by borrowing rather than taxation. Here were patterns for the future. Lend-lease also signaled the waning of the

New Deal struggle with big business. Roosevelt was no longer talking, as in 1938, about using government plants to produce munitions. Lend-lease confirmed the decisions taken in mid-1940 to remove the restraints on private industry and to privilege a few leading contractors. In 1940 the biggest one hundred companies in the United States produced about 30 percent of the country's manufacturing output; by 1943, though total production had doubled, the top one hundred held contracts amounting to 70 percent of total output. One of the attractions of big business was its capacity to apply mass-production techniques used in the manufacture of civilian goods, such as autos, to weapons of war. Perhaps the most celebrated war tycoon, Henry J. Kaiser, revolutionized shipbuilding by using prefabricated components and by riveting not welding. In 1941 it was still taking East Coast yards about a year to build a standard ten-thousand-ton cargo vessel (the so-called Liberty Ship). By 1942 Kaiser's West Coast yards could do it in two weeks.

Despite its limited immediate effect, therefore, lend-lease had immense symbolic and long-term importance. It underlined the commitment of the United States to the Allied cause, and did so by an Act of Congress rather than an executive agreement (as in the Destroyers Deal). It also set profound precedents, particularly for funding the wartime Atlantic alliance and in laying the foundations of America's military-industrial complex of the postwar era.

THE CHANGING RELATIONSHIP WITH BRITAIN

On January 29, 1941, the House Foreign Affairs Committee was holding its last full day of hearings on the Lend-Lease Bill. At the other end of Pennsylvania Avenue there began a series of secret meetings that could have torpedoed the bill if news had leaked. In the Navy Department next to the White House, a group of Britain's top military planners were conferring with their U.S. counterparts. Dressed in civilian clothes, they were officially described as "technical advisers to the British Purchasing Commission." It took two months for these "American-British Conversations" to hammer out a basic agreement on strategy *in the event* the United States entered the war. This document, known as ABC-1, was signed on March 29.

For months the British had been pressing for staff talks: it was in their interests to entangle the Americans as closely as possible in their war effort. The British renewed the proposal in November, and this time it was taken up by Marshall and Stark, the army chief of staff and the chief of naval operations. Both could see the growing possibility that the United States might be drawn into the war; equally both recognized the difficulty of getting clear direction from the president in such politically sensitive circumstances. Stark's Plan Dog in November 1940 had been an outline attempt to define global strategy, but it also highlighted the need to compare notes with the British. Not to do so risked being unprepared for coalition warfare; yet by doing so U.S. policymakers risked being accused of wanting war. Consequently FDR kept completely aloof from the staff talks. But Admiral Stark testified after the war that the president expressed approval of the agreement, though "he was not willing to do it officially until we got into the war."

The ABC-1 agreement fleshed out the ideas in Plan Dog. Both sides concurred that the main priority was to defeat Germany and Italy, and that the Atlantic lifeline to Britain must be secured. The logical corollary was therefore a defensive, deterrent posture against Japan. These broad axioms were uncontentious. Their precise implications for policy toward Japan were not. The British continued to press the Americans to send a fleet to Singapore, Britain's main naval base in Asian waters. The U.S. delegates refused to do this, concerned about their limited resources and the political sensitivity of appearing to fight for British colonies. They remained committed to the defense of the

Philippines, using their small Asiatic Fleet but no more. After heated argument, a compromise was thrashed out at the end of February. The United States would keep its main fleet at Pearl Harbor to deter Japan but would gradually shift some ships to the Atlantic. This would relieve the Royal Navy and allow it to send a fleet to Singapore. The British accepted this convoluted swap, aware that they were not in a position to push the United States too hard and confident, like the Americans, that Japan could be deterred from serious aggression. "The first thing is to get the United States into the war," Churchill instructed his ABC delegates. "We can then settle how to fight it afterwards." Both governments would pay dearly for such complacency.

The ABC-1 agreement was explicitly a contingency plan, to take effect only if the United States entered the war. But it outlined the basic "Germany First" strategy that both countries were to pursue after Pearl Harbor. And it was also the basis for their strategic dispositions during 1941. Robert Sherwood, in his 1948 biography of Harry Hopkins, commented that these talks, and the exchange of information on which they were based, "provided the highest degree of *strategic preparedness* that the United States or probably any other nonaggressor nation has ever had before entry into war." For Sherwood it was one instance of the "common-law alliance" that was taking shape between the United States and Great Britain in 1941, meaning a tacit and unofficial partnership rather than a formal alliance.

In most partnerships, one partner is usually stronger than the other. In the 1930s, with a depression-ridden America apparently scared of any entanglements in Europe, British diplomats had often privately likened America to a young woman just entering international society, who needed the solicitude and support of an older man. By 1941 the balance had shifted. In the embryonic common-law alliance, the United States was emerging as the senior partner. The origins of lend-lease had already made this clear. As Morgenthau told a British Treasury official in December 1940: "It gets down to a question of Mr. Churchill putting himself in Mr. Roosevelt's hands with complete confidence. Then it is up to Mr. Roosevelt to say what he will do." This was a novel position for British leaders, and a painful one too, as demonstrated by two other aspects of Anglo-American relations in early 1941—the talks about U.S. bases in the Western Atlantic and the recompense that Britain would offer in return for lend-lease.

The day before the staff talks commenced in Washington, another Anglo-American conference began in London, in a room from which a portrait of King George III had been hurriedly removed. (The Foreign Office decided that was preferable to putting up a picture of George Washington as well.) These talks would determine the extent and terms of the leased areas that the United States would receive in part payment for the fifty destroyers transferred under the agreement signed in September 1940. That agreement had been framed in extremely general terms, and there was consternation in London when American demands became clear. They wanted ninety-nine-year leases, which British opponents claimed was tantamount to a permanent handover. The territory demanded in Trinidad was also contentious: the United States wanted a naval and air base as well as some eighteen square miles of prime land in the center of the island to house two divisions, some twenty thousand men.

Lord Lloyd, the colonial secretary, viewed all this as the thin end of an American imperialist wedge into the Caribbean. "These people are gangsters," he told the Foreign Office. Even Anthony Eden, the foreign secretary, admitted that the bases deal had struck "a grievous blow at our authority and ultimately I have no doubt at our sovereignty, in all these places." But he and Churchill agreed that the British were in no position to argue. Churchill warned Lloyd on March 4: "You can easily have a first-class row with the United States of America about these matters, and this will be particularly vexatious at a time when the

Lease and Lend Bill is on its passage." On their own admission, the British gave way on "practically everything," and the Bases Agreement was signed on March 27, just as the staff talks were being finalized in Washington. The U.S. ambassador in London, "Gil" Winant, told Roosevelt that the powers conveyed to the United States were "probably more far-reaching than any British Government has ever given anyone over British territory before."

Another sign of the shifting balance of the Anglo-American relationship was the debate about how to pay for lend-lease. A leading opponent of the act, Republican Senator Robert Taft of Ohio, remarked that lending war equipment was "a good deal like lending chewing gum. You don't want it back." Indeed; but the administration did want some other candy in return. Section 3b of the act stated that the compensation to the United States "may be payment or repayment in kind or property, or any other direct or indirect benefit which the President deems satisfactory." Initially FDR delegated responsibility for drawing up precise proposals to the U.S. Treasury Department. Personally Morgenthau was inclined to write the goods off, saying to the British in effect, "Here, take it; you're doing the fighting; it's your men and your blood that you're shedding and we're in your debt." But that was deemed politically impossible. So his staff followed the lines of Roosevelt's original loan proposal: where the original goods could not be returned, the British should provide comparable defense articles of similar value or useful raw materials. The president even mentioned rare books, manuscripts, and paintings. But there was no intention of taking over some of Britain's colonies in part payment. The benefits of informal empire, such as Caribbean bases, were more attractive than the practical burdens and ideological stigma of colonial rule.

In May, however, FDR passed the matter from the Treasury to the State Department on the grounds that it involved political rather than financial issues. State was anxious to avoid another unpaid war debt, this time in goods rather than cash. Instead, Hull, Berle, and Welles wanted the "consideration" for lend-lease to take the form of a policy commitment by Britain to U.S. Open Door trade and financial policies. This built on the philosophy enunciated during debate on the extension of the Reciprocal Trade Agreements Act in 1940, namely that freer trade would be an essential part of U.S. postwar planning. As Dean Acheson, one of the assistant secretaries of state, put it to Morgenthau, the consideration offered a once-and-for-all opportunity to "make" the British agree to end Imperial Preference and the Sterling Area in return for breaking down America's "outrageously high tariff schedules." In 1941–1942 this was to become a major theme of State Department policy.

Roosevelt's own interest in the matter ebbed and flowed. In May he was concerned because he wanted to say something about the consideration in his first ninety-day report about lend-lease to Congress. But he eventually decided that it was sufficient simply to state that talks had started with the British, and the issue then slipped off the policy agenda until late July and August. It is also clear that Roosevelt was not as keen as State on driving a hard bargain with the British, particularly when they were fighting for their lives. And he related the lend-lease consideration to his larger vision of Anglo-American relations.

Like Hull, but in different ways, Roosevelt was already looking toward the end of a war that the United States had not even entered. On May 28 he spoke with the economist John Maynard Keynes, who was in Washington on behalf of the British Treasury to discuss lend-lease issues. FDR emphasized two points about the postwar era. The first was that Britain and America should function as international policemen. Whereas postwar Europe must be totally deprived of all offensive weapons, these two countries must retain sufficient arms "to act as policemen of Europe." (When Keynes mentioned Russia, Roosevelt smiled: "Now you are making things difficult.") The president was equally emphatic that, unlike after 1918, "America would not pull out." According to Keynes, "he refused to consider the possibility that America would not take her full share of responsibility for the post-war situation in Europe, political and economic." Building on these ideas, in early June the president told Hopkins and Acheson that one way to fulfill the consideration was for the British to contribute items to "a mutual defense pool," which would support "the British and United States military force."

Both Roosevelt and Hull were, in different ways, looking beyond the "common-law alliance" to a long-term Anglo-American partnership in the interests of world peace and prosperity. But, as the Bases Agreement and the consideration debate made clear, the relationship would be very different from that in the 1930s. U.S. policymakers were now keen to assert America's wealth and power on the international stage, whether or not the country was a formal belligerent. Although the publisher Henry R. Luce was no Democrat, the ideas he expressed in his famous article on "The American Century," published in *Life* on February 17, 1941, found echoes in official Washington.

Luce insisted that the United States was already, for practical purposes, "in the war," and that it had got there for reasons that went beyond basic defense. ("No man can say that that picture of America as an impregnable armed camp is false.") Larger issues were at stake than strict "necessity and survival," because the United States was belatedly accepting its twentieth-century destiny as "the most powerful and vital nation in the world." To create this American Century, Luce offered a fourfold agenda. First, the United States must ensure the triumph of "a system of free economic enterprise." It must also "send out through the world its technical and artistic skills," be they those of engineers or doctors, teachers or filmmakers. Third, said Luce, it should become "the Good Samaritan of the entire world," providing food and relief to the victims of "this worldwide collapse of civilization." Above all, America must be "the powerhouse of the ideals of Freedom and Justice." These, claimed Luce, would be the hallmarks of the American Century, as isolationism was replaced by "a truly *American* internationalism." Franklin Roosevelt might have put it differently, but the essential ideology was the same—"a vision of America as a world power" that was "authentically American." Moreover these ideas were being voiced not in 1945, but in 1941.

THE ATLANTIC CRISIS

But Adolf Hitler also had a vision. His was even more grandiose, spanning a whole millennium. The American Century could not be realized without victory over Hitler's Thousand-year Reich. In the spring of 1941 such a victory seemed even less likely than in mid-1940.

On April 6, 1941, Hitler launched invasions of Greece and Yugoslavia. The Yugoslavs capitulated in less than a fortnight, and by the end of April Greece was also under Nazi control. During March, Churchill had diverted British troops to Greece, hoping to forestall a German attack. Instead he succeeded only in weakening his forces in North Africa against a combined German-Italian campaign mounted by the new German commander, Erwin Rommel. By the end of March, Libya was in Axis hands, and the road to Cairo and the Suez Canal lay open. In British black humor the initials BEF no longer signified "British Expeditionary Force" but "Back Every Friday."

As April turned into May, the gloom in London deepened. Britain's hold over the Eastern Mediterranean slipped further when German paratroops captured the strategically vital island of Crete. Lack of RAF support for the British army and navy, which lost several major capital ships, showed up again Britain's incompetence in combined operations. Meanwhile the German Blitz against British cities intensified with better weather. Major ports, such as Plymouth, Glasgow, Liverpool, and London, suffered some of their heaviest raids of the war. On the night of May 11, the chamber of the House of Commons, symbol of British liberties, went up in flames.

Shipping losses also increased remorselessly, from a winter average of 365,000 tons a month to 687,000 in April. If sinking continued at this rate it would mean a net annual loss of a quarter of Britain's merchant fleet. Churchill later confessed that he had been far more anxious about the Battle of the Atlantic than about the Battle of Britain, adding, "The only thing that ever really frightened me during the war was the U-boat peril." Although Allied merchantmen were often the unsung heroes of the war, the Battle of the Atlantic hit the headlines in America in late May as the British hunted Germany's greatest battleship, the *Bismarck*. In London and Washington that spring there was also grave concern that Hitler would suddenly pounce on some of the key mid-Atlantic islands, such as the Cape Verdes and the Azores, or on the vital French West African port of Dakar. This would further threaten Britain's lifelines and bring the Nazi threat much closer to the Western Hemisphere.

Even Churchill's own political position seemed shaky. Although now regarded as the embodiment of Britain's bulldog spirit and the country's uncontested wartime leader, Churchill in the 1930s had been on the fringe of the Conservative party. Even after he became prime minister he lacked a firm political base and was acutely conscious that Conservative loyalty depended on military success. In April 1941 a whispering campaign developed in and around the House of Commons. Churchill was surrounded by "yes men," it was said; he meddled incessantly in the conduct of the war—too much "cigar stump diplomacy," too many "midnight follies." When Churchill put the opposition to the test in a formal votes of confidence, on May 7, he won handsomely by 447 votes to 3. But that did not still the undercurrent of criticism. Arguably Churchill's political position was not fully secure until the British army won its first major victory over the Germans, in November 1942 at Alamein in Egypt.

Britain's predicament was viewed with mounting alarm in Washington. Stimson, Ickes, and other senior policymakers anticipated that the bombing and sinkings were prelude to a full-scale invasion of Britain, accompanied by poison gas. Most were pessimistic about British chances of holding North Africa: they are "damned near licked in the Mediterranean Area," noted Breckinridge Long of the State Department in his diary on May 22. After the debacle in Crete, Hull wrote that everything was going "hellward." The crisis in the Atlantic accentuated fears for the security of the Western Hemisphere. Roosevelt viewed islands such as the Azores as being of decisive importance to the United States in the air age. The threat to Britain itself, and the insecurity of Churchill, reopened fears of renewed appeasement, the fall of Churchill, and a bid for a compromise peace. When Hitler's deputy, Rudolf Hess, landed in Scotland on May 10, rumor and speculation ran riot. Although the British quickly concluded that Hess was acting on his own in a crazy one-man peace mission, even Roosevelt was not sure what was going on.

In short, the spring of 1941 was a critical moment in the war. Even before the Lend-Lease Bill had passed, FDR had made contingency plans. In mid-January he ordered the U.S. navy to be ready by April 1 to escort convoys all the way to Britain, and he also instructed it to create a new "Atlantic Fleet," though this started as little more than an inexperienced squadron. At the beginning of April the president seemed ready to implement the convoy plan. He gave instructions to transfer a carrier, three battleships, four cruisers, and supporting destroyers from Pearl Harbor to strengthen the Atlantic Fleet.

But then he backed off. One reason may have been the state of the U.S. navy. It would take months to fit ships and train crews for the challenging tasks of naval escort. Many of the vessels, particularly essential destroyers, were of World War I vintage; crucial equipment, such as sonar detectors, was in short supply. And the Atlantic Fleet was still an inchoate entity, operating out of a variety of bases from Norfolk, Virginia, to Newport, Rhode Island. On the other hand the navy was keen for action—in part because Stark and other senior admirals knew that, given Britain's plight, the alternative to fighting a naval war in the Atlantic was likely to be a demand to lend-lease U.S. warships to Britain. As the historian Waldo Heinrichs has put it, "There is some truth in the notion that the navy [felt it] had to join the battle to save its ships."

More important in explaining Roosevelt's renewed caution than the state of the navy was the high-profile domestic opposition. On April 1 seventy-one members of Congress attended a meeting to plan further opposition to administration foreign policy now that lend-lease had passed. They decided to focus their energies on the naval issue, and Republican Senator Charles W. Tobey of New Hampshire introduced an anti-convoy resolution. Sobered by his mail, which thanks to America First was overwhelmingly against convoying, Roosevelt told his advisers that if he tried to push the matter through Congress he would probably be defeated. The president's other concern was Japan's likely reaction to a reduction in the Pacific Fleet. On April 13, to the surprise of U.S. intelligence, the Japanese suddenly concluded a nonaggression pact with the Soviet Union. With Japan's northern flank secure, this left its leaders, in principle, freer to move south. Reducing the U.S. Pacific Fleet at such a time would send all the wrong signals, as Hull kept reminding the president.

To the distress of Atlanticists such as Stimson, FDR therefore curtailed the redeployment from Pearl Harbor to one carrier and four destroyers, which slipped through the Panama Canal in early May. The three battleships, four cruisers, and accompanying destroyers that were originally slated for transfer did not do so until early June. Instead of full-scale convoying, Roosevelt chose to extend the "Western Hemisphere Neutrality Patrol," which had been in existence since the start of the European war in 1939. During April the president settled on a line drawn north-south down the twenty-sixth meridian. This ran midway between Brazil and West Africa and included the Azores and most of Greenland, which the Danish government in exile had just handed over to U.S. protection. Within this area U.S. naval task forces would monitor the movement of Axis vessels, reporting them to the British. They could use force if there was a threat to shipping under the U.S. flag or to the territory of the Western Hemisphere, including Greenland. Following these instructions, naval planners developed Western Hemisphere Defense Plan One.

It was a typical Roosevelt compromise, pouring new wine in old wineskins. In this case, the skin of a traditional concept, the Western Hemisphere, was being stretched far more widely than ever before. In doing so the president was both reflecting and also influencing a larger intellectual debate. Interventionist spokesmen were now attacking the conventional equation of "the Western Hemisphere" with "the Americas." Articles in the journal *Foreign Affairs*—organ of the Council on Foreign Relations in New York—during 1941 help measure the shift. One essay, in January, sought to argue on strict geographical grounds that Greenland and Iceland belonged to the North American continent. Another, in April, started from the insistence on hemisphere defense by Philip La Follette, the former governor of Wisconsin. It pointed out that every European capital, including Moscow, was closer to La Follette's hometown of Madison, Wisconsin, than the Argentine capital of Buenos Aires. And a brief essay in July 1941, entitled simply "The Atlantic Area," was accompanied by a map centered on mid-Atlantic, with distances between key points delineated in red. This highlighted the sense of connection rather than separation between Western Europe and North America.

The most influential exponent of the new Atlanticism was the columnist Walter Lippmann, who had first used the term "the Atlantic World" back in February 1917. On April 7, 1941, he contributed a feature article to Henry Luce's widely read *Life* magazine, under the title "The Atlantic and America." Lippmann's aim was to reinterpret U.S. entry into the war in 1917. It had not been, he said, an exercise in misguided idealism but a hardheaded attempt to preserve the security of the Atlantic, in which the United States had a vital interest. Instead of eschewing parallels with 1917, Lippmann was therefore keen to underline them. In 1941, as in 1917, he insisted, the Atlantic was in danger. This theme was developed later in the year by the journalist Forrest Davis. His book *The Atlantic System* traced an Anglo-American community of interest back to the Founding Fathers. The chapter on U.S. belligerency in 1917 was entitled "The First Battle of the Atlantic." Davis propounded what he called "the law of the opposite shores," namely that "the United States cannot tolerate the establishment of a hostile Sea Power on the European side of the Atlantic." Roosevelt was more concerned about airpower, but his grand strategy revolved around a similar Atlanticist framework.

Such talk about an "Atlantic Area" signaled a sea change in what the historian Alan Henrikson has called Americans' "Mental Maps"—how they viewed their relationship with the outside world. Another conceptual shift was the growing use of the language of "national security"—a term FDR had himself employed in his momentous fireside chat of December 29, 1940. The phrase had been developed by academics, notably the Princeton political scientist Edward Mead Earle in articles since 1938. In 1940–1941 Earle ran an influential seminar on the relationship between military affairs and foreign policy, using the term "national security" to connect the two. One participant, the historian Felix Gilbert, recalled that this was partly to critique classical Wilsonianism—to advance the case that if the United

States entered *this* war it would be for reasons of self-interest rather than idealism. But these new definitions of self-interest went beyond conventional concepts of national defense of the sort still employed by America First. As Earle, who was refining his argument all through 1940 and 1941, declared in November 1941: "Security involves more than defense. It is active, not passive; it demands foresight and initiative" aimed at "measures that prevent trouble" rather than "those which salvage what one can from disaster." The new Atlanticism was an example of this. Although FDR still chose to mask his policy in the language of Western Hemisphere Defense, his elastic definition of the hemisphere and his extended naval patrolling reflected this preemptive concept of national security.

The discourse of U.S. foreign relations was therefore in flux in 1941, well before Pearl Harbor, let alone Hiroshima. But words did nothing to deter Hitler. After lend-lease had been announced, Churchill's tactic had been to wait on Roosevelt and not put the president under pressure. But on May 4 the beleaguered British prime minister sent a telegram to Roosevelt asking explicitly for a U.S. declaration of war—the first time he had done so since the dark days of June 1940. Churchill added: "I shall await with deep anxiety the new broadcast which you contemplate. It may be the supreme turning point." When, a few days later, Hess landed in Scotland, Churchill kept silent and did nothing to allay American fears of a possible compromise peace.

May 1941 was one of the most miserable months of Franklin Roosevelt's twelve-year presidency. The British seemed close to collapse and were demanding that he enter the war. Many of his senior advisers also felt that there was little choice, including Morgenthau and Berle who had previously held back. Ickes was so despondent at the apparent lack of American leadership that he considered resignation. Stimson, the cabinet's elder statesman, urged the president face-to-face to marshal the country and, indeed, a world divided "into two camps, [of] one of which he is the leader." Yet FDR judged that the opposition in Congress was too substantial, and that the American public, whose whole-hearted commitment was essential to sustain any war effort, still had no real grasp of the issues at stake. In early May his health, never robust, collapsed with intestinal flu and acute anemia. For two weeks the president took to his bed, ill but also acutely frustrated. The speech on current policy to which Churchill had alluded, scheduled for May 14, was postponed. That only heightened the sense of national and international anticipation.

By the third week of May the president had regained his strength. On Pan American Day, May 27, he gave his long-delayed speech, as the British hunted the *Bismarck* and the battle for Crete neared its climax. Roosevelt set out his enlarged definition of the Western Hemisphere. He depicted a Nazi threat to "the island outposts of the New World" such as the Azores, Greenland, and even Iceland, whose loss would "directly endanger the freedom of the Atlantic and our own American physical security." He also summarized his concept of national security, noting in the days of tanks and bombing planes, "if you hold your fire until you see the whites of his eyes, you will never know what hit you! Our Bunker Hill of tomorrow may be several thousand miles from Boston, Massachusetts." Reiterating the Four Freedoms and also American determination to "give every possible assistance to Britain," he concluded by announcing a state of "unlimited national emergency."

At press conferences the next day, however, it became clear that FDR had no plans to escort convoys or seek repeal of the Neutrality Act. Privately the U.S. attorney general admitted that the unlimited national emergency lacked legal specificity and was being proclaimed "primarily for its psychological effect in impressing on the country the threat of aggression." At that level it appears to have succeeded. As with the reaction to earlier sensitive speeches, FDR was elated by the telegrams he received. "They're ninety-five percent favorable," he exclaimed. "And I figured I'd be lucky to get an even break on this speech."

Moreover the broad definition of the hemisphere helped justify further steps. In the speech FDR stretched it quietly to include Iceland. (On a map torn from the *National Geographic* magazine and given to Hopkins, the president had penciled in the twenty-sixth meridian, but then his line turned sharp right to include Iceland within the boundaries of U.S. naval patrolling.) He told the British ambassador that within the next month he would send U.S. troops to take over the defense of Iceland, currently in British hands, if the British and Icelandic governments agreed. This would justify U.S. naval and merchant vessels in assuming responsibility for the whole Western Atlantic, thereby assisting the British without what he called "a dog fight with Congress."

Privately FDR periodically hinted to the British that he was seeking a naval "incident" that might justify asking Congress for a declaration of war. But the president did not respond when news reached Washington on June 11 that an unarmed U.S. merchantman, the *Robin Moor,* had been sunk by a U-boat in the South Atlantic. Although he announced the freezing of German and Italian assets, and ordered the two Axis powers to close their consulates by July 10, these measures had been planned for some time. The sinking of the *Robin Moor* was a pretext, not the cause. It remains a matter of debate whether FDR's talk about seeking an "incident" was genuine or an effort to bolster British morale. What *is* clear is that by early June 1941 Roosevelt knew that the immediate pressures on Britain, and thus on him, were abating because of the widening war.

This widening was strikingly reflected in his vocabulary. Like many Americans, Roosevelt often referred to the conflict of 1914–1918 as "the World War." Germans used the same term—*Weltkrieg*—as one can see, for instance, in Hitler's *Mein Kampf.* When the international scene darkened in the early 1930s, there were predictions of "the Second World War." The journalist Johannes Steel used this as the title for his 1934 book on the state of Europe. The idea was even more popular in Asia. After Japan invaded Manchuria, Chiang Kai-shek foresaw a "Second World War" by 1936, and this prediction was taken up by Japanese pundits as well. Such talk died away in the late 1930s, during the era of appeasement, but Roosevelt returned to it in 1940–1941 as his globalist vision took shape.

On May 31, 1940—with Hitler's armies at the English Channel, Italy on the brink of belligerency, and Japan plotting further moves in Asia—he warned Congress of the possibility "that all countries may become involved in a worldwide war." In his annual budget message on January 3, 1941, he referred simply to "a world at war." By the spring he was explicitly making the verbal link with 1914–1918. In a radio address on March 8, when lend-lease had virtually been approved by Congress, he spoke of "the first World War" and then started a sentence with the phrase "When the second World War began a year and a half ago. . . ." In his radio speech on May 27 he also referred to "the first World War" and "this second World War," arguing that "what started as a European war has developed, just as the Nazis always intended it should develop, into a war for world domination."

Why did Roosevelt start using the term "second World War" in public? There is no clear evidence, but some inferences may be made. In part it was probably a response to signs of growing Axis collaboration. The Tripartite Pact of September 1940 had been particularly significant here. Perhaps the president also judged, like Walter Lippmann, that it was no longer politically necessary to avoid analogies with 1917. The Lend-Lease Act had given congressional approval to the popular conviction that America's security and values were bound up with Britain's survival. There may have been another reason for FDR's growing talk about "this second World War," which he was not yet at liberty to reveal. Secret intelligence told him that a new and titanic conflict was about to engulf Eastern Europe and much of Eurasia.

6

Projecting American Power and Values (June to December 1941)

WHEN HITLER invaded the Soviet Union on June 22, 1941, he opened up what we now recognize as the decisive battle-front of the European war. But in mid-1941 Soviet survival seemed unlikely. Roosevelt's gamble that the Soviet Union would not succumb and his decision to provide material help were acts of presidential leadership, paralleling his bet on Britain in 1940. The policy of aid to Stalinist Russia, which ran contrary to America's inclusive image of totalitarianism, also obliged FDR to define more clearly his ideological vision—hence the "Atlantic Charter" of August 1941.

During the autumn the president was projecting American power as well as American values. In the Western Atlantic there developed something close to an undeclared naval war. In the Pacific, where the German attack on Russia gave Japan a freer hand, the president approved tougher "deterrent" measures, including oil sanctions against Japan and reinforcement of the Philippines. What the Americans conceived of as deterrence, however, Japan saw as encirclement. In Tokyo plans were completed for a series of combined operations across Southeast Asia and the Western Pacific, which would turn Roosevelt's prediction of a world war into a reality.

THE SOVIET UNION AND THE GLOBAL CRISIS

Hitler's buildup in Eastern Europe had been evident for months. It is, after all, hard to conceal 3.6 million troops, 3,600 tanks, and 2,500 combat aircraft. In addition the U.S. embassy in Berlin had a highly placed source who provided accurate information about Hitler's plans (codenamed Operation Barbarossa) for a short, decisive war. But the consensus in Washington was that Hitler would play the same game as he had over Czechoslovakia and Poland, using the buildup as part of a diplomatic war of nerves to force Soviet concessions. Few expected him to attack without warning, especially while still waging war against Britain.* When he did so, with devastating success, few expected the Soviet Union to survive for long. Hitler's victories in 1940 had created an image of Nazi invincibility. By contrast, the Red Army had been decimated by Stalin's purges in 1937–1938; it had performed lamentably in 1939–1940 in the "Winter War" against Finland.

Most of the Soviet air force was destroyed on the ground, and the Wehrmacht advanced more than two hundred miles in the first five days. The U.S. ambassador in Moscow, Laurence Steinhardt, reckoned that the Soviet capital would fall in considerably less than sixty days; the War Department's prediction was between one and three months. Conveying this assessment to Roosevelt, Stimson urged him to use "this precious and unforeseen period of respite" to "push with the utmost vigor our movements in the Atlantic theater of operations." This was "the right way to

---

*This was also Stalin's view. Ten days before Barbarossa he told his top generals: "Germany is busy up to her ears with the war in the West and I am certain that Hitler will not risk creating a second front by attacking the Soviet Union. Hitler is not such an idiot. . . ."

help Britain, to discourage Germany, and to strengthen our own position of defense."

But Roosevelt's gut instinct was more optimistic. "Now comes this Russian diversion," he wrote on June 26 to his ambassador in Vichy France. "If it is more than that it will mean the liberation of Europe from Nazi domination—and at the same time I do not think we need worry about any possibility of Russian domination." Contrary to the preferences of the War Department (and the British), he was ready to give more than token aid to the Soviet Union. Contrary to the advice of the State Department, he also hoped to build a working relationship with Stalin and the Russians. He did not share, for instance, the view of Ambassador Steinhardt that the psychology of Soviet policymakers recognized "only firmness, power and force, and reflects primitive instincts and reactions that are entirely devoid of the restraints of civilization." Roosevelt's military and political gamble on the Soviet Union proved to be a decisive moment in the war.

That was clearer in retrospect than at the time, however. Churchill spoke out on June 22 in a radio broadcast that was relayed to the United States. While arguing that Nazism was "indistinguishable from the worst features of Communism," he insisted that this consideration was secondary to Britain's "single, irrevocable purpose" which was "to destroy Hitler and every vestige of the Nazi regime." He went on: "It therefore follows that we shall give whatever help we can give to Russia and to the Russian people." Roosevelt made no similar statement. As the historian Ralph Levering has suggested, FDR seemed happy to hide behind Churchill, whose growing stature in America (and past record as a vehement anti-Communist) made him a far more compelling spokesman for aid to Russia than anyone in Washington. The State Department issued a press release the next day, expressing the same sense of priorities: given Hitler's "plan for universal conquest," the United States welcomed "any defense against Hitlerism" as a benefit to its security. The president endorsed this statement, when asked, at a press conference on June 24. He said the United States would "give all the aid we possibly can to Russia," but evaded a question about including the Russians within lend-lease.

Roosevelt's public caution is explicable on two levels. One was simple pragmatism. Like other observers, he was waiting to see how Barbarossa would unfold. By early July it was clear that, despite appalling losses of men and territory, the Red Army would not surrender abjectly. On July 10 the president saw the Soviet ambassador, Konstantin Umansky (their first meeting to date in 1941), and promised to fill some of Moscow's most urgent requests for supplies, if Britain agreed. It was Russian resistance more than the German attack itself that opened up new policy opportunities for the United States.

Equally important, Roosevelt was waiting for public opinion to congeal. For two years, since the Nazi-Soviet Pact, the Soviet Union had been absorbed within America's image of totalitarianism. Some conservative commentators argued that the German invasion had changed nothing. According to the *Wall Street Journal,* in a June 25 editorial entitled "Tweedledum and Tweedledee," the American people knew that "the principal difference between Mr. Hitler and Mr. Stalin is the size of their respective mustaches." The previous day Senator Harry Truman of Missouri had stated: "If we see that Germany is winning we ought to help Russia, and if Russia is winning we ought to help Germany, and that way let them kill as many as possible." But a Gallup poll published on July 13 indicated that only 4 percent of respondents wanted Germany to win, compared with 72 percent favoring Russia. Dr. George Gallup summed up their reasoning: "Russia is not imperialistic, but Germany is. Russia, even if she won, would not invade the United States, whereas Germany probably would."

This interpretation of the situation testifies to the success of Roosevelt and his supporters in establishing a new foreign policy consensus based on the arguments that Hitler was bent on world conquest and that Britain and any other foes of Nazism constituted America's front line. Hitler had reinforced this argument by his brutal, unprovoked attack on the Soviet Union. At a deeper level there were also subtle differences in American perceptions of Russian and German totalitarianism, despite the horrors of both regimes. Put simply, in contrast to Nazi Germany the Soviet Union seemed to be moving away from expansionism and revolution. The Bolshevik coup of 1917, with its rhetoric of world revolution, was receding into history. Many American conservatives judged that the Soviet Union was becoming a personal dictatorship; liberals, including FDR, played up signs that it was evolving into a socialist state. On both sides there was a growing consensus that the USSR was maturing into a conventional great power, motivated mainly by concerns about national security. Hence the predominant use of the term "Russia" rather than "Soviet Union."

On the other hand, the image of "totalitarianism" still lurked in the background of opinion and debate. Roosevelt had used the term on occasions in 1940–1941, usually about Germany or Italy. After Barbarossa it disappeared from his political vocabulary and also, in large measure, from general public discussion. Yet as the historian Abbott Gleason has argued, "privately a strong residue of belief in Soviet totalitarianism remained in many circles," and this surfaced in literary newspapers and intellectual journals. This helps explain Roosevelt's repeated efforts to distinguish the Soviet Union from conventional indicators of totalitarianism. The question of religious persecution was particularly important, because the Catholic church was a leading opponent of Bolshevik atheism. In September 1941 FDR wrote a public letter to the pope asserting that "churches in Russia are open" and that freedom of religion was a "real possibility in Russia," unlike Nazi Germany.

As Russian resistance hardened and American opinion took

shape, Roosevelt began to move decisively. In mid-July Harry Hopkins flew to England to review the major war issues with Churchill and his advisers. It became clear that planning in many areas, including lend-lease, depended crucially on assessments of how long Russia could survive. Hopkins cabled Roosevelt on July 25 asking for permission to visit Moscow. (The British RAF had just opened a hazardous flying-boat route from Scotland around Norway to Archangel.) The president immediately agreed and sent Hopkins a letter for Stalin. As Roosevelt's personal emissary, Hopkins was able to go right to the top—just as he had on his first visit to England in January. Stalin rarely met foreign ambassadors, but on July 30 and 31 Hopkins had two long meetings with the Soviet leader. He saw nothing of the battlefronts but came back deeply impressed with Stalin—terse, controlled, and totally determined to win. "Give us anti-aircraft guns and the aluminum and we can fight for three or four years," was an exclamation that particularly stuck in Hopkins's memory. Stalin also employed language surely intended to fit Roosevelt's ideological framework, opening for instance with the need for "a minimum moral standard between all nations" and insisting that "the President and the United States had more influence with the common people of the world than any other force."

Once again Hopkins served as Roosevelt's eyes and ears. More than any formal intelligence data, his reports on Stalin persuaded the president to move decisively on aid to Russia. On August 1 FDR lectured his cabinet for forty-five minutes, accusing Stimson and the War Department in particular of foot-dragging on key Soviet supplies. "Get the planes off with a bang next week," he ordered. Stimson's resistance reflected the dilemmas of U.S. rearmament. War production in 1941 was a mere 10 percent of total output and only two-thirds of total British and Canadian munitions. Already forced to share this limited production with the British, Marshall and his colleagues objected strongly to a three-way cut. When Morgenthau remarked that with Hopkins away there was no one able to cut through the red tape, FDR charged Wayne Coy of the Office of Emergency Management with a rare written directive: "Act as a burr under the saddle and get things moving."

Roosevelt's basic concern was clear. As long as Hitler was occupied in the East, he could not turn back against Britain and perhaps the United States. Yet Russia was also an Asian power. Operation Barbarossa also had profound implications for Japan, and thence the United States.

For months the foreign minister, Matsuoka Yōsuke, had been seeking to construct a full-scale alliance between Germany, Italy, and Japan (already partners in the Tripartite Pact) and the Soviet Union. This would range them against Anglo-American hegemony. Matsuoka intended his visit to Berlin and Moscow in March–April 1941 to consummate this alliance. Hitler would not cooperate. While saying nothing about Barbarossa, he intimated that relations with the Soviet Union were deteriorating. In Moscow, however, Matsuoka found Stalin ready to conclude a neutrality pact. The Russians now feared a combined German-Japanese attack and were ready to recognize Japan's conquest of Manchuria. The neutrality pact was better than nothing for Matsuoka; it was signed on April 13. But then the opening of Barbarossa on June 22, about which Tokyo was not forewarned, destroyed what was left of the Japanese foreign minister's grand design.

It is worth reflecting for a moment on the implications of these events. Matsuoka, building on the Nazi-Soviet Pact of 1939, envisaged an international divide along geopolitical lines, between the established hegemonial powers and the revisionists. What transpired in June 1941 looked more like the split on ideological lines that the left had urged in the mid-1930s—between the fascist powers and the anti-fascists. That was how it figured in Soviet war propaganda. From the American perspective,

1939–1941 was a period in which Roosevelt had gradually crystallized the image of a bipolar struggle between the forces of democracy and totalitarianism. After June 1941, "totalitarianism" slipped from the diplomatic lexicon, and FDR exaggerated signs of liberalism in the Soviet Union to make Stalin's Russia fit the democratic stereotype. Geopolitically, Barbarossa's impact on Europe and Asia vindicated FDR's insistence that this was a global struggle—the "second world war." U.S. policy in one theater clearly had implications in the other. Yet Barbarossa might also have called into question Roosevelt's stereotype of a unified Axis. In June 1941, as in August 1939, Japan's leaders were totally surprised by the twists of German policy toward the USSR. At a time when the Anglo-American common-law alliance was tightening, the Berlin-Tokyo Axis again showed its hollowness. But U.S. policymakers were now locked into their worldview.

Late June 1941 saw a great debate among Japan's factionalized policymakers. Matsuoka, together with Prime Minister Konoe, favored a drive north against the embattled Soviet Union, in breach of the recent neutrality pact. The navy preferred renewed "southward advance" by diplomatic and, if necessary, military means to secure essential oil and raw materials from the colonial powers. Army strategists split between the two groups. At an imperial conference on July 2, a memorandum entitled "Outlines of Future National Policy" committed the country to both southward expansion and preparedness against the Soviet Union, while spelling out the southern strategy in more detail. Concretely, the Japanese got ready to take over southern Indochina during July while also concentrating up to 850,000 men in Manchuria for a possible Russo-Japanese war by September 1.

There was still support for reducing the chances of U.S. involvement. Since February, the new Japanese ambassador in Washington, Admiral Nomura Kichisaburō, had been engaged in talks with Hull to see if they could find the basis of an Asian settlement. Konoe, anxious to avoid war with the United States, had encouraged these behind Matsuoka's back as a counterbalance to the foreign minister's pro-Axis policy. In July Konoe sought to resume the talks in an effort to keep the United States at bay, forcing out Matsuoka to show Washington that Tokyo was in earnest about improved relations. On July 18 a new Konoe cabinet was formed. But the southward advance continued. Japanese troops occupied southern Indochina, a colony of Vichy France, at the end of the month. The leadership in Tokyo assumed that U.S. warnings were merely rhetoric. That was a serious mistake.

In September 1940, U.S. army and navy cryptanalysts, in a rare display of cooperation, had cracked Japan's high-grade diplomatic code, known as "Purple." The successful team was dubbed the "magicians," and the name stuck: "Magic" became the official codeword for Japanese decrypts. During July 1941 Magic showed how the Japanese were putting pressure on the Vichy authorities. It also gave an erroneous impression of single-minded Japanese policy; the flux of debate in Tokyo was impenetrable now that the U.S. embassy was shunned by almost all its influential Japanese contacts. In service jargon there was no humint to illuminate the sigint—no human intelligence to help interpret the signals intelligence.

During the winter of 1940–1941 the Japanese had been buying up oil in California. Once Magic made clear their intentions in Indochina, the pressure for oil sanctions became overwhelming. The cabinet "hawks"—Stimson, Morgenthau, and Ickes—who had secured a partial cutback in July 1940, now demanded a total embargo, confident that Japan would be cowed. Hull and the Navy Department still disagreed, fearing this would spark a Pacific war.

The president shared their caution: his core question about economic pressure was, would it work as a deterrent? At a cabinet meeting on July 24 Roosevelt announced that he would freeze Japanese assets in the United States, just as he had frozen those of Germany and Italy in June. This meant that Japan would not only need an export license to purchase any product related to national defense (as had been required since July 1940), it would also have to secure another license to unblock dollars for payment. These dual controls would harass Tokyo, leaving it uncertain of what could be obtained, and they could be applied flexibly to reduce but not cut off Japan's oil. That, at least, was the president's intent. It was an extension of the existing, if controversial, policy of only limited sanctions. As FDR told a press conference that day: "There is a world war going on, and has been for some time—nearly two years. One of our war efforts, from the very beginning, was to prevent the spread of that world war in certain areas where it hadn't started." Southeast Asia was especially sensitive because its raw materials were essential to Britain and it lay astride Britain's imperial communications to Australasia. "If we had cut the oil off," Roosevelt added, the Japanese "probably would have gone down to the Dutch East Indies a year ago, and you would have had war."

To complement this deterrent policy, U.S. policymakers also intended to reinforce the Philippines. That same day, July 24, Roosevelt announced the formation of a full-scale Philippine army command, and called General Douglas MacArthur out of retirement to head it. This was a major reversal of earlier thinking, evident for instance in Stark's Plan Dog memorandum of November 1940, which favored a tactical withdrawal from the Western Pacific. The Philippines, a sprawling archipelago of seven thousand islands spread out over one thousand miles of ocean, had seemed both untenable and unnecessary. In part this policy shift was testimony to the intensifying ideology of all-or-nothing global war, in which retreat was tantamount to defeat. But it also reflected the growing faith in airpower. An improved version of the new B-17 heavy bomber (the Flying Fortress) was coming off the Boeing production line in Seattle. B-17Es, flying from the Philippines, could reach the southern Japanese home island of Kyushu. Operating from a range of bases, from Manila to Singapore, they might deter attack on Southeast Asia. During August and September, army planners, previously skeptical about the Western Pacific, changed their minds. Stimson was a dramatic convert. He talked of airpower as the "big stick" that had "revolutionized" Pacific strategy. "From being impotent to influence events in that area," he wrote Roosevelt, "we suddenly find ourselves vested with the possibility of great effective power." The United States had found its technological "super-weapon." Stimson and his colleagues assumed Japan would be cowed.

But Stimson's strategic revolution could not be accomplished overnight. As usual, logistics was America's Achilles' heel. The buildup of B-17s in the Philippines, planned from July 1941, would be completed only in March 1942. By then 165 B-17s, about half of total U.S. strength, were scheduled to be based there, but the first one did not arrive until September 1941. Stimson, like Teddy Roosevelt before him, recognized that the United States needed to talk softly while preparing its big stick. In line with its new Pacific strategy, the War Department therefore now became one of the keenest supporters of the Hull-Nomura conversations. These had been terminated on July 23 in view of the Japanese move into Indochina. Stimson favored their resumption, if only to play for time until the deterrent was in place. The president agreed.

The end of July 1941 was therefore a turning point in U.S. diplomacy. As Soviet resistance made the USSR a significant factor in the war, Roosevelt was freed from the policy paralysis of May 1941. The Hopkins visit convinced the president that aid to Russia made strategic and political sense. Japan's response to the Soviet crisis prompted a new deterrent policy of oil sanctions and reinforcement of the Philippines, backed by a readiness to keep talking to gain time. The energy with which Roosevelt acted at the end of July also owed something to another international event. On the evening of August 2 he slipped out of Washington, ostensibly bound for a fishing trip off New England. In fact he was en route for his first wartime meeting with Churchill. Firming up U.S. policy toward the Soviet Union and Japan was essential so that Roosevelt could deal effectively with his British partner.

THE "FIRST SUMMIT" AND THE ATLANTIC CHARTER

Roosevelt and Churchill had met only once before—in London in 1918—and by 1941 Churchill had forgotten their brief encounter. After Churchill became first lord of the admiralty in September 1939 they had developed a personal correspondence through telegrams and letters, totaling 110 from Churchill and 52 from Roosevelt by August 1941. But, as Roosevelt told Admiral Ernest King, "those friendly relations were not the same as a heart-to-heart talk." In January 1941 Harry Hopkins had flown to London to help FDR get the measure of Churchill. Hopkins said off the record that he was acting as "a catalytic agent between two prima donnas." The next step was a direct meeting. Both leaders keenly desired this, but it had to be postponed on several occasions, first because of the lend-lease debate and then due to the successive British crises over the Balkans, Libya, and Crete. Eventually they settled on a shipboard conference in Placentia Bay, off Newfoundland—British territory where the United States was building an air station as part of the destroyers-for-bases deal. Hitler's decision to go east gave them both an opportunity and a further reason for the meeting. Although Roosevelt and Churchill were both primarily interested in their personal encounter, they brought with them a range of military and diplomatic advisers who held their own specialist meetings.

On a personal level the Atlantic Conference (August 9–12) was a great success. The two leaders dispelled their lingering doubts about each other and cemented their relationship. Close ties were also forged among the service personnel, especially between General George Marshall and his British counterpart, Sir John Dill. These helped lubricate the machinery of Anglo-American cooperation throughout the war. But the significance of the Atlantic meeting was as much symbolic. In Sunday worship on the sunlit quarterdeck of the British battleship *Prince of Wales,* British and Americans intermingled. They shared in readings from the King James Bible and sung familiar hymns in the same language, such as "Onward Christian Soldiers," while British and American chaplains read prayers from a pulpit draped with the Stars and Stripes and the Union Jack. Film of this service went around the world. Capping the whole edifice was the declaration of eight war aims. This was quickly dubbed the "Atlantic Charter"—a community of Anglo-American values to complement the new Atlanticist framework for U.S. security.

The global impact of the declaration was profound. In early August, Hitler was still rambling about an eventual combination of Britain and Germany against the United States. Shaken by the Atlantic Charter, he refused to let Propaganda Minister Josef Goebbels publish it. But privately he reminded Goebbels of his January 1939 "prophecy" that if the Jews succeeded in starting a world war, the result would be the annihilation of European Jewry. In Japan the leading Tokyo newspaper, *Asahi,* said that the declaration aimed to maintain "a system of world domination on the basis of Anglo-American world views." Privately one senior Japanese staff officer commented that it was tantamount to America's declaration of war. Just as policymakers in Washington tended to exaggerate the unity of the Tripartite Pact, imagining secret military protocols whenever German and Japanese leaders met, so Axis leaders assumed that the Atlantic Charter was merely the public face of detailed war planning. For many Japanese policymakers, in particular, the Atlantic meeting confirmed their sense of encirclement. Combined with the American freezing order, it had the effect of ending plans for an attack on the Soviet Union. Southward advance became the agreed strategy, by diplomacy if possible, by force if necessary.

The Anglo-American common-law alliance was, however, less cohesive than its opponents imagined. Churchill had come to Placentia Bay hopeful that FDR was ready to declare war. In consequence the British delegation was chiefly military, with Sir Alexander Cadogan from the Foreign Office added at the last minute. Churchill was therefore bitterly disappointed to return, almost like Neville Chamberlain, with little more than a piece of paper. That paper was indeed forced on him without warning. There had been no prior discussion about a statement of war aims. Roosevelt suggested the idea at one of the first meetings on August 9; Sumner Welles had already jotted down key American ideas before leaving Washington. Seeking to draw the British out, Roosevelt invited Churchill to offer a first draft. Cadogan hastily penned something next morning, on *Prince of Wales* notepaper, while eating his eggs and bacon before the Sunday worship. This was the unlikely genesis of one of the most important ideological documents of the war.

Motivating Roosevelt was the Wilsonian problem of associating the United States with a country whose aims, though similar when measured by global criteria of democracy versus totalitarianism, differed in signal respects from those of his administration. Although Roosevelt had aligned himself clearly with Churchill, he was also anxious to tie the British down to American goals, particularly now that Soviet Russia complicated the ideological picture.

Egged on by Welles, Roosevelt had two definite concerns, and probably one other. Each was about "imperialism." First, the two men wanted assurances that the British had not and would not sign "secret treaties" akin to those with France and Russia in 1914–1917. After Soviet entry into the war, rumors were rife about clandestine territorial deals, for instance to acknowledge Soviet hegemony in eastern Poland and the Baltic states. Roosevelt had cabled Churchill on July 15 asking brazenly that Britain make "no secret commitments to any of its Allies" without "the agreement of the United States." The Americans had been disturbed to receive no reply.

Second, Roosevelt and Welles wanted to make progress on the lend-lease "consideration," which they intended should take the form of British commitments to a liberalized regime of international trade. During the summer this effort had become bogged down in bureaucratic discussions with the British, particularly the wily Keynes. In the flurry of activity in Washington in late July, before departure for the Atlantic meeting, Roosevelt had approved a tough new State Department draft about an end to trade discrimination, which Keynes strenuously opposed. At the Atlantic meeting Welles tried to pin down Churchill himself.

A third issue, certainly for Welles, was the American desire that Britain concede dominion status, or semi-independence, to India. Although couched as a concern about the effect of Indian discontent on the British war effort, it reflected underlying American animosity to formal empire. The issue was very likely in Welles's mind as he reworked Cadogan's draft.

Churchill was able to consult his own cabinet and the dominion governments by telegram. Sensing that Roosevelt would compromise on details rather than delay issuing the declaration, he was able to water down some of the contentious language. Nevertheless the eight-point statement of common principles became a benchmark for Anglo-American diplomacy throughout the war. The second article rejected territorial changes that did not "accord with the freely expressed wishes of the peoples concerned." The fourth contained a pledge that both governments would try to promote access by all states "on equal terms" to the world's trade and raw materials. (The British desire to retain Imperial Preference, at least until the nature of the postwar economy became clear, was safeguarded by the clause "with due respect for their existing obligations.") There were references to other Rooseveltian ideas, such as "freedom from fear and want," and to his qualified Wilsonian approach to disarmament as a long-term goal for all nations and an immediate necessity for the vanquished aggressors.

The potency of the declaration was demonstrated by international reaction to article three about the rights of national sovereignty and self-government. This was immediately seized on by nationalist politicians in India, Burma, and Ceylon in their battle against British imperial rule. Churchill insisted in Parliament that article three was intended to apply to the subject nations of Europe—"a quite separate problem from the progressive evolution of self-governing institutions" within the British Empire. But soon after Pearl Harbor FDR was insisting publicly that the Atlantic Charter "applies not only to those parts of the world that border the Atlantic but to the whole world." It became the ideological basis of America's wartime globalism.

Many in London felt that Churchill had made sweeping pledges to Roosevelt and had gained little in return. With justification the prime minister told his cabinet that the readiness of the United States, "still technically a neutral," to join with a belligerent power in a commitment to "the final destruction of Nazi tyranny" was "astonishing." But it is likely that he regarded a declaration of war aims as a poor surrogate for a declaration of war. The British delegation at Placentia Bay was also sobered by news during the conference that renewal of America's draft beyond the first year had passed the House of Representatives by only one vote (203 to 202). Although owing much to poor Democratic management and the lack of a clear lead from the president, the vote seemed to confirm the strength of noninterventionist opinion.

In the Atlantic, all Churchill could extract was a promise that the U.S. navy would take over escort of all Allied convoys in the area west of Iceland and the Azores. Repeatedly the president left Churchill with the impression that he hoped to provoke a naval "incident" that would justify asking Congress to declare war. According to Churchill, FDR said that "if he were to put the issue of peace or war to the Congress, they would debate it for three months. The President had said he would wage war, but not declare it, and that he would become more and more provocative. If the Germans did not like it, they could attack American forces." According to Churchill's account: "Everything was to be done to force an incident."

But then nothing seemed to happen. The president did not even implement the new escort policy, and Churchill cabled Hopkins plaintively on August 28 about a "wave of depression" in his cabinet. Hopkins in turn warned Roosevelt that Churchill and British policymakers assumed that "ultimately we will get into the war on some basis or other." If they came to doubt this assumption, said Hopkins, the result would be a resurgence of appeasement and "a very critical moment in the war."

On the other big issue, Japan, the British also felt that FDR had backtracked after the meeting. For months Churchill and his colleagues had been concerned at their exposed position in the Pacific: the United States was handling the diplomacy, particularly the Hull-Nomura talks, while sharing little information. If diplomacy failed and Japan went to war, British colonies, notably Malaya and Singapore, would be the main target, with no U.S. commitment to their defense. Churchill took up these concerns with Roosevelt at the Atlantic meeting. He wanted firm parallel warnings from the two governments that Japanese expansion in the Southwest Pacific could lead to war. He also sought a public guarantee that if another power (in other words Britain) were attacked by Japan, the president would ask Congress for war.

On both counts Roosevelt was unmoved. He considered a guarantee of support to be politically out of the question, and he preferred to continue talking and gain time. Churchill left their meeting with what he believed to be a firm promise that Roosevelt would issue a private warning to Japan on the lines of a firm British draft, but the president, encouraged by Hull, emasculated that as soon as he returned to Washington. Meeting with Ambassador Nomura on August 17, the president made a general statement that further Japanese military action would oblige the United States to take such steps as it deemed necessary to safeguard *American* interests. He made no reference to other countries, and the impact of his remarks was further reduced because he went on to discuss the resumption of talks. When the British (with considerable difficulty) obtained details of the Roosevelt-Nomura meeting, this added to their despondency.

The momentum of U.S. policy picked up again in September, however. On the 4th a U.S. destroyer, the *Greer,* was attacked by a U-boat off Iceland. This gave Roosevelt a peg on which to hang the new policy in the Atlantic. His fireside chat on September 11 distorted the details of the incident. In emphasizing that the Germans fired first, FDR omitted to mention that the destroyer and British aircraft had been trailing the U-boat for several hours. The *Greer* was used as another piece in his jigsaw—further evidence that the Nazis wanted to "seize control of the oceans," destabilize the Western Hemisphere, and ultimately establish "world mastery." Consequently the U.S. navy would now protect merchantmen "of any flag" within "the waters we deem necessary for our own defense" and would no longer wait for Axis vessels to strike first. The press dubbed this the "shoot-on-sight" speech. Although he mentioned Iceland, the president did not make explicit that most of the Atlantic, up to about four hundred miles from the north coast of Scotland, was now defined as American waters. Escorts began on September 17.

With regard to Japan, policy had also hardened—though not as the British would have liked. The United States issued no warning to Japan and no guarantee to Britain; Hull resumed his talks with Nomura. Behind the scenes, however, the oil sanctions imposed in late July had congealed into a total, if unofficial, embargo on all shipments to Japan. Some scholars, notably Jonathan Utley and Irving Anderson, claim that this embargo developed behind FDR's back through the covert efforts of hawks in the bureaucracy, particularly Dean Acheson in the State Department. They argue that when Roosevelt and Hull found out about the de facto embargo, in early September, it was too late to reverse the policy without a disastrous loss of face for the United States. Waldo Heinrichs, by contrast, believes that Roosevelt knew and approved of this hardening of policy. It fitted his preference for covert pressure rather than public confrontation.

Either way, the effects of the new policy are important as its origins. The July restrictions had prompted Tokyo to stop all plans for a buildup against the Soviet Union. The southward thrust, already implicit in the July 2 imperial conference, now became firm policy. Faced by a complete cessation of oil supplies, Japanese policymakers judged that they had no course but to secure the raw materials they needed for Southeast Asia by force. De facto or de jure, approved by Roosevelt or contrived behind his back, oil sanctions served not to deter Japan but to start the final planning for Pacific war.

STALEMATE IN THE ATLANTIC

In the fall of 1941, U.S. policy toward the European war revolved around the twin issues of aid to Britain and aid to Russia. The two were related: because of the limits of the American arsenal, there had to be a decision on priorities. And in either case the main casualty would be the U.S. military, whose own rearmament program was still in its infancy. The fall of 1941 saw major efforts to reconcile these three competing demands on U.S. production as the Nazi advance surged on across the Soviet Union.

By August the German high command recognized that its hopes of a quick victory in the Soviet Union were illusory. Its three-pronged offensive could not be maintained at the same intensity because of supply shortages, and Hitler decided to concentrate on destroying enemy strength in the north and south. Not until the beginning of October was Army Group Center allowed to resume its main thrust to Moscow. Its rapid success forced the Soviet government in mid-October to evacuate the capital for Kuibyshev, five hundred miles east. Even the mummified body of Lenin was moved from its resting place in Red Square and sent east in a refrigerated train. The official evacuation sparked panic among Muscovites: some fled, others looted the empty shops and offices. It took several days to restore order. Stalin, who himself had planned to leave, decided to stay put, rally morale, and bring his best commander, General Georgii Zhukov, from the embattled city of Leningrad in a last-ditch effort to defend the capital. There was, however, a glimmer of hope. Already the autumn rains were turning the ground into mud, and the first snow had fallen.

Compared with the combined efforts of General Zhukov and "General Winter" (historic savior of Russia against Napoleon), aid from the allies was of minuscule material significance in 1941. (Sixty percent of U.S. wartime supplies to the USSR did not arrive until 1943–1944, after the German tide had been turned at Stalingrad and Kursk.) But aid to Russia did matter in 1941–1942 as a boost to popular morale and as an earnest of diplomatic support. In Washington and London there were lingering fears that Stalin might once again make a deal with Hitler (indeed there are signs that he extended peace feelers through the Bulgarian government in the crisis of mid-October). In September 1941, therefore, Roosevelt sent his lend-lease "expediter," Averell Harriman, to London to thrash out a common policy on Soviet supplies. Harriman went on to Moscow as part of a joint Anglo-American mission, which concluded a supply protocol on

October 1. For the nine-month period to June 30, 1942, the two governments pledged about 1.5 million tons of supplies, ranging from tanks to army boots, worth about $1 billion. Such was the state of U.S. rearmament that in the key areas of aircraft and tanks, the British and U.S. contributions were equal—each promised 200 planes and 250 tanks a month.

The War Department, desperate to complete its Protective Mobilization Plan (PMP) for a fully equipped combat force of 1.8 million by mid-1942, wanted aid to Russia to be at the expense of aid to Britain. The British fought strenuously against this—they were already diverting some of their own scarce munitions—and Roosevelt and Hopkins agreed. In a first effort at long-term logistical planning, the army and navy had produced what became known as the "Victory Program" in late September. The army assumed that victory over Hitler would require full-scale U.S. entry into the war and another major American Expeditionary Force (AEF) in Europe. Its initial estimates put the AEF figure at 5 million troops, and peak army manpower strength at 8.8 million. These figures were close to what were eventually needed by 1945.

Yet Roosevelt put the army's expansion, even for the PMP program, on hold all through the fall of 1941. That was mainly because he was still committed to his policy of using Britain (and now Russia) as America's front line of defense. But it also reflected his aversion to waging a ground war in Europe. Not only did he continue to believe that it would be politically impossible to send another AEF, he also hoped that strategic bombing would make land warfare on the scale of 1914–1918 unnecessary. At the Atlantic meeting Hopkins told the British that the president was "a believer in bombing as the only means of gaining a victory."

Moreover there were already signs, at least to Roosevelt and a few advisers, that a bomb of unprecedented power might eventually be available. In June 1941 the president had approved a more effective organization for U.S. research into the military implications of atomic energy. This was the Office of Scientific Research and Development, headed by Vannevar Bush, a former vice president of MIT. But U.S. atomic research remained low-key; indeed the whole program was in danger in mid-1941. What saved it was a top-secret British report, which landed on Bush's desk on October 3 (though its conclusions had been fore-shadowed in the summer). The British had passed on their radar secrets in 1940; now they shared their conclusions that an atomic bomb was scientifically feasible and "likely to lead to decisive re-sults in the war."* Bush took the report to Roosevelt on October 9, urging a major research and development program. The pres-ident established what became known as the "Top Policy Group," including Bush, Stimson, and Marshall. Two days later he wrote Churchill suggesting that future work on the project "be coordinated or even jointly conducted."

Although these were important decisions, preparing the ground for the wartime "Manhattan Project," their results lay years in the future. What mattered in October 1941 was not an atomic bomb but Soviet resistance. Under the terms of the Lend-Lease Act, the president could decide which countries were vital to the defense of the United States. Nevertheless FDR bided his time, hoping that opinion would move clearly in his direction. His efforts to play up religious freedom in the Soviet Union were part of this endeavor. Critics such as Representative Martin Dies of the House Un-American Activities Committee objected to his bid "to dress up the Soviet wolf in the sheep's clothing of the four freedoms." But on October 10 the House, voting on the second lend-lease appropriations bill, rejected by 217 votes to 162 an amendment banning the use of such funds for the USSR. This followed a more organized effort by Democratic managers than

*A copy of the report was also provided to Moscow by a Soviet agent in the British Cabinet Office, John Cairncross.

over draft extension in August. The Senate rejected a similar amendment two weeks later, and on November 7 the president declared the Soviet Union to be eligible for lend-lease assistance. Stalin accepted an interest-free loan of $1 billion to cover the supplies listed in the Moscow Protocol of October 1. This loan would be repaid over a ten-year period, starting five years after the end of the war. A tacit alliance with Russia was now taking shape.

Yet the United States was still formally operating under the framework of the 1939 Neutrality Act. A Gallup poll on October 5 indicated that 70 percent of the public thought it more important to defeat Hitler than to stay out of war, but noninterventionist opinion in Congress appeared to have hardened as America First mounted a new campaign to preserve the Neutrality Act. Roosevelt remained mindful that it took only a few lawmakers, under Senate rules, to filibuster a bill into oblivion. Consequently the administration tested the water by asking only for repeal of article six of the act, which banned the arming of U.S. merchant ships. Given the escort policy already under way, this change was the least contentious, and on October 9 FDR laid the matter before the House. It was, he insisted, not a declaration of war "any more than the Lend-Lease Act called for a declaration of war. This is a matter of essential defense of American rights." On October 17 the House approved repeal of article six by 259 votes to 138, largely on partisan lines.

The night before the House voted, a U.S. destroyer, the *Kearny,* lost eleven men in a torpedo attack off Iceland. The destroyer had gone to the aid of an eastbound convoy under U-boat attack off Iceland. In a Navy Day address on October 27, Roosevelt insisted that the *Kearny* "is not just a Navy ship. She belongs to every man, woman, and child in this Nation." He added that he had in his possession a secret Nazi map showing South America as Hitler proposed to reorganize it into five vassal states, including one that engrossed "our great life line—the

Panama Canal." (Although FDR apparently did not know it, this map was a forgery concocted by British intelligence.)

Emboldened by the House vote on article six, Democratic managers asked the Senate to repeal this and two other articles (prohibiting U.S. vessels from entering belligerent ports and allowing the president to proclaim combat zones around belligerent countries). But on October 31 the U.S. destroyer *Reuben James* was sunk by a U-boat near Iceland with the loss of 115 lives. The combined effect of Roosevelt's rhetoric and these two naval incidents made the noninterventionists more irreconcilable. The full package passed the Senate on November 7 by only 50 votes to 37—the narrowest administration victory on a foreign policy issue since the beginning of the European war. Although the House confirmed this resolution six days later, the margin was also very close (212 to 194), with more Democrats in opposition than over lend-lease.

Roosevelt had secured repeal of the key provisions of the Neutrality Act, but, conscious of the close votes, he did not rush to implement a new policy. Pressed by Hopkins and the navy, the president agreed on November 25 that U.S. merchant ships should go all the way to Britain "as they became available but that this procedure progress gradually with only a small number of ships being so routed in the beginning." No mention of it was made in public. Once again the president was proceeding by small steps, convinced that small steps were better than none. The voting figures over neutrality revision had made him more pessimistic about the mood on Capitol Hill. He had told Churchill in August that, if he asked Congress to declare war, it would debate the issue for three months. On November 3, according to the Canadian prime minister, Mackenzie King, FDR said that a war message would actually be defeated, possibly by a margin of two or even three to one. That same day, asked at a press conference whether maintaining diplomatic relations with

Germany was not "a form of dishonesty," he answered "completely off the record": "We don't want a declared war with Germany because we are acting in defense—self-defense—every action. And to break off diplomatic relations—why, that won't do any good. It might be more useful to keep them the way they are."

This was not mere rhetoric. FDR had several reasons for not rushing into formal war. As we have just seen, he believed that America's contribution would be as the provider of arms, not armies. This conformed with what seems to have been his genuine aversion to go down in history as a war president. Furthermore Roosevelt was convinced that if the United States became a full belligerent, public opinion would demand a massive cutback in foreign aid. This could have devastating consequences for Britain and thus, FDR believed, for the security of the United States. British leaders disagreed, believing that U.S. belligerency would be a massive boost to Allied morale. According to Churchill: "At the Atlantic Meeting I told his circle I would rather have an American declaration of war now and no supplies for six months than double the supplies and no declaration. When this was repeated to him he thought it a hard saying." Another reason for avoiding formal war was Roosevelt's interpretation of the Tripartite Pact. On November 3 he told the Canadian premier "that he was convinced that if the United States came into the war against Germany, Japan would enter the war immediately on Germany's side. That was a consideration which had to be carefully weighed in determining policy." A Pacific war ran directly counter to the policy of avoiding hostilities with Japan, or at least postponing them until Germany had been defeated. It would also arouse the domestic clamor he feared for a reallocation of supplies to U.S. forces instead of to Britain and the Soviet Union.

On all these grounds FDR was not anxious to force the issue

in the Atlantic in November 1941. Moreover he was still hoping
to avoid war with Japan. But U.S. diplomacy in Asia was increasingly at odds with U.S. strategy.

COUNTDOWN IN THE PACIFIC

The de facto U.S. oil embargo had concentrated the
minds of Japan's policymakers on the southward advance. But it
had not totally ended the debate over peace or war. The navy still
entertained hopes of achieving Japan's goals by diplomatic pressure on the European colonial powers. This was also the aim of
Prime Minister Konoe, who now staked all on a summit with
Roosevelt. An imperial conference on September 6 hammered
out another convoluted policy compromise. Preparations for war
with the United States and European powers would be completed by early October. If no diplomatic solution had been
reached by then, Japan would take a decision for war.

The proposal for a Roosevelt-Konoe meeting was broached by
Ambassador Nomura when he met the president on August 17,
soon after his summit with Churchill. FDR initially accepted.
The idea accorded with his predilection for personal diplomacy
and also with his strategy of gaining time while the United States
built up its deterrent strength in the Philippines. The U.S. ambassador in Tokyo, Joseph Grew, was also enthusiastic. But in the
State Department, Hull and his Far Eastern specialists disagreed. They persuaded Roosevelt that no summit meeting
should take place until agreement had been reached on basic
principles.

Japan had clearly established its diplomatic bottom line at the
imperial conference. The Anglo-American powers must stop
aiding the Chinese Nationalists in their war with Japan. They
must establish no military facilities in China, Thailand, and the
Dutch East Indies. They must also restore trading relations with
Japan and provide the country with essential resources. In return

for these concessions, Japan would promise no further military expansion in Asia. It would withdraw its troops from Indochina once a "just peace" had been achieved, and guarantee the neutrality of the Philippines.

These terms were totally unacceptable to the State Department. Hull was not willing to sacrifice his basic principles, the Wilsonian agenda of open trade and self-determination that had been his credo throughout his tenure as secretary of state. During 1938–1939 Roosevelt had taken control of European policy, believing that Hull's program of trade agreements was essentially irrelevant to a continent on the brink of war. But policy toward Japan remained largely in Hull's hands, with some critical exceptions (notably the oil sanctions tangle in July and August 1941). Although Hull had been marginalized from the European war, except on postwar planning issues, he remained central to the Asia-Pacific region, where diplomacy still had a role to play.

Hull's insistence on legalistic fundamentals was not the best way to gain time. Back in April, at an early stage in his talks with Nomura, the secretary of state had put on the table his basic "Four Principles." These comprised:

—respect for the sovereignty and territorial integrity of every nation;
—noninterference in other countries' internal affairs;
—the principle of equality, including equal commercial opportunity;
—acceptance of the territorial status quo, except where changed by peaceful means.

These essentially Wilsonian principles were not unique to America's relations with Japan. Hull was also adapting them concurrently to Britain in proposals for the lend-lease consideration. They also featured in the Roosevelt-Welles drafts of the Atlantic Charter. But those documents were proposals to a quasi-ally about the postwar order. Hull's Four Principles were submitted to a potential adversary as part of an effort to stop, or at least, postpone its declaration of war. Hard dogma is not the best tool for subtle diplomacy.

In talks with Nomura that fall, Hull kept reverting to the Four Principles. He also highlighted two corollaries. First, Japan must withdraw its one million troops from China. This was not simply a statement of principle (Hull was willing to concede Japan's presence in Manchuria). It was also intended to humiliate and discredit the Japanese military, a move that the State Department deemed essential for the "regeneration" of Japan as a liberal polity. The second sticking point was Japan's adherence to the Tripartite Pact. This, in Hull's view, aligned Japan clearly with an aggressive, expansionist power bent on establishing by force a New Order that was inimical to America's basic principles. In talks in the summer of 1941 Hull had targeted Foreign Minister Matsuoka, the main advocate of ties with Berlin. Even after Konoe squeezed him out, Hull wanted public renunciation of the Tripartite Pact.

In the fall of 1941 these two issues—China and the Tripartite Pact—marked out the great divide between Tokyo and Washington. What Hull considered essential, most Japanese policymakers found intolerable. During September, in discussions about the preliminaries to a possible summit, the divide became clear. In a note dated October 2, the State Department told Japan that there was no point in a summit until it accepted America's fundamentals. Although Konoe urged the army to accept token troop withdrawals from China, Army Minister General Tōjō Hideki was implacable. To do so, he argued, would be a return to the 1920s when Britain and America determined the security order in the Pacific, thereby negating all the gains Japan had made in the 1930s by war in China. The army, Tōjō insisted, would not tolerate a return to "Little Japan before the Manchurian Incident." Here, for Japanese hawks, was an issue as fundamental as the Four Principles to Hull.

By now the grace period agreed at the imperial conference of

September 6 had long passed. On October 16 the Konoe cabinet fell. Next day Tōjō started forming a new government. In deference to the emperor, however, he continued to explore the diplomatic option while war plans were prepared. Both the army and the navy were now determined to bring matters to a head. A sixteen-hour liaison conference on November 1–2 agreed to give the new foreign minister, Tōgō Shigenori, until November 30. If no agreement were reached, war would follow soon afterward. Thus, in crabwise fashion, Japan's factional leadership continued to edge nearer to the brink.

Tōgō came up with a two-pronged approach. Plan A set out Japan's terms for a comprehensive settlement with the United States, including China. As expected, Hull would have nothing to do with it. On November 20 the Japanese therefore presented Plan B—essentially a return to the situation before July 26, namely an end to the U.S. freezing order and the oil embargo in return for Japanese withdrawal from southern Indochina. The "China Incident" was left for Japan and China to resolve (in other words by continued war).

The State Department was more responsive to Plan B. Hull's Far Eastern desk officers prepared their own modus vivendi— Japanese withdrawal from most of Indochina and a reduction in U.S. oil sanctions for a three-month trial period while efforts continued for a general settlement, including China. But hawkish bureaucrats in other interested departments watered down these concessions, and Chiang Kai-shek's emissaries were strident in their criticism. If America relaxed its pressure while Japanese troops remained in China, they said, the Chinese people would feel "completely sacrificed." This would show that America was ready "to appease Japan at the expense of China" and would encourage Chinese defeatists to urge "oriental solidarity against occidental treachery." Hull was shaken by China's warnings, to which Churchill also lent his voice. At this stage in the war, when the Red Army had been driven back to the gates of

Moscow, a Chinese collapse would be disastrous. Hull did not feel inclined to call Chiang's bluff.

With the proposal already leaking to the U.S. press (courtesy of the Chinese), Hull abandoned the modus vivendi. Yet it was still in America's interests to buy time. The buildup in the Philippines was far from complete, and most of the B-17s still had not arrived. But Hull was ill and exhausted: the storm of criticism that greeted his modus vivendi draft was too much. In any case, he knew from Magic intercepts that Plan A would be followed by Plan B and that Tokyo had set a deadline for further negotiations. By November 25 it was also clear that a large Japanese expeditionary force had embarked at Shanghai and was now moving south toward Indochina and the Malay peninsula. Faced with this evidence of Japanese perfidy, Hull threw in the towel. On November 26 he gave the Japanese an unyielding ten-point program for a comprehensive settlement, centered on China. Next day he told Stimson that he had washed his hands of the Pacific: "It is now in the hands of you and Knox—the Army and the Navy." Although Roosevelt still toyed with the idea of a final appeal to the emperor, in practice the administration now braced itself for a Pacific war. But where would it break out? And what would be the U.S. reaction?

At noon on Tuesday, November 25, a major policy meeting convened at the White House. It included Hull, Stimson, Knox, Marshall, and Stark. According to Stimson's diary, the president said "that we were likely to be attacked perhaps next Monday for the Japanese are notorious for making an attack without warning, and the question was what we should do. The question was how we should maneuver them into the position of firing the first shot without allowing too much danger to ourselves."

That last sentence has been the centerpiece of conspiracy theories ever since it was revealed to the 1946 congressional inquiry into Pearl Harbor. It provided the title for the culminating chapter of Charles Beard's massive indictment of *President Roosevelt and the Coming of War 1941,* published in 1948. As a variant on the persistent charges, particularly in popularized histories, that FDR permitted the Japanese attack on Pearl Harbor in order to get the United States into war, there is the more recent claim that Churchill was the culprit. According to James Rusbridger and Eric Nave in 1991, he concealed intelligence about the imminent attack on Pearl Harbor from the president in order to consummate the Anglo-American wartime alliance.

What did Roosevelt mean when he talked of maneuvering the Japanese into firing the first shot? What did he and Churchill know of Japanese intentions, and what plans had they made? Although there remain many dark corners to the Pearl Harbor story, the evidence points to confusion and complacency, not conspiracy, in Washington. But the confusion and complacency are deeply revealing.

When Roosevelt and Churchill braced themselves in early December for Japanese belligerency, their eyes were firmly on Southeast Asia. From its new stronghold in Indochina, Japan could move west into nearby Thailand and south into Malaya and the Dutch East Indies—all sources of vital raw materials. Magic intercepts, such as those about the troop convoy from Shanghai, clearly indicated a thrust into Southeast Asia. Yet none of these were U.S. possessions. For months U.S. policymakers had avoided any promise to fight if European colonies in Asia were under attack. In line with the ABC-1 agreement on strategy, back in March, the U.S. movements of ships to the Atlantic would allow the British to reinforce their own defenses in Southeast Asia. This was now taking place: in November 1941 a small British Far Eastern Fleet was steaming to Singapore. On land, plans were in place for a preemptive British move into Thailand to strengthen the defenses of Malaya.

But Churchill would not sanction the implementation of these plans without pledges of U.S. support. Otherwise Britain might have to fight Japan on its own. By the end of November 1941,

Roosevelt could sit on the fence no longer. Just as Hull judged that showing solidarity with China was more important than buying time with Japan, so Roosevelt felt obliged to make clear military commitments to Britain. On December 1 the president (with studied casualness) mentioned to Lord Halifax, the British ambassador, that in the event of an attack on British and Dutch possessions, "we should obviously be all together." According to Ambassador Halifax, he added later that if Japan attacked Thailand, Britain "could certainly count on their support, though it might take a short time, he spoke of a few days, to get things into political shape here." Churchill and his Defence Committee were still wary. Two decades of British suspicions about American grandiloquence could not be dispelled overnight. Did the president mean "armed support"? Yes, FDR told Halifax on December 3, he did. In such eventualities, he had no doubt "you can count on [the] armed support of [the] United States."

On November 28 Roosevelt had already agreed on this position with his principal military and naval advisers. But he could only propose war; the Congress had to declare it. From a purely diplomatic point of view, Pearl Harbor was therefore a godsend. That is why some writers have convinced themselves that Roosevelt allowed it to happen. As the intelligence archives have been opened, a fuller picture has emerged. It confirms, in modified form, the orthodox account of intelligence failure.

It is now clear that U.S. and British cryptanalysts had achieved some success with the Japanese naval code JN-25. From that cable traffic the attack on Pearl Harbor *could* have been deduced. But the decisive messages were in the improved JN-25b code, which remained largely impenetrable to both governments. U.S. intelligence had concentrated on the diplomatic messages, which generated the Magic intercepts. At the end of 1941 only eight cryptanalysts were working on JN-25b. The material was available but not the resources to penetrate it.

Even the Magic intercepts could have been exploited more effectively had U.S. intelligence been better organized. Because of interservice rivalry, an absurd arrangement developed whereby the army would decode material on days with an even-numbered date and the navy on odd-numbered days. For a time in 1941 the president was getting Magic from the navy one month and the army the next. That nonsense ended in early November, but the army-navy division of labor for daily decoding continued to the very end. It delayed transmission to FDR of intercepts of Tokyo's final messages to Ambassador Nomura. These rejected Hull's note of November 26, indicated there was no point in further negotiations, and instructed Nomura to deliver them to Hull exactly at 1 p.m. on Sunday, December 7. This was just after dawn on December 8 in Hawaii, and roughly forty-five minutes before the attack was due to begin.

Greater attention to naval codes and better coordination of intelligence would have helped immensely. But, as many historians have concluded, the failure was as much a matter of perceptions as information. Preoccupied with East Asia, Washington policymakers simply did not expect an attack on Pearl Harbor—five thousand miles from the Philippines. Indeed, they thought it unlikely that Japan, already bogged down in the China war, would also take on the United States and Britain in simultaneous attacks. Churchill referred to the Japanese privately as the "Wops of the Pacific"—adapting the derogatory term used by the British about the Italians. In other words, if the Japanese went to war, they would be a nuisance but not a real threat. U.S. policymakers thought in a similar vein. When General Douglas MacArthur heard the news that Pearl Harbor had been attacked by carrier-based aircraft, he assumed that the pilots must have been white mercenaries. At Pearl Harbor most of the fleet rode at anchor in "Battleship Row." U.S. commanders reckoned that the main security threat was sabotage, not bombing, and concentrated their planes in the middle of airfields, away from the perimeter fence.

For many in the U.S. army and navy in November 1941, the looming conflict was not between America and Japan but between themselves. The annual bitterly fought Army-Navy football game was scheduled for November 29. The game program pictured a battleship with the caption: "A bow-on view of the U.S.S. *Arizona* as she plows into a huge swell." The caption added: "It is significant that despite the claims of air enthusiasts, no battleship has yet been sunk by bombs." Eight days later the 600-foot, 31,000-ton *Arizona* lay at the bottom of Pearl Harbor, sunk in less than ten minutes by Japan's airborne task force.

WORLD WAR

In 1946 a joint congressional investigating committee described Pearl Harbor as "the greatest military and naval disaster in our Nation's history." Many commentators and scholars have echoed its language. Yet as the historian John Mueller has noted, in military terms Pearl Harbor was not a catastrophe. The fleet's vital aircraft carriers were out on patrol. Although all eight battleships were hit, three were returned to service within three weeks and three more within three years. In any case, all were World War I vessels whose useful days were already numbered. Four new, state-of-the-art battleships were commissioned in 1942 alone. Similarly, in cruisers and destroyers, bombers and fighters, the United States soon eclipsed with new production what it had lost on that Sunday morning.

But 2,400 servicemen and civilians could not be replaced. And the sense of national humiliation was indelible. That evening the cabinet convened in the president's study. Labor Secretary Frances Perkins recalled that Roosevelt's face had "a queer gray, drawn look." Such was his pride in the navy that, said Perkins, "he was having actual physical difficulty in getting out the words" and admitting "that the Navy was caught unawares." On the other hand, FDR now had an unequivocal *casus belli*. According to Hopkins, on hearing the news about Pearl Harbor he said it took the matter "entirely out of his hands, because the Japanese had made the decision for him." At Yalta in 1945 he told Churchill and Stalin that but for the Japanese attack, "he would have had great difficulty in getting the American people into the war."

On December 8 FDR addressed a special joint session of the Congress, emphasizing not merely the gravity of Japan's attack but its "unprovoked and dastardly" character, before negotiations had been formally broken off. Little more than half an hour later both houses had approved his request for a declaration of war against Japan. There was only one dissenter—Congresswoman Jeanette Rankin of Montana, a pacifist who had also voted against war in 1917. Most of Roosevelt's opponents followed the lead of the America First Committee and rallied around their commander-in-chief. Senator Arthur Vandenberg was a representative example. He wrote in his diary that "we may have *driven* her [Japan] *needlessly* into hostilities through our dogmatic diplomatic attitudes" but that was now irrelevant. "Nothing matters except VICTORY. The 'arguments' must be postponed."

The United States was now a belligerent in the war that Roosevelt had hoped to avoid, or postpone, with Japan. But the United States was not formally a belligerent in the war that he regarded as central, with Germany. It is too strong to say, with the historian Stephen Ambrose, that on December 10 the president's policy was "a dismal failure." But Ambrose is surely right that "what saved him and his policy was nothing he did, but Hitler's act of lunacy."

At the cabinet meeting on December 7, Stimson urged the president to ask for a declaration of war on Germany as well as Japan, since Hitler was undoubtedly the instigator. But no one supported him. Afterward Roosevelt told Stimson that he would "present the full matter two days later." In his fireside chat on

December 9 he insisted that Japan's attack "without warning" was part of a global Axis pattern that stretched back through Belgium in 1940, Czechoslovakia in 1939, and Ethiopia in 1935, to Japan's invasion of Manchuria a decade before. In 1941, he claimed, Axis collaboration was "so well calculated that all the continents of the world, and all the oceans" were now considered by their strategists as "one gigantic battlefield." He told the American people: "We know that Germany and Japan are conducting their military and naval operations in accordance with a joint plan," and "Germany and Italy, regardless of any formal declaration of war, consider themselves at war with the United States at this moment." But the president made no request to move from de facto to open war against the European Axis.

The Tripartite Pact of 1940 was a hollow alliance. Despite public statements of solidarity, a secret exchange of letters had preserved Japan's freedom of action to interpret whether and how the treaty obligations should be honored. Moreover the pact was a defensive alliance and did not apply if one of the signatories embarked on aggression of its own. Thus Japan had no obligations to join in Hitler's war on Russia, nor would Germany be obliged to participate if Japan attacked the United States. None of this was known in Washington.

During November 1941, however, Japan asked Germany to join in any future hostilities against the United States. Ribbentrop, the foreign minister, said that Germany would sign a no-separate-peace agreement "if Japan and Germany, regardless of the grounds, becomes involved in a war with the USA." At the beginning of December he was asked to confirm this in writing. Hitler agreed and a draft was prepared. But just as Tokyo had no advance warning of Barbarossa, so Ribbentrop learned of Pearl Harbor from the British Broadcasting Corporation (and initially dismissed the radio report as Allied propaganda). Nevertheless, on December 9 Hitler ordered unrestricted U-boat attacks on U.S. shipping. After the no-separate-peace agreement was signed on the 11th, Germany and Italy declared war on the United States.

Hitler's motives have been the subject of endless debate. He had often spoken of the United States as Germany's ultimate enemy, though usually adding that this battle would be for the next generation, after Europe had been won. His restraint in the Atlantic in 1941 was therefore a matter of tactics. He may have concluded that FDR would provoke war in the next few months and that it was better for domestic morale if he moved first. As Ribbentrop noted: "A great power does not allow itself to be declared war upon; it declares war on others." Hitler definitely did not want Tokyo to conclude a deal with Washington, because that would leave Roosevelt with a freer hand in Europe. Conversely he believed that if Japan went to war, it would tie down U.S. forces in the Pacific. At root, in fact, Hitler did not consider the United States a formidable foe. True to his racist ideology, he viewed the Americans as a degenerate, mongrel race whose bark was worse than its bite. And there was a grim racist corollary. On December 12 Hitler reminded top officials of his "prophecy" in January 1939 that if the Jews brought about another world war, they would be annihilated. "That was no empty talk," said Hitler. "The world war is there. The annihilation of the Jews must be the necessary consequence."

The events of December 8–11 must therefore be seen as a sequential whole. Japan had vindicated Roosevelt's globalist ideology. While Americans had been consistently wary about another European war, their antipathy to Japan was unequivocal and their outrage after Pearl Harbor was intense. Isolationists spoke of Pearl Harbor as the backdoor to European war, but for internationalists like Roosevelt, as the historian Frank Ninkovich observes, it was the front door to global conflict. Pearl Harbor justified FDR's insistence that this was the Second World War. That would not have been enough, however, if Hitler had not played into Roosevelt's hands strategically. By declaring war on the United States, he saved FDR from being forced to concentrate on an unwanted Pacific war, thereby salvaging the president's Germany-first strategy.

Despite this fateful convergence in December 1941, the Axis remained a hollow alliance. Although the German and Japanese navies wanted to concert their strategies, targeting British India from two sides, the two leaderships in Berlin and Tokyo went on to fight separate wars. The Allied partnership, for all its flaws, proved stronger and more effective. Within days of Pearl Harbor, Churchill was braving Atlantic storms en route to Washington to concert Anglo-American war plans. Although Hitler was at the gates of Moscow, U.S. aid was now beginning to flow to the Soviet Union. And, as the November crisis showed, the United States had also stuck by China. American perceptions of a cohesive totalitarian plot helped ease the United States into world war. But the reality of Axis divergence helped ensure eventual Allied victory.

7

From Munich to Pearl Harbor

IN THE INTRODUCTION I set out three main objectives: to
provide an interpretive overview of U.S. policy from Munich to
Pearl Harbor, to show how Roosevelt led Americans into a new
global perception of international relations, and to suggest how
some of the essentials of America's cold war worldview were
formed in this period. Policy, perceptions, and precedents form
the substance of this concluding chapter.

POLICY

Roosevelt's Washington was riven by bureaucratic politics. But, to a large extent, foreign policy was made by the president. That policy was mainly reactive—to the challenges posed
by international events and to the limitations of domestic politics.
These have been the two central themes of my account. Yet
FDR's own inclinations mattered enormously because his interpretations of events and his assessments of politics often differed
markedly from those of his advisers. Moreover his reactions were
also shaped by certain basic assumptions about the United States
and the world.

By the fall of 1937 the New Deal was on the defensive. The fiasco of Supreme Court reform and the onset of what Republicans dubbed "the Roosevelt recession" had squandered the

massive electoral victory of November 1936. The international
scene also darkened dramatically during 1937, with Japan's brutal aggression in China and great-power involvement in the civil
war in Spain. Unnerved by the depression and preoccupied by
economic recovery, many Americans now believed that entry
into the European war in 1917 had been a profound mistake.
Successive Neutrality Acts from 1935 were an attempt to avoid
that mistake again by minimizing the danger of U.S. economic
and emotional entanglement in a future European war.

In the mid-1930s Roosevelt accepted the basic framework of
the new neutrality. He shared the national aversion to another
war. But he still believed that the United States should play a
constructive role in world affairs. Although repudiating the
League of Nations, he retained the essentials of a Wilsonian
worldview, convinced that imperialism, militarism, and economic nationalism were at the root of most international problems. Influenced by his kinsman, Teddy Roosevelt, and by
Wilson's experiences in 1917–1919, he also believed that great-
power cooperation was essential to peace and security, particularly cooperation with Britain, the premier sea power.

In 1937–1938 he began to express these underlying ideas in
more concrete form. His "quarantine the aggressors" speech in
October 1937 was a globalist diagnosis of world problems, likening international lawlessness to a contagious disease. In private
he talked of naval pressure and economic sanctions as instruments of quarantine, laying the intellectual basis for his attempted containment of Japan. In Europe, Roosevelt had less to
offer, because the great-power structure was still firmly in place.
At times in 1937–1938 he picked up the Wilsonian ideas of his
close adviser, Sumner Welles, for a new international conference
to establish principles of disarmament and freer trade. But during the Czech crisis of September 1938 he was largely a by-
stander.

Nevertheless the crisis proved a turning point in Roosevelt's thinking, in several respects. Insider reports of the European summit conferences convinced the president that there could be no negotiation with Hitler. He never took that view of the other dictators, Mussolini and Stalin, let alone the leaders of Japan. Hitler's bloodless victory, handed to him by Britain and France, also shook FDR's assumption that the established powers of Western Europe would take the lead in stabilizing the Old World. Henceforth he envisaged a larger U.S. role in Europe, albeit well short of war. Privately he talked of a massive campaign of air rearmament to give him the clout he needed in international diplomacy.

Roosevelt told his advisers in November 1938 that he wanted to "sell or lend" planes and other munitions to Britain and France. Here, at the level of gut instinct, was the essential theme of his policy toward Europe over the next three years. But FDR's attempt to mobilize consent for his ideas in the spring and summer of 1939 was an abject failure. His rhetoric was too alarmist; his attempts to amend the Neutrality Act were ineffectual. A strong bipartisan coalition had now been mobilized in Congress. Although formed around opposition to the New Deal, it was inspired by general suspicion of the president and his "dictatorial" tendencies. In mid-1939 FDR was unwilling to test its cohesion on foreign affairs by a head-on confrontation. Nor was the international situation propitious. War scares in Europe had come and gone. There seemed no clear and immediate danger to the United States.

Once war broke out in Europe in September 1939, however, the situation changed dramatically. American opinion turned more amenable to Roosevelt's policy of biased neutrality, and this time Democratic managers were more effective than in the summer. In November Congress repealed the embargo on selling arms to countries at war, and placed all trade with belligerents on a "cash-and-carry" basis. This benefited Britain, with a large navy and financial reserves, while preserving Americans' insula-

tion from direct contact with the billigerents. Although FDR
made clear that his countrymen should not feel "neutral in
thought," he still talked the language of legal neutrality. He reiterated his determination to keep America out of the war and his
confidence that he could do so. But at that stage his presidency
was scheduled to end in January 1941.

If Munich was the first major turning point in the evolution of
Roosevelt's foreign policy, the fall of France was the second. In
the autumn of 1939 it seemed reasonable to anticipate a long
struggle, akin to that of 1914–1918. No one—certainly not Roosevelt, and not even Hitler—expected the stunning German successes of May and June, which left Britain alone, fighting for
survival. Munich had cracked the American image of European
power; the fall of France shattered it. U.S. policy was never the
same again.

There were two plausible responses from the U.S. perspective.
One was to accelerate America's limited rearmament and concentrate on defending the Western Hemisphere. A large body of
opinion, spearheaded by the America First Committee, advocated this policy. The other response was to extend aid to Britain
alone. Given the fate of France and the state of Britain's defenses,
that was a real gamble. But, after some hesitation, FDR took the
risk, against the preferences of the War Department and the inclinations of many in his administration. International events by
themselves were not decisive: much depended on Roosevelt himself.

His motives for backing Britain were typically mixed. He believed that British resistance bought time for American rearmament. He undoubtedly felt some measure of kinship with
Britain. And he could not envisage Europe, the cradle of American civilization, being dominated by alien values. But he responded to Churchill's pleas for U.S. destroyers only when he
was confident of Britain's survival and was advised that he could
act without congressional approval. Characteristically he also

tried to strengthen America's own defenses with bases in the Western Atlantic and an assurance that the British fleet would never be surrendered.

Although carefully balanced, the destroyers-for-bases deal of September 1940 was a milestone in U.S. policy. It signaled a new commitment to Britain Alone as America's front line. The RAF's success in the Battle of Britain helped validate Roosevelt's geopolitical gamble, while the new images of British heroism and egalitarian sacrifice during the Blitz confirmed the impression he wanted to convey of the country's ideological compatibility with the values of Americanism. The American image of Britain was changing from empire to democracy.

The destroyers deal also deepened the global divide. Berlin, Rome, and Tokyo responded with their Tripartite Pact, intended to deter the United States from further commitments to Britain in Europe or Asia. In private, unknown to Roosevelt, the Japanese retained the freedom to judge when and whether to enter a war with Germany. But the public appearance of Axis solidarity strengthened the American perception of a global totalitarian threat.

The summer of 1940 redefined American politics as well as the country's geopolitical position. The fall of France persuaded FDR to seek reelection instead of retirement. In November 1940 he became the first U.S. president to breach the no-third-term tradition. With four more years ahead of him, he enjoyed a freedom of political maneuver undreamed of in the dog days of 1939.

First fruit of the new politics was the Lend-Lease Act of March 1941. This implemented ideas that Roosevelt had enunciated, albeit vaguely, back in November 1938. The United States would lend munitions to those countries, particularly Britain but also China, whose survival was deemed to be in the national interest. It took FDR two months to secure congressional assent, but he could now claim that he had a legislative mandate for a policy that had previously been handled by executive authority.

Since the munitions had to be produced, the act was also a way of galvanizing domestic rearmament through substantial government investment.

But it was no use producing and lending supplies if they did not arrive safely. The United States had to help carry the goods as well as provide the cash. During the spring and summer FDR extended U.S. naval operations in the Atlantic, taking in Iceland in July and operating what became a "shoot-on-sight" policy from September onward. Ignoring some of his advisers, he did this without going to Congress, using his powers as commander-in-chief. From the autumn the U.S. navy was helping escort British and Canadian convoys across most of the Atlantic. In November the president secured repeal of some of the key remaining provisions of the Neutrality Act, including those that banned American vessels from entering British ports. But despite incidents with German U-boats, he remained wary of forcing the issue.

One reason why Roosevelt maintained an undeclared naval warfare in the Atlantic was the changed international situation. Hitler's invasion of Russia in June 1941 constituted the third great turning point of the years 1938–1941. It took some of the heat off Britain and therefore the United States. FDR decided to extend aid to the Soviet Union because its continued resistance diverted Hitler from Western Europe and the Atlantic. As in the summer of 1940 with Britain, he took a gamble—and one that was again strongly opposed by the War Department, still struggling with U.S. mobilization. But the gamble paid off. Russia's survival into the winter, despite massive losses, marked a major respite in the war in the West.

There were other reasons for Roosevelt's caution in the Atlantic. He judged that U.S. public and congressional opinion had, if anything, hardened against full belligerency since the Soviet entry. He also feared that if the United States formally declared war, Americans would demand that aid to Britain and

Russia take second place to the needs of U.S. forces. In addition he intended that America's main role in a war, declared or not, should be as the provider of arms rather than armies. His new passion for airpower reflected the hope that, in modern warfare, technology could replace manpower. Budgets were politically less contentious than body bags. FDR also feared that a formal war with Germany would precipitate Japanese belligerency in the Pacific. Although a mistaken reading of the Axis pact, that fear reflected his conviction that America faced a cohesive global threat. During 1940–1941 the administration's aim was to contain Japan without war, yet opinions differed as to which measures would deter and which would provoke. FDR was less in command of policy toward Asia, partly because he was preoccupied with Europe but also because the splits over Japan were more serious. Hull wanted to keep talking while reiterating Wilsonian principles. The "hawks," led by Morgenthau and Stimson, favored tougher economic controls.

Hitler's invasion of Russia in June 1941 removed a major restraint on Japanese policymakers. They decided to continue their "southward advance" and occupy the whole of Indochina. FDR responded by tightening controls over Japanese oil imports, but, perhaps without his full knowledge, administration hawks developed these into a full oil embargo. This pushed Japanese leaders toward a final decision for war. America's putative deterrents—the main fleet left uneasily at Pearl Harbor, the new buildup of airpower in the Philippines—were ineffectual and even counterproductive. In other ways, too, the implementation of U.S. policy was faulty. Roosevelt was fascinated by human intelligence—firsthand reports had decisively influenced his policy after Munich, the fall of France, and the invasion of Russia. Unlike Churchill, he was much less interested in signals intelligence and failed to ensure its proper provision and analysis. For that Americans paid a high price on December 7, 1941.

But Pearl Harbor was ultimately the result of mistaken assumptions. Roosevelt's focus was on Europe: he naturally assumed that the powers of the Old World and the New were the movers and shakers of world affairs. Like most of his advisers, he underestimated Japan's desperation and its capacity. By December 1941 he was expecting a war in Southeast Asia but not a daring air attack on the U.S. fleet more than five thousand miles to the east. This plunged America into a Pacific war that the administration had tried to avoid and for which it was woefully unprepared. If Germany had not declared war on the United States, the whole balance of Roosevelt's Germany-first policy would have been upset. After the humiliation of Pearl Harbor, domestic pressure for a Japan-first policy would have become overwhelming. Hitler saved Roosevelt from that predicament.

PERCEPTIONS

Japan's attack and Hitler's declaration of war were just the latest of a series of unexpected international events going back to Munich that shook the foundations of U.S. policy. But, as I have suggested, FDR might have reacted very differently to these events, notably the fall of France and the invasion of Russia. In both cases he could have intensified a policy of Western Hemisphere defense, as many Americans wished. He did not do so, but nor did he challenge the proponents of hemisphere defense head-on. Instead he and his internationalist supporters gradually "educated" (in their phrase) the American public into a new globalist conception of international affairs. This developed at two levels—the geopolitical and the ideological.

Franklin Roosevelt, like TR, was a disciple of Admiral Mahan. He was alert to the significance of sea power in world affairs and, for most of his life, an advocate of Anglo-American naval cooperation. Munich opened his eyes to airpower. This then became an obsession. He believed that the bomber had made America's oceanic barriers obsolescent and had invalidated the concept of a secure Western Hemisphere. German subversion in Latin America might enable Hitler to build air bases within range of U.S. cities. If he gained control of West Africa or European colonies in the Caribbean, these might become jumping-off points for an attack on the United States. Hence the importance of the British Isles and the British fleet. They had become, for Roosevelt, America's front line. Given the new geography of power in the air age, the front line might well prove the last line of defense.

In keeping with his cautious view of U.S. opinion, Roosevelt stuck with the traditional conceptual framework of a discrete Western Hemisphere. He simply stretched it farther and farther eastward. By 1941, however, pro-administration intellectuals such as Walter Lippmann were promulgating the concept of an "Atlantic Area." This offered a new "mental map" to conceptualize Roosevelt's expanded definition of U.S. interests. Also entering circulation was the concept of "national security"—a term used by the president himself though particularly associated with Edward Mead Earle of Princeton. Unlike traditional concepts such as "defense," national security was active rather than passive—a combination of diplomacy and strategy to preempt trouble rather than simply respond to attack. This was what FDR was doing as he pushed the Western Hemisphere eastward by extended naval patrolling or the occupation of Iceland.

Although the Atlantic was deemed the center of danger, Roosevelt and his allies saw the threat as global in scope. From the spring of 1940 the main U.S. fleet was kept halfway across the Pacific at Hawaii in an attempt to deter Japan. By the fall of 1941 the United States was reinforcing the Philippines rather than planning their evacuation. Moreover the administration saw the Atlantic and Pacific challenges as interconnected. The Tripartite Pact of September 1940 strengthened its fears of an interconnected Axis, and the combined declarations of war in December 1941 served to confirm them.

Each Axis power sought an empire of its own, built around the principles of self-sufficiency. The Roosevelt administration was convinced that, to survive in such a world, the United States would have to change fundamentally its trading patterns and set itself on a permanent war footing, even if it remained nominally at peace. The term for this, already used by academics such as Harold Lasswell, was "the garrison state." The administration argued that the United States could avoid such an outcome only by preempting Axis imperialism through aid to countries such as Britain and China. In direct contrast, noninterventionist critics argued that a policy of hemisphere defense was the answer. In their view it was Roosevelt's "war policy" that would turn America into a garrison state.

Although a new geopolitics was at the heart of FDR's reconceptualization of U.S. foreign policy, it was not axiomatic. As Lindbergh and others insisted, the air age had the potential to make the United States stronger, not weaker, if air rearmament for *defense* was given priority. Moreover the Axis were much less cohesive than Washington believed. Although the secret protocols of the Tripartite Pact were unknown to the administration, it was clear, for instance, that Japan had been totally surprised in August 1939 and again in June 1941 by the zigzags of Hitler's policy toward Russia.

The president's new foreign policy was in fact founded on ideology as much as geopolitics. FDR's speeches in 1940 and 1941 were replete with statements of ideals and values. Roosevelt believed, and was at pains to say, that the Axis stood for principles inimical to those of America's liberal capitalist democracy rooted in Christian values. Ideologically his Wilsonianism remained profound. It provided the basis for major wartime statements such as the Four Freedoms. But FDR was applying Wilsonian values to new international circumstances.

In the late 1930s the most influential ideological conceptualization of world affairs emanated from Moscow. This centered on a divide between the "fascists" and the "anti-fascists" which the Comintern expounded as part of the Soviet attempt to build a Popular Front against Hitler. The Nazi-Soviet Pact of 1939 exploded that idea. In the United States the term "totalitarianism"—already in use to cover Germany, Italy, and Japan—was now extended to embrace the Soviet Union as well. This helped Roosevelt set out a stark bipolar ideological divide. The totalitarians, seeking to bring all of society under the control of the state, were depicted as antithetical to the basic freedoms embodied in the United States.

There were other ways of conceptualizing the world, however. Wilsonianism was an amorphous ideology, but one of its central tenets was the condemnation of imperialism. Britain, France, and Russia were three of the world's leading empires, and Wilson's ambivalence about them was reflected in his description of the United States in 1917 as an "associate" power rather than an "ally." Roosevelt shared some of that ambivalence, but the crisis of 1940 was far worse than 1917. British imperialism became a minor concern. During the Blitz of 1940–1941 the administration and a sympathetic media helped portray Britain in a more favorable light. The erosion of class barriers under Hitler's aerial pounding was taken as evidence of a social revolution. The new image of Britain was that of democracy, not empire—a country belatedly moving toward the American way.

The repackaging of Stalin's Russia after June 1941 was much more difficult. On security grounds, Roosevelt welcomed the Soviet Union to the American camp, and most Americans concurred. For the moment the language of totalitarianism was dropped. But the idea lurked under the surface of political discussion. Roosevelt's efforts to turn the USSR into a proto-democracy, particularly by talking up freedom of religion, were not convincing. There seemed a danger in the summer of 1941 that agreements between Britain and the Soviet Union might preempt Roosevelt's vision for a postwar world. In August,

therefore, Roosevelt pinned Churchill down to a major statement of war aims—the Atlantic Charter. This eschewed secret
treaties of the sort that the administration feared might be brew-
ing in London and Moscow. It also committed the evasive British
to a Wilsonian agenda. Churchill ensured plenty of loopholes,
but in a broad sense he had signed up to American goals. Although Moscow revived the concept of an anti-fascist coalition,
Washington continued to describe the emerging alliance in the
language of democratic values. Roosevelt did not talk of making
the world safe for democracy, but that was his intention.

"World" is the operative term, for the new geopolitics and ideology constituted a statement of American globalism. This can
be seen clearly in the evolution of the term "Second World War,"
which we now use without a moment's thought.

In the 1920s and 1930s the British had referred to the European conflict of 1914–1918 as "The Great War"—a term first
used of their titanic, quarter-century conflict with France in the
era of Napoleon. A few, notably Winston Churchill, situated the
Great War within what he called "The World Crisis," but the
term "World War" was largely a German and American inven-
tion. For the Germans it connoted a war in which the British and
Americans were involved, unlike the continental European conflicts of the Bismarck era. From an American viewpoint, Europe
was at least three thousand miles from Washington, D.C., and
the conflict of 1914–1918 also had reverberations in Asia and
Africa as well as reordering the Near East. The term "World
War" was therefore apt. It lodged in American political terminology, even though Wilsonian globalism was soon discredited.

For much of the 1930s FDR considered it essential to distance
himself from Wilson. He accepted the basic framework of neutrality legislation and came close to saying that U.S. belligerency
in 1917 had been a mistake. In 1938, 1939, and 1940 his more forward policy in Europe was presented as an effort to *avoid* war,
not to enter it. But by the spring of 1941 his line had begun to

change. He had redefined America's national security to include much of the Atlantic and (more covertly) the Pacific. He was citing the Tripartite Pact as evidence of a global conspiracy, and the looming invasion of Russia accentuated the global ramifications of the European conflict. In the spring of 1941 he therefore began talking publicly about "this second World War"—picking up a phrase that had been bandied about in the United States and China in the mid-1930s. At the same time, by aiding Britain and Russia, by pressuring Japan and not abandoning China, he inserted the United States into the widening conflict at critical points. Because of its hinge position as an emerging power in the Atlantic *and* the Pacific, the United States was crucial to the fusion of the separate regional conflicts. Of course it was in large measure decisions made in Berlin and Tokyo that turned the European war of September 1939 into a global conflagration by the end of 1941. But Roosevelt's discourse and his policies also contributed. In both respects one can say that "the Second World War" was partly an American construction.

PRECEDENTS

During the cold war, World War II slipped from the gaze of many U.S. diplomatic historians. Understandably, their prime concern was Soviet-American relations. Roosevelt figured to the extent that scholars debated whether or not he was an "appeaser" who had laid the basis for Soviet hegemony in postwar Eastern Europe. U.S. entry into the war was largely irrelevant to this debate. Although conspiracy theories about Pearl Harbor persisted, the general consensus about World War II as "the good war" discouraged close analysis of U.S. intervention.

The cold war is now history, however. As it recedes into the distance, one can look past it and discern more easily the meaning of World War II. From this vantage point the redefinition of U.S. policy and discourse about foreign affairs in 1940–1941 may be seen as an important and neglected stage in the emergence of America as a superpower and in the delineation of its cold war worldview. Of course 1941 was not 1945 or 1950. The transformation of the Soviet Union from ally to enemy occurred slowly in the mid-1940s; the formation of a vast peacetime defense establishment was a product of the Korean War more than World War II. But key concepts had been formed, basic practices established, in 1940–1941, *long before* they were applied to the Soviet Union.

The new globalism was particularly influential. As early as 1943 Walter Lippmann was writing about "the Atlantic Community." That term became fundamental to U.S. strategy after 1949 with the creation of the North Atlantic Treaty Organization. The basic concepts of Atlanticism—about the geopolitical and ideological significance of a friendly Western Europe for the United States—were outlined in the months before Pearl Harbor. By this time the term "national security" had entered the vocabulary of Roosevelt and other internationalists. In due course, historians such as Daniel Yergin and Michael Hogan would depict the national security state as the defining structure of America's cold war. Moreover the concept of totalitarianism, though sublimated after Russia entered the war, had already been firmly lodged in American thinking. Roosevelt's attempt to detach the USSR from it did not succeed, and by 1947 the Truman Doctrine equated Stalinism with totalitarianism once again. Atlanticism, national security, and totalitarianism all became part of the cold war worldview of bipolarity. But that bipolar framework was established by Roosevelt, not Truman. In speech after speech in 1939, 1940, and 1941, FDR depicted a world polarized between the forces of light and darkness. Bipolarity was not a product of the cold war but a precedent. Roosevelt had predisposed Americans to think in terms of a world divided into two ways of life.

The new globalism was only one of the legacies of these years.

Roosevelt's bypassing of Congress on some crucial issues in 1940–1941 was another harbinger of things to come. The destroyers deal was couched as an executive agreement, exploiting Supreme Court decisions in the 1930s. The president conducted his undeclared naval war in the Atlantic under his powers as commander-in-chief. Here were the origins of what would later be called the Imperial Presidency, enabling Lyndon Johnson and Richard Nixon to wage a massive, undeclared war in Vietnam.

An important facet of the Imperial Presidency was a vast network of military intelligence. Here the era of 1938–1941 also set precedents, albeit more of a negative kind. Roosevelt's neglect of signals intelligence had contributed to the Pearl Harbor debacle. Although he continued to be more interested in spies than signals, the handling of sigint was transformed over the next few months. Roosevelt also recognized the need for a more integrated management of intelligence: hence the Office of Strategic Services established in June 1942. True to form, he refused to give OSS real autonomy, and bureaucratic turf wars continued to bedevil U.S. intelligence gathering and analysis. But OSS was the precursor of the cold war CIA.

Roosevelt's conception of war was also significant. After November 1938 he imagined airpower as a potent deterrent, a way of averting war. That doctrine was applied in earnest in late 1941 with the reinforcement of the Philippines by B-17s. He also envisaged airpower as a war-winning weapon—one that might even obviate the need for large and politically sensitive armies. The War Department contested that idea in its "Victory Program," rightly predicting the need for large land forces slogging their way across Western Europe. Although exaggerated, FDR's hopes for airpower were a foretaste of things to come. B-17s became the prime instrument of wartime strategic bombing; the research into atomic energy that FDR commissioned in October 1941 laid the foundations for the atomic bomb. After 1945 cold war strategy centered on aerial bombing, especially using nuclear weapons. Roosevelt was the pioneer of technowar: massive firepower applied with the intent of minimizing U.S. casualties.

Modern war was total war, requiring the mobilization of the whole of society. By aiding the Allies Roosevelt sought to avoid "a garrison state"; the political scientist Aaron Friedberg has argued that what actually emerged was a "contract state"—one that was less burdensome and directive than the totalitarian system and relied on contracts rather than coercion to harness private resources. Both the enhanced mobilization of resources and the contract mechanism were pioneered in the era between Munich and Pearl Harbor.

One early example was the decision for a peacetime draft: the Selective Service Act of September 1940. Truman tried to dispose of the draft in 1947 but then restored it in 1948 as the cold war deepened. Thereafter it was part of American life for three decades. Yet FDR had rejected the idea of Universal Military Training for all citizens, as advocated by Henry Stimson and other veterans of the World War I Plattsburg movement. That would have entailed a more radical militarization of American life. A second example was the galvanizing of American industry for air rearmament. Roosevelt's targets of 10,000 planes a year (November 1938) and 50,000 a year (May 1940) were pulled, as it were, from the air, and soon had to be brought down to earth. But in 1942 U.S. industry produced 48,000 planes, and in 1943 another 86,000. Dreams were exceeded by reality. In 1938 FDR had talked of building planes in government plants paid for by New Deal programs, but by the summer of 1940 he accepted that rearmament on such a scale would depend on private industry operating on favorable contracts.

An active policy of national security, even if operated on a contract basis, also required an activist state. During the 1940s the U.S. government gradually assumed a far greater role in the macro-management of the economy. The New Deal had breached the norms of balanced budgets, but in a limited and temporary way. The deficit spending that got under way seriously with lend-lease marked a major shift in the U.S. political economy. Expanded after Pearl Harbor, this military Keynesianism legitimated government spending and helped promote economic recovery. It also had larger political significance. As the historian Alan Brinkley has argued, the era of "reform liberalism" was waning. Since the Progressive Era, American reformers had been preoccupied with economic structures, especially the danger of monopolies. Now their focus shifted to fiscal policy and the gospel of growth. The pioneering application of Keynesianism to national security rather than social security helped ensure acceptance of this radically new economic philosophy.

The 1930s were a time of depression, economically and psychologically. The war years were an era of boom and renewed confidence. The historian Mark Leff has observed: "War is hell, but for millions of Americans on the booming home front, World War II was also a hell of a war." The years 1940–1941 are the cusp of that transition. Rearmament and full employment (in war industry and the armed forces) boosted economic recovery, which in turn inspired a new confidence. This was enhanced by the astounding collapse of the European powers, which had dominated world politics and haunted the American imagination for centuries. It was a time of threat, yes, but also a time of promise. For internationalists, the New World had an opportunity and a duty to reform the Old, to redeem the West and the Rest. Here was a decisive moment in the ideologizing of what Henry Luce called the American Century.

Roosevelt, Lippmann, and Luce were not Lindbergh, Wheeler, and Vandenberg. The active proponents of the new American globalism were a minority in 1940–1941. But, as historians have shown, the reshaping of U.S. policy in the early cold war was also the work of a small minority of Washington insiders who managed to build a consensus around what they wanted.

In the summer of 1939 a small group of obdurate congressmen, particularly in the Senate, were able to stymie Roosevelt's attempts at neutrality revision. In the summer of 1940 even smaller groups of determined internationalists promoted the destroyers deal and the peacetime draft. They helped give a cautious president the intellectual arguments and political momentum he needed to shift policy and change attitudes. Despite all the larger international, economic, and social pressures, the making and remaking of foreign policy is disproportionately an elite activity.

There was also continuity in America's foreign policy elite in the 1940s. Some of those who helped created the national security state in the early cold war had participated in the policy reorientation of 1940–1941. They included the diplomats Dean Acheson and Averell Harriman; Robert Lovett, Robert Patterson, and John J. McCloy in Stimson's War Department; and James Forrestal as Knox's undersecretary of the navy. For all these policymakers—the so-called Wise Men of America's cold war establishment—the eighteen months before Pearl Harbor constituted a turning point in their careers and their outlook.

That moment is also embodied in the architecture of America's capital. At the beginning of 1939 the Department of State, the War Department, and the Navy Department were all accommodated in a single building immediately west of the White House. In the summer of 1939 the War Department moved down to the Munitions Building on Constitution Avenue. As its civilian employees swelled to manage rearmament and the draft, so the department colonized another twenty buildings all over the District of Columbia. The Navy and State departments were also expanding, albeit less dramatically. In early 1941 the army was allocated a new federal office building, near completion, in a southwest backwater of the city known as Foggy Bottom. But Henry Stimson considered it too pokey: the façade, he said, looked like the entrance to a provincial opera house. On August 14—just as the Atlantic Charter was being broadcast to the world—Congress voted appropriations for a new, purpose-built War Department across the Potomac. On September 11—the day FDR delivered his "shoot-on-sight" radio address about the attack on the *USS Greer*—construction began on this massive, five-sided edifice, a mile around its perimeter.

Roosevelt was deeply unhappy. In August he had moved the site three-quarters of a mile downriver to avoid impeding the view of the nation's capital from Arlington National Cemetery. Nor did he like the design, proposing unsuccessfully a square, windowless monolith with artificial light and ventilation. After the war, he said, when the military had shrunk back to its proper size, the building could be used for storage. As we now know, it wasn't. Over the next decade the Pentagon became the permanent home for an integrated Department of Defense, the State Department took over Stimson's reject in Foggy Bottom, and the president's new National Security Council moved into the old State-War-Navy building. None of this FDR had imagined, let alone desired. But this architectural footnote is another reminder that Franklin Roosevelt helped lay the foundations of America's national security state.

A Note on Sources

THIS BOOK is rooted in my own primary research, particularly in the Franklin D. Roosevelt Library (Hyde Park, New York), and in the National Archives and Library of Congress. It also draws on a large and varied historiography produced by several generations of historians. What follows is a brief guide to the writing I have found particularly useful and stimulating.

Essential published collections of primary material include Samuel I. Rosenman, ed., *The Public Papers and the Addresses of Franklin D. Roosevelt*, 13 vols. (New York, 1938–1950); *Complete Presidential Press Conferences of Franklin D. Roosevelt, 1933–1945*, 25 vols. (New York, 1972); Edgar B. Nixon, ed., *Franklin D. Roosevelt and Foreign Affairs, 1933–1937*, 3 vols. (Cambridge, Mass., 1969); and Donald B. Schewe, ed., *Franklin D. Roosevelt and Foreign Affairs, 1937–1939*, 14 vols. (New York, 1979–1983).

Changing interpretations of this period may be traced through a series of historiographical articles. See particularly Wayne S. Cole, "American Entry into World War II: A Historiographical Appraisal," *Mississippi Valley Historical Review*, 43 (1957), 595–617; Gerald K. Haines, "Roads to War: United States Foreign Policy, 1931–1941," in Gerald K. Haines and J. Samuel Walker, eds., *American Foreign Relations: A Historiographical Review* (Westport, Conn., 1981); and complementary essays by Justus D. Doenecke, "U.S. Policy and the European War, 1939–1941," *Diplomatic History*, 19 (1995), 669–698, and Michael A. Barnhart, "The Origins of World War II in Asia and the Pacific: Synthesis Impossible?," *Diplomatic History*, 20 (1996), 241–260.

Overviews of U.S. foreign policy in this period include Robert A. Divine, *The Reluctant Belligerent: American Entry into World War II*, 2nd ed. (New York, 1979), and Patrick J. Hearden, *Roosevelt Con-*

192   A NOTE ON SOURCES

fronts Hitler: America's Entry into World War II (DeKalb, Ill., 1987).
Whereas Divine stresses the cautious, reactive nature of U.S. policy,
Hearden offers a more proactive, "New Left" interpretation, em-
phasizing the concern of American leaders about the threat posed
by Germany to the free enterprise system. Justus D. Doenecke and
John E. Wilz, *From Isolation to War, 1931–1941* (Arlington Heights,
Ill., 1991) updates Wilz's earlier narrative.

Among "classics" of earlier historiography, mention should be
made of the revisionist writings of Charles A. Beard, *American Foreign Policy in the Making, 1932–1940* (New Haven, 1946); his sequel,
President Roosevelt and the Coming of the War, 1941 (New Haven,
1948); and Charles Callan Tansill, *Back Door to War: The Roosevelt
Foreign Policy, 1933–1941* (Chicago, 1952). Those whom Tansill
damned as "court historians" include Robert E. Sherwood, *Roosevelt and Hopkins: An Intimate History* (New York, 1948); Herbert
Feis, *The Road to Pearl Harbor: The Coming of the War between the
United States and Japan* (Princeton, 1950); and the massive two-
volume semi-official history by William L. Langer and S. Everett
Gleason, *The Challenge to Isolation, 1937–1940* (New York, 1952),
and *The Undeclared War, 1940–1941* (New York, 1953).

For the international dimensions, see P. M. H. Bell, *The Origins of
the Second World War in Europe*, 2nd ed. (New York, 1997); Akira
Iriye, *The Origins of the Second World War in Asia and the Pacific*
(New York, 1987); and, for both continents, William Carr, *Poland to
Pearl Harbor: The Making of the Second World War* (Baltimore,
1985). Pierre Grosser, *Pourqoui la 2e Guerre Mondiale?* (Paris, 1999)
is a stimulating recent overview, richly annotated. Donald Cameron
Watt, *How War Came* (New York, 1989) provides a meticulous examination of the immediate origins of the European war in
1938–1939. The story of the whole conflict is told in vast and fascinating detail by Gerhard L. Weinberg, *A World at Arms: A Global
History of World War II* (New York, 1994).

Biographical studies of FDR include the two volumes by James
MacGregor Burns, *Roosevelt: The Lion and the Fox, 1882–1940*
(New York, 1956), and *Roosevelt: The Soldier of Freedom, 1940–1945*
(New York, 1970); Frank Freidel, *Franklin D. Roosevelt: A Ren-*

dezvous with Destiny (Boston, 1990); and Doris Kearns Goodwin, *No Ordinary Time: Franklin and Eleanor Roosevelt: The Home Front in World War II* (New York, 1994). For overviews of FDR's foreign policy, consult the incisive essays in Robert A. Divine, *Roosevelt and World War II* (Baltimore, 1969); Robert Dallek's detailed study, *Franklin D. Roosevelt and American Foreign Policy, 1932–1945* (New York, 1979); the highly critical assessment by Frederick W. Marks III, *Wind over Sand: The Diplomacy of Franklin Roosevelt* (Athens, Ga., 1988); and collections of essays by two leading scholars of the period, Warren F. Kimball, *The Juggler: Franklin Roosevelt as Wartime Statesman* (Princeton, 1991), and Lloyd C. Gardner, *Spheres of Influence: The Partition of Europe from Munich to Yalta* (Chicago, 1993). Some of the intellectual influences on FDR are examined in the last chapter of John Milton Cooper, Jr., *The Warrior and the Priest: Woodrow Wilson and Theodore Roosevelt* (Cambridge, Mass., 1983), and in the first part of John Lamberton Harper, *American Visions of Europe: Franklin D. Roosevelt, George F. Kennan, and Dean G. Acheson* (New York, 1994).

For domestic background, readers should turn to Anthony J. Badger, *The New Deal: The Depression Years, 1933–1940* (New York, 1979). Barry Eichengreen offers a stimulating reinterpretation in "The Nature and Origins of the Great Slump Revisited," *Economic History Review*, 45 (1992), 213–239. See also Michael A. Bernstein, *The Great Depression: Delayed Recovery and Economic Change in America, 1929–1939* (New York, 1987); and, for a broader period, Peter Fearon, *War, Prosperity and Depression: The U.S. Economy 1917–45* (Lawrence, Kans., 1987). The war years are covered in John W. Jeffries, *Wartime America: The World War II Home Front* (Chicago, 1996). See also Neil A. Wynn, "The 'Good War': The Second World War and Postwar American Society," *Journal of Contemporary History*, 31 (1996), 463–482; Mark H. Leff, "The Politics of Sacrifice on the American Home Front in World War II," *Journal of American History*, 77 (1991), 1296–1318; and the iconoclastic essay by Robert Higgs, "Wartime Prosperity?: A Reassessment of the U.S. Economy in the 1940s," *Journal of Economic History*, 52 (1993), 41–60. The metamorphosis of New Deal ideology is explored in Alan Brinkley, *The End of Reform: New Deal Liberalism in Recession and War* (New York, 1995). The whole era of Hoover and Roosevelt is narrated in detail by David M. Kennedy, *Freedom from Fear: The American People in Depression and War, 1929–1945* (New York, 1999).

My thinking in the broader context has benefited from a number of incisive studies, including the Watergate-era classic by Arthur M. Schlesinger, Jr., *The Imperial Presidency* (New York, 1973); Michael S. Sherry, *In the Shadow of War: The United States Since the 1930s* (New Haven, 1995), a stimulating account of recent U.S. experience as a story of progressive militarization; and Frank Ninkovich's interpretation of American internationalism in *The Wilsonian Century: U.S. Foreign Policy Since 1900* (Chicago, 1999). On the cold war political economy, see Michael J. Hogan, *A Cross of Iron: Harry S. Truman and the Origins of the National Security State, 1945–1954* (New York, 1998), and Aaron L. Friedberg, "Why Didn't the United States Become a Garrison State?" *International Security*, 16 (1992), 109–142. For recent discussions of the notion of American "exceptionalism," see Byron E. Shafer, ed., *Is America Different: A New Look at American Exceptionalism* (New York, 1991).

The evolution of Roosevelt's thinking in the late 1930s can be followed in Robert A. Divine, *The Illusion of Neutrality: Franklin D. Roosevelt and the Struggle over the Arms Embargo* (Chicago, 1962). David G. Haglund, *Latin America and the Transformation of U.S. Strategic Thought, 1936–1940* (Albuquerque, N.M., 1984) analyzes the move away from hemisphere defense, and Barbara Rearden Farnham, *Roosevelt and the Munich Crisis: A Study of Political Decision-Making* (Princeton, 1997) focuses on the crucial months of 1938–1939 from a political science standpoint. For the impact of the fall of France, see David Reynolds, "1940: Fulcrum of the Twentieth Century?" *International Affairs*, 66 (1990), 325–350; and Marvin R. Zahniser, "Rethinking the Significance of Disaster: The United States and the Fall of France in 1940," *International History Review*, 14 (1992), 252–276. Ernest R. May, *Strange Victory: Hitler's Conquest of France* (New York, 2000) is a fascinating recent analysis.

On lend-lease, Warren F. Kimball, *The Most Unsordid Act: Lend-*

Lease, 1939–1941 (Baltimore, 1969) remains essential. On the payoff, consult Kimball's 1971 article "Lend-Lease and the Open Door: The Temptation of British Opulence, 1937–1942," reprinted in his volume *The Juggler*, and the early chapters of Alan P. Dobson, *U.S. Wartime Aid to Britain, 1940–1946* (Beckenham, Kent, England, 1986). Theodore A. Wilson, *The First Summit: Roosevelt and Churchill at Placentia Bay, 1941*, 2nd ed. (Lawrence, Kans., 1991) is superb both on the conference and on its context. There are also useful essays in Douglas Brinkley and David R. Facey-Crowther, eds., *The Atlantic Charter* (New York, 1994). Although focused on March to December 1941, Waldo Heinrichs illuminates much more in *Threshold of War: Franklin Roosevelt and American Entry into World War II* (New York, 1988).

On military aviation, see Michael S. Sherry, *The Rise of American Airpower: The Creation of Armageddon* (New Haven, 1987), chapters 3–4; and Jacob Vander Meulen, *The Politics of Aircraft: Building an American Military Industry* (Lawrence, Kans., 1991), especially chapter 7. Richard Rhodes offers a detailed account of *The Making of the Atomic Bomb* (New York, 1986). J. Garry Clifford and Samuel R. Spencer, Jr., *The First Peacetime Draft* (Lawrence, Kans., 1986) look at the enactment and implementation of Selective Service in 1940–1941. On the navy, see Patrick Abbazia, *Mr. Roosevelt's Navy: The Private War of the U.S. Atlantic Fleet, 1939–1942* (Annapolis, 1975), and James R. Leutze, *Bargaining for Supremacy: Anglo-American Naval Collaboration, 1937–1941* (Chapel Hill, 1977). Eric Larrabee, *Commander in Chief: Franklin Delano Roosevelt, His Lieutenants, and Their War* (New York, 1987), though focused on 1941–1945, contains much interesting background. Mark A. Stoler provides the broad strategic picture in *Allies and Adversaries: The Joint Chiefs of Staff, the Grand Alliance, and U.S. Strategy in World War II* (Chapel Hill, 2000).

Walter Johnson, *The Battle Against Isolationism* (New York, 1944) is a wartime study of the Committee to Defend America by Aiding the Allies. Mark Lincoln Chadwin, *The Warhawks: American Interventionists Before Pearl Harbor* (New York, 1970) focuses on the more extreme "Century Group" and the "Fight for Freedom"

Committee. Nicholas John Cull, *Selling War: The British Propaganda Campaign Against American "Neutrality" in World War II* (New York, 1995) offers an excellent study of how the British tried to shape American opinion.

On isolationism, see Wayne S. Cole, *Roosevelt and the Isolationists, 1932–1945* (Lincoln, Nebr., 1983) and his earlier study of the principal anti-war pressure group in 1940–1941, *America First: The Battle Against Intervention* (New York, 1953). On a broader canvas is Thomas N. Guinsburg, *The Pursuit of Isolationism in the United States Senate from Versailles to Pearl Harbor* (New York, 1982). Also illuminating are Justus D. Doenecke, ed., *In Danger Undaunted: The Anti-Interventionist Movement of 1940–1941 as Revealed in the Papers of the America First Committee* (Stanford, 1990), and the study by James C. Schneider, *Should America Go to War?: The Debate over Foreign Policy in Chicago, 1939–1941* (Chapel Hill, 1989).

Several scholars have developed anti-interventionist ideas into a renewed critique of the "national security" argument for U.S. belligerency in 1941. See Bruce M. Russett, *No Clear and Present Danger: A Skeptical View of the U.S. Entry into World War II* (New York, 1972); Melvin Small, *Was War Necessary?: National Security and U.S. Entry into War* (Beverly Hills, Calif., 1980); and two articles by John A. Thompson, "Another Look at the Downfall of 'Fortress America,'" *Journal of American Studies*, 26 (1992), 393–408, and "Did the United States Enter World War II for Reasons of National Security?" *Odense American Studies International Series*, Working Paper 45 (August 2000).

For contemporary use of the term "national security," see the essays of Edward Mead Earle, for instance, "The Threat to American Security," *Yale Review*, 30 (Spring 1941), 454–480, and "American Security—Its Changing Conditions," *Annals of the American Academy of Political and Social Science*, 218 (November 1941), 186–193. On the wartime revolution in Americans' "mental maps" that began in 1940–1941, see the pioneering article by Alan Henrikson, "The Map as an 'Idea': The Role of Cartographic Imagery During the Second World War," *American Cartographer*, 2 (1975), 19–53. Suggestive examples are Walter Lippmann, "The Atlantic and

America," *Life*, April 7, 1941, 84–88, and Francis Pickens Miller, "The Atlantic Area," *Foreign Affairs*, 19/4 (July 1941), 726–728.

There is a wealth of bilateral studies of U.S. relations with key countries in this period. On Nazi Germany, see Arnold A. Offner, *American Appeasement: United States Foreign Policy and Germany, 1933–1938* (New York, 1969); Hans L. Trefousse, *Germany and American Neutrality, 1939–1941* (New York, 1951); Saul Friedländer, *Prelude to Downfall: Hitler and the United States, 1939–1941* (London, 1967); and James V. Compton, *The Swastika and the Eagle: Hitler, the United States, and the Origins of the Second World War* (London, 1968). An insightful review essay on Trefousse, Friedländer, and Compton by Ernest R. May, entitled "Nazi Germany and the United States," was published in *Journal of Modern History*, 41 (1969), 207–214. See also Gerhard L. Weinberg, "Hitler's Image of the United States," *American Historical Review*, 69 (1964), 1006–1021; Milan Hauner, "Did Hitler Want a World Dominion?" *Journal of Contemporary History*, 13 (1978), 15–32; and Holger H. Herwig, "Prelude to *Weltblitzkrieg*: Germany's Naval Policy Toward the United States of America, 1939–1941," *Journal of Modern History*, 43 (1971), 649–668. An important recent study is Norman J. W. Goda's *Tomorrow the World: Hitler, Northwest Africa, and the Path Toward America* (College Station, Tex., 1998).

Aside from Goda's work, however, the focus for studies of German-American relations has shifted to the Jewish question. See, for instance, Hans Mommsen, "Hitler's Reichstag Speech of 30 January 1939," *History and Memory*, 9 (1997), 147–169; and the provocative piece by Tobias Jersak, "Die Interaktion von Kriegverlauf und Judenvernichtung: Ein Blick aug Hitler's Strategie im Spätsommer 1941," *Historische Zeitschrift*, 268 (1999), 311–374. The major new biography by Ian Kershaw, *Hitler, 1936–1945: Nemesis* (New York, 2000) also contains relevant material. Among older studies, David S. Wyman, *Paper Walls: America and the Refugee Crisis, 1938–1941* (Amherst, 1968) remains useful.

Relations with Britain are touched on in many of the other works mentioned in this note. For general bilateral studies, consult C. A. MacDonald, *The United States, Britain and Appeasement, 1936–1939*

(London, 1981); William R. Rock, *Chamberlain and Roosevelt: British Foreign Policy and the United States, 1937–1940* (Columbus, Ohio, 1988); and David Reynolds, *The Creation of the Anglo-American Alliance, 1937–1941: A Study in Competitive Cooperation* (Chapel Hill, 1982). The endnotes to the latter contain references to many of the sources used in this volume. B. J. C. McKercher surveys a longer period, mainly from the British side, in *Britain's Loss of Global Pre-Eminence to the United States, 1930–1945* (New York, 1999). On the Anglo-American leadership, see Warren F. Kimball, *Forged in War: Roosevelt, Churchill, and the Second World War* (New York, 1997), and his essential documentary collection, *Churchill and Roosevelt: The Complete Correspondence* (Princeton, 1984), vol. 1. John Charmley offers a deeply skeptical view of the relationship in *Churchill's Grand Alliance: The Anglo-American Special Relationship, 1940–1957* (1995).

On policy toward the Soviet Union, see Thomas R. Maddux, *Years of Estrangement: American Relations with the Soviet Union 1933–1941* (Tallahassee, Fla., 1980); the opening chapters of George C. Herring, Jr., *Aid to Russia, 1941–1946: Strategy, Diplomacy, and the Origins of the Cold War* (New York, 1973); John Daniel Langer, "The Harriman-Beaverbrook Mission and the Debate over Unconditional Aid for the Soviet Union," *Journal of Contemporary History*, 14 (1979), 463–482; and Kimball, *The Juggler*, chapter 2. The older study by Raymond H. Dawson, *The Decision to Aid Russia, 1941: Foreign Policy and Domestic Politics* (Chapel Hill, 1959) remains useful. On U.S. perceptions, see Ralph B. Levering, *American Opinion and the Russian Alliance, 1939–1945* (Chapel Hill, 1976), and the suggestive analysis by Eduard Mark, "October or Thermidor? Interpretations of Stalinism and the Perception of Soviet Foreign Policy in the United States, 1927–1947," *American Historical Review*, 94 (1989), 937–962. On the concept of totalitarianism, see Thomas R. Maddux, "Red Fascism, Brown Bolshevism: The American Image of Totalitarianism in the 1930s," *Historian*, 40 (1977), 85–103, and Abbott Gleason, *Totalitarianism: The Inner History of the Cold War* (New York, 1995).

On Asia and the Pacific, see generally the studies by Iriye and

Eric Nave, *Betrayal at Pearl Harbor: How Churchill Lured Roosevε* *into World War II* (New York, 1991). To this, Richard J. Aldrich, *In* *telligence and the War Against Japan: Britain, America and the Politics* *of Secret Service* (New York, 2000), chapter 5, offers a rounded corrective. Roosevelt's general indifference to signals intelligence in the approach to Pearl Harbor is exposed in Christopher Andrew, *For* *the President's Eyes Only: Secret Intelligence and the American Presidency from Washington to Bush* (London, 1995), chapter 3.

Henrichs cited earlier. The essays in Dorothy Borg and Shumpei Okamato, eds., *Pearl Harbor as History: Japanese-American Relations, 1931–1941* (New York, 1973) remain essential for closer study. The State Department is at the center of James H. Herzog, *Closing the Open Door: American-Japanese Diplomatic Negotiations, 1936–1941* (Annapolis, 1973), and Jonathan G. Utley, *Going to War with Japan, 1937–1941* (Knoxville, Tenn., 1985). On oil, see Utley, and also Irvine H. Anderson, Jr., *The Standard-Vacuum Oil Company and United States East Asian Policy, 1933–1941* (Princeton, 1975). Jonathan Marshall argues against the image of U.S. self-sufficiency in *To Have and Have Not: Southeast Asian Raw Materials and the Origins of the Pacific War* (Berkeley, 1995). The broader background is covered in Michael A. Barnhart, *Japan Prepares for Total War: The Search for Economic Security, 1919–1941* (Ithaca, 1987). An interesting assessment of Chinese diplomacy, based on recent documentation from Taiwan, is Youli Sun's *China and the Origins of the Pacific War, 1931–1941* (New York, 1993).

The Axis connection is examined in Paul W. Schroeder, *The Axis Alliance and Japanese-American Relations, 1941* (Ithaca, 1958); Hosoya Chihiro, "The Tripartite Pact, 1939–1940," in James William Morley, ed., *Deterrent Diplomacy: Japan, Germany, and the USSR, 1935–1940* (New York, 1976), 191–257; Gerhard L. Weinberg, "Pearl Harbor: The German Perspective," in Weinberg's *Germany, Hitler and World War II: Essays in Modern German and W* History* (New York, 1995); and Gerhard Krebs, "Deutschland Pearl Harbor," *Historiche Zeitschrift*, 253 (1991), 313–369. For term "hollow alliance," see Johanna M. Meskell, *Hitler and The Hollow Alliance* (New York, 1966).

On Pearl Harbor, see the works of Gordon W. Prange, es *At Dawn We Slept* (New York, 1981), and *Pearl Harbor: The of History* (New York, 1986). Robert W. Love, Jr., ed., *Pea Revisited* (New York, 1995) is one of several sets of fiftieth sary conference essays. The effects are reassessed by Joh "Pearl Harbor: Military Inconvenience, Political Disast *tional Security*, 16 (Winter 1991/2), 172–203. For a va conspiracy theory, indicting the British, see James R

Index

A NOTE ON THE AUTHOR

David Reynolds is a Fellow of Christ's College, Cambridge University. He has also held visiting appointments at Harvard University and at Nihon University in Tokyo. He is the author of two prize-winning works on the United States and Britain in World War II: *The Creation of the Anglo-American Alliance, 1937–1941: A Study in Competitive Cooperation* (1981) and *Rich Relations: The American Occupation of Britain, 1942–1945* (1995). His other books include *An Ocean Apart: The Relationship Between Britain and America in the Twentieth Century* (co-author, 1988), which accompanied the BBC/PBS TV series for which he was principal historical adviser; *Britannia Overruled: British Policy and World Power in the Twentieth Century* (2nd ed., 2000); and *The Origins of the Cold War in Europe: International Perspectives* (editor, 1994). A collection of essays entitled *Allies at War: The Soviet, American, and British Experience, 1939–1945* (1994), which he co-edited, was the result of a joint project by historians from the three countries. It was also published in Russian. His most recent book, on a broader plane, is *One World Divisible: A Global History Since 1945* (2000).

973.917   Reynolds, David,
REY   1952-

           From Munich to Pearl
           Harbor.

$24.95

DATE			